The Secrets of Syndication

The Secrets of Syndication

How to Make Money with Other People's Money

RICHARD H. BEGUELIN

LITTLE, BROWN AND COMPANY • BOSTON • TORONTO

FIRST EDITION

This book was previously published as *Syndication Secrets: How to Create Wealth Using Other People's Money.*

Library of Congress Cataloging in Publication Data

Beguelin, Richard H., 1937–
The secrets of syndication.

Rev. ed. of: Syndication secrets. c1983.
1. Syndicates (Finance) — Handbooks, manuals, etc.
2. Venture capital — Handbooks, manuals, etc. I. Beguelin, Richard H., 1937– . Syndication secrets. II. Title.
HG6021.B4 1985 658′.044 85-5157
ISBN 0-316-08783-1

MV

Designed by Dede Cummings

Published simultaneously in Canada by Little, Brown & Company (Canada) Limited

PRINTED IN THE UNITED STATES OF AMERICA

To three very special people in my life . . .
my wife, Dyan
my sons, Todd and Michael

Preface

THIS BOOK IS about job security, *true* job security — the ability to earn a very large income whenever and wherever you choose.

We live in the most affluent country in the world; yet, the vast majority of Americans spend their entire lives struggling to survive financially. Most can just barely make ends meet. Even executives, engineers, and professionals with decent incomes find it's tough to get ahead. They are too busy earning a living to accumulate any lasting wealth.

But then, there are those who enjoy the good life, who never need to worry about where the next dollar is coming from. They are financially independent, and they answer to no one but themselves. They can generate an income whenever and wherever desired; they are called syndicators.

For the first time ever, here is a "womb to tomb" guide to becoming a syndicator. This tells you in detail how to use other people's money to make money for yourself, whenever and wherever you choose. And, it tells you how to become financially independent in the process. They don't teach this in school, but you *can* learn everything about it right here in these pages. This book takes the mystery out of a seemingly mysterious, yet very lucrative method to accumulate wealth. By knowing how to use this method, you quickly can join those who answer only to themselves.

You've always been told to "put away 10 percent of what you earn and make it grow." It's true, the 10 percent can grow, but the problem always has been earning enough to end up with the 10 percent to put away! That's why this book is so important. It tells you exactly how to earn large sums of money, exactly how to create wealth without putting up one penny of your own.

This book will make you knowledgeable in a field that's becoming the money-maker of the eighties. It offers all my experience as a syndicator. I've used other people's money over and over again — forty-four times so far — to make money for myself, to create a large personal net worth. The case studies, examples, step-by-step instructions, and model documentation packages make it easy for you to do the same for yourself. This book will give you the motivation to act, to pull yourself up to real affluence and independence, regardless of where you are or what you are doing now.

You can move into millionaire status in only a few short years through persistent application of the instructions in this book. Don't be a sheep; don't follow the masses who just eke out a living, who have to answer to others. Take your desire to get ahead and put it to work with my detailed road map to wealth that's contained in this book. Work *smarter,* not harder, and be one of those who finish first! Begin now!

Table of Contents

The Secrets of Syndication

CHAPTER 1

One Hundred Percent Return Every Time

WELCOME TO THE world of syndication: the world of using other people's money to make money for yourself. It gives you a 100 percent return on investment every time!

The system works because it takes advantage of something inside every human being — a burning desire, a NEED, to get ahead. Every one of us wants to make money. Every one of us wants to enjoy the good things available to those with enough money to buy them. Yet, most people earn barely enough to support themselves or their family. So, all of us are open to that special opportunity, that once-in-a-lifetime deal that will give us extra income. We want "in" when we hear about it. You can cash in on this basic human desire; you can put $5,000 to $200,000 and more into your pocket each time you use the system.

Reading this book could be the most important step in your life concerning your efforts to earn a livelihood. Earning a good living is just a small part of the story, however. The rest deals with the potential of monetary wealth far exceeding anything you thought possible.

This exciting system for making money gives you a 100 percent return every time because your dollar investment is *zero* — you use dollars belonging to others. And, you have no obligation to repay these dollars in the traditional sense because they are not "loaned" to you. Using this system can give you complete financial independence. You will not have to depend on your boss or anyone else for an income ever again. You will have real job security. Most exciting, it makes sense for you right now, regardless of your present station in life.

It does not matter whether you are unemployed, or have a job just letting you make ends meet, or are an executive with high income. You can earn as much as or more than the other person regardless of which of these three categories you are in. Best of all, you can say good-bye to job subservience: no more answering to a boss. You answer only to yourself.

The ability to use other people's money ("OPM") is like finding the proverbial pot of gold at the end of the rainbow. This is especially true in today's world of high interest rates and restrictive terms on traditional bank loans. With OPM, you can acquire property and other assets, start any kind of business, or invest in thousands of other different ways while retaining complete control in every case. Your use of OPM can be good for everyone involved, too. The people putting up the money can receive good returns on their funds. And, you unquestionably can receive big rewards for your efforts as the following example shows.

Results from Using the System One Time

In June 1976, two friends and I opened a fitness club business. We used OPM to build it and open it; not a penny was put in by the three of us. We sold the business five years later, in June 1981. This is what I personally earned from this transaction:

Front end organization fee	$ 5,000
Fund-raising fee	17,463
Steady cash flow from five years of operating the business (approximately $1,000 per month)	60,000

Sales fee from sale of business	28,500
Profit (from my 13.3 percent ownership share)	68,590
Approximate interest from note (on profit still being paid out)	18,000
TOTAL EARNINGS:	$197,553

That's right. I earned a minimum of $197,553 by using the system just one time. Yet, I continued to use the system over and over again while this one was earning me these dollars.

I would classify this as a medium-size project. A larger project could have earned me much more. Even the very small projects — the size you may begin with — can earn you thousands of dollars in fees and other earnings.

What about investors who put up the money for these ventures? Well, they can make out very nicely, too, and that is what makes the whole process work. There are millions of people with both small and large amounts of money to invest. They have neither the time nor the inclination to work on properly investing their funds. But, they still have that human desire to get ahead, that NEED to get in on "a good one." So, they are more than willing to have someone else do the legwork for them. This is where you and I come into the picture.

In the example above, how did the people that put up all the money come out? You know what my earnings were, and I certainly did well. How could I make this much money for myself with their funds, and still have them as satisfied investors and friends? Let's take a quick look at their side of the project, which will give you a clear understanding of why all of this works so well.

The investors in the example put up a total of $175,000. This is what they earned as a result of their investment:

Steady cash flow during operations (approximate)	$270,000
Profit from sale of business	283,000
Approximate interest from note (on profit still being paid out)	85,000
TOTAL EARNINGS:	$638,000

These people put up $175,000 for earnings of about $638,000, almost four times the amount of their investment! And this is not the whole story. They also received significant tax deductions, which made much of their earnings tax-free while the business was operating. Then, they were given favorable capital gains tax treatment on the profit from the sale. On their own, these investors could not hope to make their funds grow this way. Yet, with someone else creating a business opportunity with their money, their funds multiplied several times. They also received attractive tax benefits as icing on the cake.

Many Ways to Line Your Pockets

Using OPM can make money for you in many different ways every time you apply the system. Some of the ways available to you are listed below:

- a packaging fee
- a healthy front end organization fee
- a substantial fee as a percentage of funds raised
- a front end finder's fee, or sales commission, depending on the project
- a percentage share of the ownership at no cost (which allows you to build equities in different businesses without using any of your own funds)
- regular cash flow from operations, depending upon the nature of the project
- a management fee
- sales commissions/fees when the project is sold
- profit from the sale of a project (from your percentage ownership)
- compounded earnings from the reinvested fees and profits received from the above sources
- fees, profits, and compounded earnings from the "fallout" of using OPM (more on this later)

Thousands — sometimes hundreds of thousands — of dollars from some or all of these sources can flow each time you use the system, and you can use it several times each year. Like most careers, the more you put in, the more you can expect to get out. But unlike most careers, you do not need any special skills or education to have success here. The tremendous potential for wealth is open to men and women from all walks of life, young or old. And that makes this system one of the best games in town for making money, and a lot of it.

This book unveils the secrets of the system of using OPM. Many are aware of the concept and have heard of others who have made it this way. But, you cannot sit in a classroom to study it, nor can you find books with it laid out in detail. Because of this, the concept remains mysterious and confusing for the great majority of the public.

In this book, you will find the system spelled out in detail. In essence, this book is a road map, complete with all the examples, forms, and directions — including two complete model documentation packages — needed for you to start earning money immediately. The book even will tell you, in detail, how to go about acquiring the funds of others. But it helps you the most by eliminating all the years of trial and error and frustration through which I had to struggle. My efforts were worth it, though, as the previous example and others in this book show. A little effort on your part can dramatically change your life, too.

My Knowledge Will Become Yours

In these pages, I share all that I have learned about the intricacies and techniques of how to become wealthy and independent by using OPM. My experience and knowledge will become yours so that you can start out quickly and easily in the pursuit of your own financial security. My main objective is to keep you from fumbling, from making the mistakes that people always make when embarking on a new venture.

Since we will be working together closely, you should know a little about me. A short time ago, I was typical of a majority of Americans. I had a decent job with a large aerospace industry corporation, and I worked hard for my annual 5 percent to 8 percent salary increases. As my company was in aerospace, however, layoffs were always in progress because of changing government contracts. I had to tread lightly in my work; the threat of a "pink notice" constantly reminded me of just how insecure my "job security" really was.

I could not seem to get ahead financially, either. I slowly was able to buy furniture, get a "newer" used car, and rent a house instead of an apartment. Finally, I even managed a down payment for a small house (with borrowed funds). But I could never accumulate any savings for a real vacation, or for financial emergencies. All the money I earned was spent just to provide a decent level of existence for myself and my family.

Then I discovered what I thought was a good, existing business for sale, one that would give me independence and a better income. I borrowed money for the business, quit my job, and jumped into it. (Remember, I put *my own* borrowed funds into this business because I knew nothing at this point about using OPM.) The business transaction failed, and suddenly I was without either funds or a job. It was one of the lowest points in my life.

Desperate for income at this point, I decided to try to raise investment money, from private individuals, on a commission basis. This fund-raising job was for a man who happened to be raising a large sum of OPM that he would use to purchase an avocado ranch. It was difficult for me, because I worked with no direction; however, the months I spent working for him and others in this field were eye-openers for me. I saw the tremendous potential for personal profit there was by using the funds of others, rather than my own, for business ventures.

Deciding to try this OPM business myself, an old school friend and I teamed up. We used OPM to get our first small project off the ground. It was a nineteen-unit apartment building that required only $50,000 in OPM to cover the down payment, all fees, and working capital. Even though it was small, this first project still earned us $3,000 in organizational fees, $7,975 in purchase and sales commissions, and $2,200 in profit and interest. And some years later, I ended up buying the building for my own account. It now gives me monthly cash flow plus good tax benefits, and I own it outright.

Since that humble beginning, I have used OPM to make money for myself over and over again. I have been a consultant on countless other projects trying to utilize the same system. My projects have involved ranches, oil refineries and oil exploration, apartment buildings, vacation properties, restaurants, new homes and existing homes, automobiles, office buildings, tennis clubs, fitness centers, book publishing, and other businesses. There really is no limit to the various types of projects that can be put together with the funds of others.

My use of the system forty-four times and "fallout" from the system also have given me the millionaire status that I was originally seeking when I left that salaried job. I now have what every man and woman thinks about for him- or herself: a large home; a second vacation home; expensive cars; a boat; rental houses, apartment buildings, and other income-producing investments; and healthy savings accounts. Most important, I have time with my family, time to travel, time just to enjoy life in general.

In my case, I fell into this exciting field by accident. I had no special education, no money behind me, and no one to show me the way. Yet, I still found real job security and independence.

When I started out, I had nothing more than you have, maybe a lot less. I did have that desire to get ahead and the persistence to keep trying during the rough spots. But then, you also have the desire to get ahead or you would not be reading this book. And because of this book, you should be able to miss all of the rough waters through which I had to wade because no one laid things out for me. No one was there with a road map to success as this book is designed to be for you.

CHAPTER 2

To Hell with Just Making Ends Meet!

IN CHAPTER 3, you will begin to see exactly why this system works. By the time you are into Chapter 4, you will be deeply involved in the step-by-step details that will enable you to reap the rewards of using OPM. And the rewards are many, as this chapter points out.

The Rewards of Syndication

While I was still buried in my salaried aerospace job, I used to think constantly about how to break out of my no-win rut. I didn't want to just barely scratch out a living for the rest of my life. Finally, I realized why financially successful people do so well. They work SMARTER, not harder. They cash in on the rewards of using their brain for THEMSELVES, instead of for their boss or the company.

Every time you use OPM to put together something, you're using your brain to benefit yourself. You directly reap the rewards of each deal. And, each deal has the same common denominator, that of putting immediate and potential future dollars in your pockets. But, many of these transactions have other benefits, too. You end up with new friends and new business associates. You will find that new opportunities will be continually referred to you. Most important, you will back into some of that all-important "fallout" mentioned earlier.

So, if your appetite for personal wealth and independence is not yet whetted, it will be after this chapter. In the next few pages are several short, descriptive case studies of how OPM actually was used in different ways to earn the dollars and benefits just described. Some specific fallout cases are also included to show how these can quickly pyramid your buildup of net worth.

A Small Project Nets Good Returns

In Chapter 1, we reviewed an example of a medium-size project. Here is an example of a small project and the monetary results it produced. This was one of the first times I used OPM to put together a deal. It involved an income property, a twenty-unit apartment building. The transaction took only $40,000 of other people's money, and very little time. Here is what I earned along with some partners I worked with on this one:

Front end organizational fee	$ 4,000
Front end administrative fee	8,000
Sales fee upon sale of property	9,750
Profit (from 15 percent ownership share)	1,795
TOTAL EARNINGS:	$23,545

Using the system netted us almost $24,000 on a very small project. The investors who put up the funds came out nicely, too. Those in the 50 percent tax bracket earned a total of $79,794 which, after deducting their original investment, netted them $39,794. Their average return over the three-year holding period was 33.2 percent per year (as a percentage of their original $40,000 investment). This was better performance than they could have realized on their own, so both sides were pleased with the results.

This building was sold in three years because we already had received our major tax benefits, plus we received a good sales price. As an interesting sidelight, the buyer was another investor group, which held the building about four more years. This second group of investors also made good profits. Then, I purchased the property for my own account because I knew its history and potential. I now earn positive cash flow which is more than offset by tax benefits from depreciation, and I have an asset that is becoming more valuable each day. So, for the last nine years, this income property has been kicking out very nice profits and tax benefits for its three different owners.

Ten Times as Much from a Larger Project

As with most investments, the bigger the deal, the greater the potential for big profits. This next investment opportunity called for $245,000 to be put up by other people for the purchase of a 170-unit apartment complex. Again, not a penny was put in by me or my partners. Yet, we took out the following earnings:

Front end organizational fee	$ 1,000
Front end administrative fee	34,000
Sales fee upon sale of property	39,600
Profit (from 20 percent ownership share)	166,116
TOTAL EARNINGS:	$240,716

This time the system gave us $240,716. The individuals coming up with the cash came out very well, too. Again assuming 50 percent tax bracket investors, they earned a total of $1,131,828. After deducting their original cash investment of $245,000, they cleared $886,828. Over the fifty-nine-month holding period, their average return on invested dollars was a very healthy 73.6 percent per year.

(Actual tax savings are realized by investors to varying degrees depending upon their income tax bracket. The 50 percent tax bracket investors mentioned here and in the previous example are used as a standard base for calculation purposes only. In fact, investors in these two examples were of varying means, as well as tax bracket levels. Exactly how tax bracket level is used in dealing with investors, and why, is spelled out in Chapter 5.)

Converting a Closed-Down Plant into a Thriving New Business

OPM can be used to buy just about anything, or to start just about any type of business. The only limit to its use is your imagination.

This time OPM was used in two different stages to create a new, exciting business out of an old, abandoned chemical plant. This was a large project, but the size is meaningless; the system works the same for any size project, big or small. As with many of these projects, I used partners to help create and operate the investment opportunity. There are both advantages and disadvantages to using partners, which we will discuss later in this book.

We wanted to buy a large chemical plant that had been closed down by Shell Chemical for economic reasons. Our intent was to convert it into a low sulfur fuel oil refinery, the products from which could be sold to public electrical utility companies at a good profit. We needed $2,250,000 total to purchase the plant, offices, and surrounding acreage. Shell Chemical required a $100,000 good faith cash deposit to open a purchase escrow.

First, we used OPM from one small group of investors to come up with the $100,000 deposit requirement. Second, we used approximately $2,350,000 in OPM from a second group to fund the purchase price, reimburse the deposit to the first investors, and pay closing costs and fees. Because the funds put up by these groups of investors paid for everything, we did not have to use any of our own money. This transaction put the following earnings directly in my pocket:

Front end organizational fee	$20,000
Financing fee	20,000
Profit (from sale proceeds of my 1 percent ownership share)	59,064
TOTAL EARNINGS:	$99,064

Now, here is what the investors earned. The people in the first group had no ownership promised in return for their $100,000 escrow deposit. But, they did have a double-their-money-back promise (from my other syndicator partners and me) if the purchase transaction went through. It did go through, and they did receive double their money back. They received their original capital plus their profit in just four months, a whopping 300 percent return on an annual basis! These investors obviously became good sources of money for subsequent deals.

And the other group that put up approximately $2,350,000? They still own and operate the business. They acquired more land, built additional facilities, converted the chemical plant into a gasoline refinery, and have made millions of dollars in profits. Again, the creators of the investment opportunity and the people who put up all the funds both made out very well.

Creating Investment Opportunities in Hot Industries

Chapter 1 described a business two friends and I started with OPM. This business had looked to be very profitable shortly after opening the doors, so we decided to duplicate it in another city. Do you remember the racquetball club business in the late seventies? Right, it was a hot industry. It seemed as if everyone was trying to get in on the profits. Well, both of these businesses were in the racquetball/fitness club field, which still does well depending upon club amenities and management.

We held this second racquetball/fitness club about three and one-half years versus five years for the first, but this one also earned significant dollars for me:

Front end organization fee	$ 5,000
Fund-raising fee	23,500
Steady cash flow during operations (approximately $850 per month)	35,700
Sales fee upon sale of business	8,693
Profit (from my 13.3 percent ownership share)	18,080
Approximate interest (on profit being paid out)	4,300
TOTAL EARNINGS:	$95,273

Not too bad. Now the investors. They put up $274,000 and were pleased with their return, too. They enjoyed cash flow from operations, profit from the sale of the business, tax benefits, and are receiving good interest income on some of the profit still being paid out. After recovering their original capital, their average return on investment was 19.45 percent per year, plus tax benefits.

An Office Building Gold Mine

Occasionally, I invest my own personal funds right along with investors. In this next case, I felt that a particular location held promise for an office building. So, I negotiated the purchase of some appropriately zoned land. I used the funds of four other persons in equal shares with mine to buy the land, and to design and build a 24,150-square-foot office building. We sold the building approximately three months after its completion. Here are the results:

Profit upon sale of building (each investor)	$114,800
Commission upon sale (to me exclusively)	52,198
TOTAL EARNINGS:	$166,998

This is an important point. Neither I nor the other people involved would have made anything on this project had we not joined together. None of us had enough money to do this on his own.* But, because I created the investment opportunity and knew how to use OPM, each of us made $114,800 profit and I made an additional $52,198 fee on the project sale. Over the two-and-one-half-year life of this venture, each of us made a 73 percent return per year on our investment, while I made another $52,198 for my initiative. Are you beginning to see why this system works so well?

Tennis, Anyone?

An existing tennis and swim club had several acres of excess land, so the owners and I worked out an attractive and logical way to utilize this land for everyone's benefit. A large lodging complex would be designed and built, and increments of time in the lodging units would be sold to tennis buffs and others for vacation purposes. Operating capital in the amount of $342,000 was required to get the project rolling. For bringing people with these funds together, I earned a $34,200 fee. But the interesting thing here is the potential "after market" for me.

This is a five- to seven-year project; however, my potential earnings from an ownership percentage I was given, and from sales fees, could be in excess of $3 million! Again, it is doubtful that this project could have been started without my help in creating the investment opportunity and bringing together the funds of others. Now, all of us have an opportunity to make very large sums of money from land that was lying fallow.

The American Dream

I think that each one of us, at one time or another, has a certain business or idea that we would give anything to have a

*Throughout this book, I've used the masculine form to eliminate cumbersome, confusing pronoun problems. This usage is not meant to be sexist; it is done simply for readability. In fact, the method presented in this book works successfully for either gender.

chance trying. Usually, we never get the chance — or we don't *take* the first step — because of fear, or lack of money, or both.

One of my recent uses of the system helped two close friends realize their lifelong dream: to own an internationally franchised restaurant and high quality ice cream parlor. Their major difficulty in not going forward had been their questionable ability to borrow the funds for this venture. The risk associated with borrowing bothered them, also. Together, these factors were enough to keep them from getting the business off the ground. They were constantly frustrated because they didn't know how to overcome their problems.

Over a period of several months, I slowly talked them into using OPM. I explained that this would eliminate the need to borrow funds from a bank or other lending institution. As such, it would eliminate the risk of borrowed funds, and would let them get started immediately. They were very excited about my suggestion, so I ended up developing an investment package and raising the required funds for them.

In this instance, I earned a fee for bringing together the funds of others, and for helping my friends develop the investment package itself. I retained no ownership and will not receive anything else. But, I profited immensely by seeing two friends develop, build, and open a business they had been dreaming about for years. I know it will be good for the investors, too. The business is steadily exceeding projections, and my friends already are negotiating a second location in a nearby community. And then, my fee for my contribution was not too bad, either. For the $395,500 of other people's money that I raised for them, I collected $42,974.

As you use the system yourself, you will find that simply raising OPM for someone who needs it for a project is a clean, quick way for you to earn a very good living. Since you are not staying in the venture, you may not have any potential for increasing your net worth beyond the fund-raising fee. But, neither do you have any of the work usually associated with staying involved with a project. You are in and out on a very clean, profitable basis. So, a balance of both methods can be good for you. The main thing is, you win either way.

Fallout

A couple of times now, I have mentioned "fallout." This is a very important aspect of this system, one that will help you on your way to becoming a wealthy, financially independent person. Fallout as used here is the incidental result of looking for and creating investment opportunities, and of working with people in the use of their funds for these opportunities.

The fallout from this profession is in two major areas. First, you will meet a great many people from all walks of life, people whom you never would have met had you not decided to get involved in bettering yourself financially. You will develop personal friendships, and probably some business relationships, too. Association with these individuals — and in some cases their advisers — will give you more self-confidence, a better self-image, a greater sense of purpose to your life. It's a nice benefit of being a syndicator, one that should continue to pay you dividends throughout your life.

The other major aspect of this fallout is the profit opportunity for yourself above and beyond the everyday syndication fees and benefits. By this I mean the good buys, opportunities, and unusual situations you will run into while you are looking to create investment opportunities for others. This fallout in itself can make you a millionaire over a relatively short period of time.

There will be times when you will not want to offer an attractive deal to others. The money required and risk associated are things you can handle on your own. You will want to keep it for yourself.

There also will be situations wherein you may tie up some property or business opportunity in preparation for offering it to others. Then, you discover that the attraction goes away because of timing, economics, or other reasons. You may end up letting the asset go. On the other hand, you may continue to stay with it because you feel the situation will reverse itself again very rapidly. In the latter instance, you suddenly can find yourself with an attractive opportunity that you may just decide to keep for yourself.

Even the apartment buildings that I originally syndicated, then bought for my own account, are examples of the fallout from this business. I originally earned substantial fees and profits from using OPM to buy, operate, and sell these properties. Then, I purchased the buildings and now keep all of the cash flow, tax benefits, and profits for myself. Having originally syndicated these properties gave me inside information on them. Consequently, I could repurchase them with an intimate knowledge of their character and potential, without fear or worry about their economic viability. Some other specific fallout examples follow.

Keeping Some for Yourself

While looking for commercial sites in one community, I found a five-acre, residentially zoned parcel of land that fronted on a major street in a commercial setting. It was a problem piece of property; the owner had attempted to rezone it several times before and had failed. However, I felt confident that I could get it rezoned, and took an option on the parcel at a good price.

I went through the several-month planning process. As expected, I was successful in rezoning the front one-fifth to "Commercial" while the rear four-fifths remained "Residential." This automatically increased the value of the entire parcel because of the radically increased value of the front Commercial portion.

Using OPM, a commercial building now could be developed because of the proper zoning. My two partners and I personally purchased the five-acre parcel at a good price, which had been based on Residential zoning. We then resold the front one-fifth to the investment group for almost what we had paid for the entire parcel. Our price to the investor group was significantly under market value, so it was a "wholesale" deal for them. Yet, we personally owned almost four acres for practically nothing but our efforts. In addition, we received a 35 percent ownership interest in the commercial operation which included the land we had just sold.

Our Land Forever

Here is a very good example of the fallout from this business. I found a Commercial 1.95 acres adjacent to a large K-Mart on the busiest street in a growing southern California community. (This site was to be used for development of another racquetball/fitness club.) I negotiated a sixty-day option to buy the land. This would give me ample time to investigate all aspects of the site, such as business location, utilities, and city requirements.

During my investigation, I discovered that the optionors (the owners) had forgotten to divide off this 1.95 acres from their large fifteen-acre K-Mart parcel. Since they could not sell me an "illegal" parcel, they agreed to perform the land division. During the land division process, I could retain my purchase option for my original $1,000 in option consideration.

The optionors encountered major difficulty and cost during the fifteen months it took them to split the 1.95 acres from their parcel. Throughout this time, racquetball clubs became less attractive as investment vehicles, so the site's future development became questionable. However, this fifteen months also resulted in the completion of a major cross-city thoroughfare, which curved to intersect the busy street at the corner of this property. This made the land a corner parcel; consequently, its value approximately tripled during the period of my option.

My partners and I exercised our purchase option, buying this acreage for only $115,000 even though it had a value of $300,000 at the time. Naturally, we did not use it for a racquetball club. In fact, we decided never to sell this land as it now is in the prime developing spot in this community, and developable land is fast becoming very scarce. We will keep it indefinitely as a continually appreciating asset.

This has become an excellent, income-producing investment. At the time of this writing, we had ground leased the parcel to an office building developer on a long-term basis for $4,150 per month. The rent escalates each year with the Consumer Price Index. (In no event can the rent increase *less than* 7 percent each year, however. This means that in just ten years, we will be receiving a minimum of $8,164 per month from this one investment.) At the end of the ground lease period, the office building complex reverts to us with no compensation going to the developer for the building.

Had I not been in the business of using OPM, I never would have been presented with this opportunity. But, I was interested in creating a good investment opportunity for others, and was actively searching out racquetball club sites for this purpose. Out of this searching effort came this fallout opportunity, this chance to make a lot of money in a way I had not previously envisioned. Are you beginning to see how fallout from this business can help speed you on your way to achieving personal wealth?

Gentlemen Ranchers

Personal relationships made during the OPM process can result in financial fallout as well. One of my investors and I became close personal friends. He and his wife asked me to sell their home and eighty-acre horse ranch in Solvang, California, which I did. After receiving a down payment from the buyer, my friends carried back a large ($975,000) promissory note for the balance of their equity, secured by a second trust deed. (Both trust deeds and mortgages make real property security for money borrowed by the owner of the property. A mortgage is a written contract, whereas a trust deed is a special form of deed.)

One year later, these friends decided to leave this country and return to their homeland, England. They wanted their cash from the note even though it would not pay off for another four years. After trying unsuccessfully to discount their note through traditional means, they asked me to help. They offered to discount the note to $600,000 if the funds could be delivered to them in thirty days.

Based on the current rate of interest being paid on their note, and also on the note payment schedule and terms, the return to purchasers of this discounted note would be almost 34 percent per year. In addition, the buyer had since borrowed an additional $760,000 from a large bank on a third trust deed basis. This made the second trust deed senior to this bank loan, and junior only to a small ($195,000) first trust deed in favor of a savings and loan association. All of these factors, plus the value of the desirable horse ranch property, made this a virtually risk-free transaction.

I personally wanted to take advantage of this high return with low risk myself, but did not have the capital to do so. I again went to the OPM system. Along with some personal funds, I used OPM to come up with the $600,000. All of us are now enjoying this unusually low risk, high return investment in a present market that pays only 8.5 to 9.0 percent for money market funds. Knowing how to use OPM created my personal friendship to begin with, then helped to enable a second investment opportunity come to fruition.

Father and Son

Another case history shows how this syndication business can mushroom. When I first began to use the dollars of others to make money for myself, I started off by working with a father and son team. The father had just quit his executive-level aerospace position. He sensed a real opportunity in buying poorly maintained apartment buildings in low-income areas of Los Angeles, then fixing them up and operating them as rental properties. His idea was to take advantage of the low prices caused by most buyers' fear of owning in these areas, then to give the tenants good quality housing and a reason to have a sense of pride in their community. The son also was in the aerospace industry working full time as a computer programmer. He helped his father initially on a part-time basis, evenings and weekends.

They already had scraped together enough money to buy their first small complex. There were more good purchases in the area that fit their formula, but they could not continue to buy without funds to do so. At this point, a friend and I joined with them. They were to find and manage the buildings; we would raise OPM with which to buy them.

Over a period of approximately three years, we acquired eight apartment complexes with OPM, all of which were very successful. We also acquired several buildings for ourselves along the way. Eventually, my partner and I sold our interests in our own buildings to the father and son, and they began to use the OPM system on their own.

They continued to find, acquire, and operate apartment buildings, but now they were capable of using OPM themselves. Their holdings grew, and the size of their acquisitions increased, too. Now they buy large, three and four hundred unit complexes that take $1.5 million or more in OPM in order to make the down payment. They own and manage almost three thousand units, which makes them one of the largest family-owned and -operated property management firms in southern California.

What about the fallout? Because of their constant searching for bargains or situations with potential, they began to run into extraordinary deals that they could purchase on their own. Some of these were apartment buildings; others involved industrial and farm lands. For example, they came upon a large ranch in San Luis Obispo County, California, which they were able to buy at a good price. By excavating and forming a small lake, and by subdividing, they measurably increased the value of the ranch. Then, they sold off a small portion of the ranch for more than they had paid for the entire parcel, leaving the remaining acreage unencumbered by debt.

Other attractive purchases and shrewd financing arrangements made each of them a multimillionaire. They live in fabulous homes, work when they want to, and are free to travel as much as they choose. They and their immediate family members still exclusively run their property management business. And, all of this was made possible by knowing how to use OPM to make money for themselves.

All right, your imagination is stimulated from these examples. You probably are mentally applying some of them to ideas you have, or to ideas some of your friends may have. You sense a money machine that's always been available to you, but one which you have never before tapped into.

It is clear that just about anything can be started with OPM, and you are beginning to see why this type of activity appeals to investors. You want to start making money with this system as soon as possible. But, before you can start applying this system to some of the ideas bouncing around in your head, you need the answer to one big question bothering you right now. The question is: How does this system work, in detail?

Let's answer your question.

CHAPTER 3

Using OPM to Make Money for Yourself – How It Works

WHENEVER YOU OR anyone else — including large corporations — wants to purchase something, it takes money to do so. Small items, such as clothing, shoes, small pieces of furniture, and groceries are usually paid for in cash, although a credit card or the store's credit for some of these items can be used. Larger purchases, such as cars, boats, houses, land, office buildings, shopping centers, and all types of businesses, also can be paid for in cash, but usually are not. Purchase of these larger items normally is made with a down payment of cash (equity). The balance of the purchase price is owed to the seller, or put up by a lender (debt).

For example, a small rental house is purchased as follows:

$90,000 purchase price
−15,000 cash down payment (equity)
$75,000 balance owed (debt)

Equity is the money value of an item that is in excess of claims against it. It is the ownership value in that item. Quite obviously, if we purchased the above rental house on a reasonable basis, our equity (money value) is $15,000. This equity should grow as the property appreciates in value, and as the loan is paid down (equity buildup). The equity and debt together equal 100 percent of the value of the house, or

$90,000, at the time of purchase. If you were making this purchase, you would have to come up with only $15,000 cash; however, you would have to make the payments on the $75,000 debt remaining against the property.

But, what if you do not have the $15,000 cash? Or, maybe you can't make the monthly payments on the rental house (the loan payments will be more than the amount of the rental income). The price is low and this is a very good deal, but you just cannot swing the transaction on your own. What can you do to preserve it?

In this very simplified illustration, you might consider getting together four of your relatives or friends who, along with you, each put up $3,000 to buy the house. Together, you could cover the monthly payment deficit, and one of you might be willing to do the minor property management and record keeping involved. Each of you would own 20 percent of the equity, and your personal cash outlay is now reduced to $3,000 instead of $15,000. True, you own only 20 percent instead of 100 percent but you still will share in the probable appreciation of the property. You will also receive 20 percent of the tax benefits of owning this rental property. And most important, you are taking advantage of this good deal; you are not letting it slip through your fingers.

Now, let's take this one step farther. Instead of five of you each putting up $3,000 and one of you doing the property management, why not have the other four people each put up one-fourth of the money needed, or $3,750. You agree to do the management for the group in return for a 20 percent ownership interest. After all, you found the rental house and negotiated the purchase price and terms. The other four people want to be passive owners anyway. They don't want to be involved in the management or decision making; they just want a good return on their dollars.

Now what do you have? You still own 20 percent of the rental house, but you have not put one cent of your own money into its purchase. In addition, if you have a real estate license, you may even make money because you can receive a commission from the seller for arranging the purchase of his home.

Taking this yet one step farther, you can have each of your

partners contribute a little more, say $4,000 each, and pay yourself a $1,000 organization fee. A management fee for renting up and maintaining the property also can be charged. Then, you may be able to receive a sales commission upon the resale of the property. Naturally, you also will receive your 20 percent of any profits that result from the property's sale.

You need not worry about having to put up any of your funds to pay any monthly deficit, either. This can be handled by raising more money initially as a reserve. Or, you can have each investor agree to contribute more money periodically for this purpose.

This is a very basic, simplified example of using OPM to make money for yourself, but I think you probably are catching on to the idea. (By the way, many people have done exactly what I have explained in this example; it's easier than you think to accomplish.) You can see now that there are two basic OPM formulas. If the investment is purchased by using all cash and no debt, then the formula is:

Equity = 100 percent of funds required

If the investment is purchased by using a cash down payment, with some debt left over as in the rental house example, then the formula is:

Equity + Debt = 100 percent of funds required

In either case, the amount of money you have to come up with personally is *zero*. All funds required are put up by others. You created the investment opportunity and will manage it. In return for these services, you receive a promotional ownership interest plus all the applicable fees and commissions.

This type of "financing" has become more important than ever before, because of the high interest rates and unattractive terms of institutional loans in today's economy. This concept allows you to put together capital sums to buy almost anything, or to start just about any business. It allows you to control assets of high value with a tie-in to the profits. It allows you to be financially successful by working with a limited clientele (friends, neighbors, relatives, work associates, referrals, etc.). And all this will help you build your estate even while you are using the system again and again.

Investor Pooling of Resources

What I have just described is the pooling of resources by several individuals and/or entities. High equity (cash) demands require a pooling of money very frequently if a project is to get off the ground. Many small businesses are started this way. You may want to start a small shoe repair shop, or a donut shop, or a shaver repair booth, but you do not have the $5,000 or $15,000 needed for inventory, rent, and working capital. So, you raise $1,000 or $2,000 or more each from some friends because your idea is good and all of you can see the potential for profits. They receive a percentage ownership and the opportunity for profits they otherwise would not have; you get a salary from the business plus an ownership percentage for creating the investment opportunity.

The possibilities are unlimited. Pooled resources can be used to sponsor a boxer or a singer, make a movie, buy equipment for leasing, purchase stocks and bonds, buy or start all kinds of businesses, acquire rental properties, raw land, and other real estate, and on and on. Just recently, pooled resources were even used to search for and recover sunken treasure from the ocean floor.

Even life insurance companies have jumped into the field. Giants such as Travelers, John Hancock, Phoenix Mutual Life, Penn Mutual, Aetna Life & Casualty, and Connecticut General are offering ownership shares in apartments, office buildings, and other real estate investments. These life insurance company offerings use pooled resources, too, although they generally involve millions of dollars in each case.

Most individuals do not have enough money, or do not have the interest or ability to do these things on their own. But every one of them has that basic human desire to get ahead, to get in on the good deal. So someone — you — pools their money and uses it for the investment opportunity found or created.

In some cases, you may find or create the opportunity and be involved in the functioning of the investment during its life. This gives you the opportunity for various fees, and also a percentage ownership in the investment. In other cases, you just may bring the investors' money together for someone else who created or has the investment opportunity. You still receive various fees, but you may or may not end up with an ownership interest. You win *either* way, however; you make out very handsomely in terms of monies earned for yourself.

Why are people willing to pool their resources and let someone else manage their money? Well, there are many good reasons for this; the main ones are described below.

- **No management responsibility.** This is the primary reason. Most investors are passive. They do not want to make decisions or be hassled with any details of the investment. They are too involved with their own jobs. They are too busy trying to make money; they don't have the time or interest to manage it. They just want to sit back and wait for their returns.
- **Limited liability.** If the investment does not turn out well, the investors can lose their money; however, if the venture is structured properly, their investment amount is the maximum they can lose. They generally are insulated from liability for loans or other debts/responsibilities of the project, except under certain unique circumstances.
- **Investment benefits.** They still can retain most all the benefits of individual investing. Yet, they do not have to put up with the aggravations of individual investing, such as research, negotiations, management, and asset liquidation.
- **Participation in high value projects.** Investors have the chance for ownership in large projects. They can receive better yields than on smaller, modestly valued, individually owned investments. The larger scale provides negotiating strength and efficiency. It also means less competition because there are fewer buyers capable of funding high value projects.
- **Profiting together.** Other than front end fees and possibly sales commissions, the investors' profit comes out before, or with, yours. If they profit, you profit, and vice versa. You can win together. Investors like this. They do not want you

to profit first, but usually are glad to have you make money if it means that they are making money, too.

There are many other reasons for investors wanting to pool their funds, including attractive tax benefits and a chance for windfall profits. Whatever the reasons, the facts are that thousands of persons let others use their money each year with the hope that they will benefit from the transaction. The facts also are that you, as the one who uses the funds of others, always should make a significant chunk of dollars each time you use the system.

There is no reason for you to sit back any longer and think about all the others you know who are making good money. There is a tremendous market — a GROWING market — at your back door that you have not had the chance to tap until now. In fact, it's an unbelievably large market, as the next two paragraphs point out.

On April 4, 1982, an article entitled "Boom in Securities Syndication Noted" appeared in the Sunday edition of the *Los Angeles Times.* It discussed comments by Kenneth Jay Gain, 1982 president of the Real Estate Securities Syndication Institute. The article stated that Mr. Gain estimated 1981 investment in public and private securities syndication at over *$14 billion,* and this during poor economic times! But the really amazing statistics in this article were that only $3,587,000,000 were invested in public syndication. Yet, *private* syndication investment dollars were estimated at *three times* that of public investment, or approximately $10,761,000,000!

Another article in the September 4, 1983, edition of the *San Francisco Examiner* revealed additional insight into this subject. The article described how this trend to pooling of investor resources for investment purposes is expanding. In the article, the National Association of Securities Dealers projected 1983 public syndication investment at $6.7 billion nationally. And, the article also pointed out that the value of private syndications was estimated at up to *four times* that of public syndications. This means that *private* syndication investment will have climbed to approximately *$26.8 billion*, or two and one-half times the amount invested privately just two years earlier! And, it is this lucrative private investment sector that I am talking to you about in this book.

Syndication Defined

There are some new words in the preceding paragraphs. Don't let them bother you. Securities, in the sense used, refers to ownership interests in investment properties, both real and personal. (Basically, real property consists of land, buildings, and everything affixed permanently to them; personal property consists of everything else.)

The term "syndication" is important because we have been talking about it all along. Syndication is the use of other people's money through the "pooling" of their money. More specifically, syndication is the uniting of the two or more persons in an association, under central management, to carry out a particular transaction for profit. As a syndicator, you create, analyze, and structure the investment opportunity, package the investment documents, raise the funds, organize and manage the investment, and share in the profits and other benefits of full involvement. (In California, persons who are syndicators must apply for and receive a certificate as a broker/dealer. There is, however, an exemption for real estate brokers acting as syndicators under certain conditions.)

On occasion, you could perform just some of these syndication functions. You might only analyze and structure an investment opportunity, package the investment documents, and raise the required funds for someone else who organizes and manages the investment. In this case, each of you is a syndicator, as each is performing part of the syndication process. You are the "packaging/fund-raising syndicator"; your client is the "organizing/managing syndicator." If you were not in the picture, however, the organizing/managing syndicator would, of course, perform all the syndication tasks.

The terms "public" and "private" refer to the way the syndication is put together. Generally, putting together a "public" syndication is a costly and lengthy process. It requires registration with the department of securities or corporations in your particular state, or with the national Securities and Exchange Commission, or with both agencies. In general, "private" syndication is exempt from these costly, cumbersome registration requirements as long as you follow the guidelines estabished. We'll look more closely at these private syndication guidelines in Chapters 7 and 11.

The above-noted articles are telling us two very important things. First, even in a dismal economic period, over *$14 billion* was invested by, basically, private individuals. Regardless of the times, people want in on that good deal. This investment then *increased* about two and one-half times in the following two-year period. Second, the great majority of syndicators shy away from the costly public syndication process; they use private syndications. They use private syndications because they are much quicker, easier, and less expensive to put together. This private method is the one we will be following throughout this book.

The Basic Road Map

You will not have to feel your way along as I did, and as others have had to do in the past. Instead, the detailed steps of the syndication process will be laid out for you beginning in the next chapter. All the instructions can be summarized into six basic steps, however. These six steps are your road map to the successful use of this system.

1. Search, see, and listen
2. Analyze and structure
3. Tie up the deal
4. Package the opportunity
5. Obtain OPM
6. Close the deal; receive fees/commissions

Six basic steps with dollars for you in the last one. And remember, these dollars are not small.

What about time? The time is somewhat variable depending upon the opportunity itself; that is, more time is required if the opportunity is large and/or complicated, or possibly if the amount of OPM needed is large. (But not necessarily; I once put together one of my largest ventures in terms of dollars needed in just over three weeks.) You probably will start out applying the system on a small basis, so I would plan on one to two months for your first project.

If two months sounds like a long time to you, don't forget that you should be collecting several thousand dollars for your efforts. Depending on what you apply the system to this first time, you also may start receiving cash flow, and be sharing in the increase in value. And, you can do this several times a year with the fees and future earnings getting larger each time as you become more confident with the use of the system.

So, two months really isn't that much time. Unless, of course, you don't do anything productive during that period. Then, it can be a lot of time — *wasted time.* And, time is one thing that can't be recaptured.

All right. You have a feeling for how many different ways there are for you to make money each time you use this system. You have seen some actual examples of the system in use, and what the results have been for me and for the people who gave me their money in each case. You have learned about the all important "fallout" that you can expect from being active in this field.

You know about investor pooling of resources (syndication), why people are willing to give you their money for investment opportunities, and how big the market for the use of this system really is. And now you have a preliminary road map for using the system. So, let's take this road map and expand it; let's dissect each item so that every step of the way is completely and clearly laid out for you. Let's get down to business.

CHAPTER 4

Getting Started—Search, See, and Listen

AT THIS POINT, some of you may be thinking that syndication looks like a lot of work. Others are thinking it may be too complicated for them. The bare fact is that some of you do not have the courage to "step up to the plate," to grab hold of this opportunity and wring out the multitude of benefits that are there for you. You just will let that inborn desire for financial security die away inside you again. Why? Because you do not think conditions are right, or you are afraid you might fail, or you are not sure, or because of any number of other reasons. But all of these are not reasons: they are excuses.

It would be great if you knew in advance exactly how things were going to turn out. But if you keep waiting for safety and certainty at every step, you can tell financial security good-bye. Turn it around. Not knowing exactly how things are going to turn out will give you the chance to discover new things, new ideas, new techniques which will lead to improvement of your position in life. In other words, you *cannot* lose by trying this system; you only can win.

The biggest hurdle most of us have to overcome in beginning something new is thinking about *how* to get started. Yet, the very first step in starting something new is to make a firm decision *to* get started. Then, once you have made this decision, stick by it and make it work. The facts and figures you will need to tell you exactly where you are going will come easily now because you have a goal, a purpose, a commitment. So make the decision to get started now. After this decision is made, all you have to do is to digest the step-by-step instructions beginning right here, then put them into action.

Where to Look and What to Look For

To use this system, you need something to apply it to; a project, an opportunity to make money, something to syndicate. Your job at this point is to search for a product.

Where should you search?

What should you search for?

The best answer to the first question is *in your own backyard*. That's right. You will find the opportunity you are looking for in your own small town, your own large city, or wherever you may live.

The answer to the second question is *anything that makes sense.* Anything that shows that the people putting up the money should make out well, and that also shows a handsome fee (and other monies) in it for you.

What about real estate? Many books have been written about how to make money in real estate. There is nothing wrong with a real estate project. In fact, one of the model packages I have included for you in this book is for a small real estate syndication. An investment opportunity similar to this model may be good for you to arrange as a syndication because it can be put together with very little money from others. It can be done rather quickly and easily. It also gives you an up-front fee, a share of profits, a management fee (if you want it), and possibly two sales commissions.

But, in no way should you restrict yourself to real estate projects solely. There are an unlimited number of other opportunities you can create or be involved in that can make big money for you and for your investors. Some of these you may create. Others may be the ideas of other people whom you are helping insofar as putting the deal together (for a fee, of course). Following is a partial list of just a few of the possibilities that you might want to think about (for you to initiate, or for you to work on with others):

1. Any new or existing small business, including but not limited to the following:

   a. Shoe shop
   b. Donut shop
   c. Car wash/polish service
   d. Delivery/courier service
   e. Small food shop (pizza, bagel, sandwich, cookie, candy, yogurt, etc.)
   f. T-shirt store
   g. Clothing boutique
   h. Batting cages
   i. Copy service
   j. Furniture repair/refinish
   k. Book shop
   l. Appliance repair
   m. Day care center
   n. Building materials
   o. Landscape service
   p. Secretarial service

2. Any new product someone wants to develop (cars, toys, fixtures, tools, games, etc.)
3. Group purchase of stocks, bonds, precious metals, etc.
4. A dinner restaurant, or a fast-food outlet (either a unique one, or a franchise such as McDonald's, Wendy's, Taco Bell).
5. An ice cream parlor franchise, or any kind of franchise
6. Small, or large, ranch of any kind (cattle, horse, citrus, fruit, nuts, nursery, even wind farming, etc.)
7. Oil drilling/production, minerals mining, etc.
8. Existing, or new, single family homes, duplexes, apartments, condos, etc.
9. Existing, or new, commercial and industrial (shopping centers, office complexes, industrial buildings, etc.)
10. Any type of raw land for future appreciation or development
11. Existing, or new, recreation facilities (e.g., aerobic dance studio, tennis courts/club, full fitness club, miniature golf, work-out/self-defense gyms)
12. Resort facility operation

13. Discount purchases of trust deeds/mortgages
14. Buying and leasing of all types of equipment
15. Publishing and marketing a book, manual, or how-to kit
16. Breeding and selling dogs, parakeets, or other animals
17. Starting up a video games arcade

Clearly, there are as many opportunities out there as there are real and personal property items, as well as business situations, in the world. That's why I have to stop the list; noting down all of the possibilities would fill this book and then some.

Your goal is to find something to syndicate which will show a projected return for the investors — a good return — and fees and profits for you. You can search out a specific kind of opportunity or project. You also can keep your eyes open and eventually see or run across an attractive project. And, you can keep your ears open as you undoubtedly will hear (and may already have) a friend, neighbor, or acquaintance say, "If only I could get some money together, I could make a fortune by developing a drag strip outside of town." The point is, you have made your decision to proceed and are attentive to what is going on around you; consequently, you will find your project much faster than you think and it will be very close to you, too.

Advertising Pays Off

In your search for a product, place an inexpensive, small classified ad in the newspaper. The ad can read something like, "Individual has dollars for product or business"; or, "Private party wants small or medium income property"; or, "Will buy trust deeds at a discount"; or, "Have capital to invest in business venture." Add your telephone number, and you will be surprised at the response.

Check out all the leads you receive, at least at first. This will increase your awareness of what is available, and will add to your storehouse of knowledge about businesses, products, and properties. Ask people to send you any descriptions/financial projections about their deals, and you will quickly see how others analyze things in which they are interested. You will be taking their deal "under advisement," of course, so you will have no obligation to proceed with anything that comes your way unless you want to. A little ad like this should cost only a few dollars, which will come back to you anyway when you put your first deal together. Be sure to use advertising as one of your methods in your search when first starting out.

Real Estate and Mortgage Brokers

If you decide you want to concentrate in the real estate area in the beginning, contact all the real estate brokers and agents you can, directly and through referrals from your friends. Get to know as many as you can. Pay particularly close attention to the ones who call you back and act as if they are interested in working with you. Let them know what you are looking for (e.g., single family dwellings, duplexes, apartment buildings, raw land, industrial or commercial income properties, business opportunities, or trust deeds at a discount). Try to look at everything they come up with. You will begin to learn a great deal, and they will know that you are serious about putting something together.

Though mortgage brokers deal mainly in "paper" (loan brokerage, trust deeds/mortgages, foreclosures, etc.), they all know and hear of good deals. They know of properties in foreclosure, and trust deeds offered at a discount. They all have clients, and know of others who want to get something off the ground and need help. They can be an excellent source of leads for product and other opportunities.

Real estate appraisers are another excellent source of help. They are constantly compiling data from previous actual sales to use as comparables for current appraisal jobs. Plus, they look at new listings of properties for sale to determine what sellers think their properties are worth. Because of this, not only do they have a vast knowledge of what's available in an area, but they quickly can tell you if the property you are considering is priced too high, or is a bargain. You'll find that they usually are willing to help you because your interest in acquiring property will probably result in a new client for them.

Scanning the classified ad section of your local newspaper can be especially rewarding, too. Look under the Income Property, Business Opportunity, Trust Deed (or Mortgage), and Houses for Sale headings. When you find something that looks promising, enlist the help of the real estate agent in analyzing it, as he will be more than glad to do so for his potential commission. Just remember that his interest is different from yours, so be thorough in asking your questions, and try to verify his answers with other agents as a check.

Your County Recorder's Office

This can be an effective way to investigate directly specific properties that interest you. It speeds up the process of finding something, and may save you on the price and commission by going direct to the owner of the property.

As you scout the areas that interest you, note the address of the property, or the location if raw land, and add any other information you can. After several locations (ten to fifteen) have been pinpointed this way, go to the County Recorder's Office where you can get names and addresses of all the owners of the properties.

At this point, you can contact the property owners by phone or by letter. Ask them if they are interested in selling their property. If the answer is no, then move on to the next prospect; if it is yes, you can begin negotiating on the property. Just because the owner did not have his property up for sale on a formal basis does not mean that he is not willing to sell it. This initiative on your part can put even more dollars in your pocket.

Listen and Ask

Keep your ears open. You are bound to hear a friend, neighbor, business associate, or someone else talk about his idea or dream. Maybe it's a piece of land that has potential, but the person cannot keep up the payments, or he needs money and a partner to develop the land to its fullest potential. You might hear one of your friends or relatives talk about that laundromat he knows will be a gold mine, if only he can get some money together to do it. (I hear probably one or two of these comments each week.) And, once you have used this system a few times, people will start coming to you with their ideas.

Do not be bashful about asking people questions either. Ask your friends if they have any ideas of how to make money from a business or product. Your use of this system of using OPM may be just the answer they are looking for.

After I first started using this system, I went back to the defense industry company where I had previously worked. I asked many of the four thousand–plus engineers and other employees if they had any money-making ideas. I was amazed! About one out of every two people had some scheme or business they knew would make money if only they had the time and funds to devote to it. I also asked a friend who works at a large government base to do the same thing, then to let me know what people told him. Again, I ended up with a lot of ideas and prospects, only I had someone else get them for me this time.

You will find that most people who are out there working for a wage have a product, service, or small business idea in their head. They know they will never get rich working for an hourly wage or salary. Again, it's that old burning desire to get ahead, to get in on that good deal. That desire is what will get you the project you need, as well as the people who will put up their money to try it.

You also should assemble a list of people you know, or know of, who own income properties — residential, commercial, or industrial. Ask them if they are interested in selling the property. If they are not, ask them for referrals of others they may know of who have similar properties they would like to sell. Keep expanding this list and working with it, because people have a habit of changing their minds more frequently than you might expect.

Collect Data

When you hear of or find an income property that may be of interest to you, always ask for a set-up (a "facts" sheet giving income, expenses, and financing data). If the project is anything other than an income property, ask for as much financial information as possible. This includes profit and loss statements (or projections of profits and losses if it is a new business, product, or service), and any information about the existing or new financing required.

You will need these data in order to analyze the project (we will cover this in the next chapter). You also can use these data for learning purposes. The more you look at and digest, the more confidence you will have. You will be able to quickly weed out the deals that do not make any sense, thereby saving you time and effort in your searching.

Summary

Very important: You do not want to make a mistake in selecting a project just because you are anxious to get that first one under your belt. It is important to make many inquiries, to investigate many properties and potential business opportunities. In other words, you do not want to end up with a bad project, one that will be bad for you and bad for the individuals putting up the money. You want winners. You will end up making more, and each new deal will become easier because you will have a stable of satisfied investors that gets larger and larger.

The first project probably will be the most sensitive for you to put together in terms of overanxiousness and lack of experience. So, be extra-cautious this first time. Do not move too quickly. Look at the opportunity from all sides. Ask many questions to draw out all the potential problems. And then sit down to analyze and structure it in detail.

CHAPTER 5

Analyzing and Structuring

LIKE A COOK preparing Thanksgiving dinner, you need the right ingredients and approach to have a successful project. Cook the bird too little, and the dinner is bad. Likewise, skimp on the time you spend evaluating a potential project, and your project may be bad.

When you have narrowed down your choice of potential projects, you need to calculate the expected return on investment several times for each one of those in the final running. Use different sets of forecasted income and expenses each time. See which project makes the most sense. "Cook" your bird well. Only then can you be relatively sure of that one project you choose to pursue.

Regardless of the type of deal at which you are looking, you want to end up with answers to the following three questions:

1. What is the probable income (if any)?
2. What are the forecasted expenses?
3. What is the forecasted return on dollars invested?

Remember, you probably will receive more than just a front end fee in most cases. You may be entitled to sales fees, part of the cash flow, management fees, a percentage of the ownership profits, and other fringe benefits. So, this analysis is just as important for you as it is for the investors.

The answer to the third question is the most important one. You need this third answer to be able to know how to structure the investment; that is, how much of the total projected return can you keep for yourself? In other words, if the total projected return is $30,000, and $20,000 of this gives the investor a good return on his invested funds, then you can cut yourself in for the $10,000 balance.

Making a nice fee or fees up front is great, but it's your percentage of profits that will keep building up your assets and net worth. Yet, it's possible to justify only so much for yourself while leaving the deal still saleable to the investors. This third answer will enable you to back into this percentage, the calculation for which I will show you later in this chapter.

A Small Coffee/Sandwich Shop

We'll go through a couple of different examples so that you are comfortable with the analyzing and structuring process. This is an example of a very small project. In this hypothetical situation, let's say that one of your friends has been talking to you about a small coffee/sandwich shop. He is confident that he can make a good living if he can come up with the funds with which to get it off the ground. He has his eye on some storefront space for lease in a good shopping center, and he's anxious to get moving. He is having difficulty obtaining a bank loan of $51,000, however. The bank is nervous about his ability to repay the loan, and he does not want to put up the equity in his home as collateral as required by the bank. And even if he did acquire the loan, the commercial loan interest rate is high. Much of his profit would be eaten up by the high monthly payments required to service the debt.

Your friend shows you some numbers that he has obtained by thoroughly investigating other comparable small coffee shops (see projections, following). The information seems reasonable, and the indicated profit is substantial. You tell him that by using other people's money, he won't need a bank loan, so his monthly debt service can be eliminated completely. He will have to give up some of the ownership in return for the funds, but he still can have complete control over the operation. He can pay himself a salary out of the gross revenues. And, if this shop is successful, he may be able to start a second one on his own.

He likes the idea. You tell him approximately how much you will want for your packaging/fund-raising services, reminding him that your fees will be paid out of the funds of others, not by him directly. You also want a small piece of his part of the profits, to which he agrees. The entire arrangement is contingent upon your analysis of his numbers, and of the project as a whole.

NOTE: This is a simplified example of a situation whereby you will only analyze, structure, and package the investment, and raise the funds for a fee. You will have no further responsibility for the venture other than to collect and spend your share of your friend's profits. In a subsequent example in this chapter, we will look at a situation wherein you will be completely involved with all syndication aspects of the venture, but your fees and profits will be much higher, too.

After you have spent some time verifying your friend's data and have collected your own, you are ready to analyze the deal. Following are the facts and figures put together by your friend, and verified by you. (His figures show the debt service that would be required in the event of a bank loan.) Your job now is to see if the venture appears to be sound, if it will support a good return for the investors, for your friend, and for you.

All data collected should be arranged in a Projected Income Statement format, as follows:

Coffee/Sandwich Shop

PROJECTED INCOME STATEMENT

(First 12 Months Operation)

Projected gross annual sales revenue (based on other shops' open hours and revenue/customer)		$178,000
Operating expenses (variable costs):		
Cost of goods sold	$49,840	
Wages, including all taxes	35,600	
Paper supplies (1½ percent)	2,670	
Cleaning, other supplies (1½ percent)	2,670	
Repair/maintenance (1 percent)	1,780	
Advertising/Promotion (2 percent)	3,560	
Outside services, other (2 percent)	3,560	
Operating Expenses (fixed costs):		
Management compensation	$24,000	
Leasehold rent	12,600	
Utilities	4,800	
Telephone	1,975	
Accounting/legal	550	
Insurance (including Workman's Compensation)	2,250	
Real/pers. prop. taxes, permits (estimate)	1,750	
Debt service ($51,000 @ 18 percent, 15 yrs.)	9,856	
TOTAL OPERATING EXPENSES:		157,461
NET OPERATING INCOME (CASH FLOW):		$ 20,539

On surface, everything looks good. You have verified his data by talking to his restaurant sources. You also have interviewed two of your friends who own similar coffee shop operations, and have copies of their detailed profit and loss statements. All the numbers check out. Since your collective numbers are based on the experience of these other owners of similar establishments, and because their expense figures have been increased to be conservative, you feel comfortable with these projections.

Your friend wants to go forward. He sees that he is able to pay himself $24,000 per year, and his forecast still shows a $20,539 net profit from operations. While all this looks good, however, he still needs some capital to make this venture a reality. His capital needs in order to open up the shop are as follows:

a. Leasehold improvements construction (including plumbing, electrical, etc.)	$17,475
b. Interior equipment and decor (tables, chairs, dishwear, stove/grill, etc.)	16,175
c. Rent and utility deposits, permits	3,800
d. Opening inventory	3,350
e. Initial insurance, advertising	3,700
f. Beginning working capital, miscellaneous	6,500
TOTAL CAPITAL REQUIRED:	$51,000

Your friend is willing to take in partners and to work for the $24,000 salary, especially if he can share in the net profit indicated. You know that his $9,856 per year debt service projection can be eliminated right off the top by using OPM, so the new indicated net profit would be $9,856 more, or $30,395. You also know that you want 12 percent of the money you raise for him, plus 12 percent of his personal share of the net profits as your fee.

With the above in mind, you continue your analysis based on the venture being a syndication:

a. Estimated legal fee for syndication legal agreement		$2,000
Estimated fee for accountant's financial review		200
Cost of printing and binding syndicate document package		300
TOTAL ADDITIONAL CASH REQUIRED:		$2,500
b. Basic cash needs	$51,000	
Additional cash needs	2,500	
NEW TOTAL CASH:	$53,500	

c. Plus: Fee of 12 percent of capital (your fee):

$$.88x = \$53{,}500$$
$$x = \frac{\$53{,}500}{.88}$$
$$x = \$60{,}800 = \text{Total OPM needed}$$

You know now that if you raised $60,800 for your friend, you would receive an immediate fee of 12 percent, or $7,296. He would be able to pay all legal, accounting, and printing costs, and would still net a total of $51,000, which would enable him to see his coffee shop project become a reality. But, you have one more very important step to go through: You must see if this whole transaction makes *sense* for the investors and your friend, and if so, on what basis. This is part of the structuring involved.

There is an indicated profit of $30,395. Some of this must be used to give the investors an attractive return on their money. The return must be more than they could get just by leaving their funds in a bank savings account, a money market fund, or some other fairly safe investment. You feel that anything over 25 percent would be attractive to friends, neighbors, and business contacts to whom you would show this venture. It would be even better if you could represent a 30 percent or 35 percent per year return, since a coffee shop operation has more risk associated with it than some other investments. It also is an asset with less sales appeal than an income property which almost certainly will appreciate in value (and this one may not), so the current return must be high to justify an investment. Consequently, you decide to use a target 35 percent return for your analysis.

Will the indicated profit support a 35 percent return to the investors? Based on the $60,800 they invest, a 35 percent return would be $21,280 a year. At least this amount can be expected to be available since there is $30,395 of indicated net profit each year. Their $21,280 is approximately 67 percent of the total profit, so by stretching a little, the overall syndication structure possibly can be 70 percent of the profits to the investors, and 30 percent to your friend. This would work as follows:

Investors:

$$\$30{,}395 \text{ profit} \times .70 = \frac{\$21{,}277}{\$60{,}800} = 34.995 \text{ percent per year}$$

Your Friend:

$30,395 profit x .30 =	$ 9,118	
	−1,094	your share
	$ 8,024	
plus salary	24,000	
TOTAL EARNINGS:	$32,024	

Under current federal tax codes, there will be a small amount of depreciation and investment tax credit on the restaurant equipment. This can be shared by the investors and your friend, or can be given to the investors. In any case, the investors reasonably can expect to receive about 35 percent per year cash return on their investment, plus some sheltering of this income through allowable deductions. This obviously is a good return on investment, especially when they do not have to lift a finger or put in any time on the business. And, it far surpasses the 8.5 percent annual money market return currently available to them.

What about your friend? Right now he is sitting in a dead-end job that may pay less than the $32,024 he can expect from this business. Or, maybe he does not have a job at all. Either way, this would give him something in which to sink his teeth, something that could develop into a chain of profitable businesses for him. He can get it off the ground with OPM, without an obligation to repay these funds, without using his house or other assets as collateral as he would have to do in order to get a bank loan. He is very happy for the chance to try this out.

And what about you? For very little work and time, you will be pocketing $7,296. You also will be setting yourself up to receive about $91.00 per month, which is your share of the owner's profit. This monthly income, although small, can go on indefinitely, and should increase with time as the restaurant business increases and prices rise. Once the funds are raised, your participation is over, too. No continuing responsibility, yet you have income as long as the business is open and profitable.

Obviously, this is a good deal for everyone concerned. From your standpoint, this is a small venture. But a small one is a good place to start. And again, you can do this in your spare time, or on a full-time basis. Most important, you can do this as many times a year as you choose. So, if you put together five little projects like this one on a part-time basis, you now are looking at $36,000 or more a year just in fees. In addition, who knows how much more in profit sharing or other cash flow benefits you may receive.

A Residential Income Property Project

This is an example of a larger project. It includes a very detailed analysis, possibly more detailed than you may actually need to perform. But, the grounding you receive here should enable you to look comfortably at anything that comes your way.

With this type of deal, your fees and profits are substantially greater than in the coffee shop example. In fact, in this example, I will show you how using this system only one time can earn you over $207,000. This is a hypothetical situation; however, we (co-partners and I) have earned in excess of this amount in similar income property ventures using this same analysis and similar structure. Much more can be earned from a project larger than the one used in this example. But, let's get into this specific example and see what it can do for you.

Being interested in possibly syndicating a residential income property, you checked with four local information sources to investigate the apartment building situation in your area. These sources were:

a. Chamber of Commerce
b. City Planning Department
c. Two professional property management firms

d. Real estate people (the Board of Realtors and several individual real estate brokers specializing in income properties)

The Chamber of Commerce gave you good, current demographic data which verified that incoming business and industry would continue to uphold this as a good rental area. The data also verified that the percentage of the total population living in apartment complexes was rising steadily. This factor was attributed to the radical slowdown in apartment house construction caused by high interest rates and a lack of suitably zoned land. At City Hall, the director of planning discussed the slowdown in construction from his viewpoint, and agreed that there was a severe shortage of rental units in the area.

Meetings with the professional property management firms' office managers gave you a wealth of information on apartment building revenues, expenses, rental rates, and vacancy factors. (They are happy to provide this information because you represent a probable client for them, once you acquire your building.) You pinned down the fact that there was only a 1 percent vacancy factor in the area. Subsequent meetings with the Board of Realtors' staff and with individual real estate brokers shed additional light on the situation. These sources verified the property management firms' data. They also verified that unattractive buildings in lower- and lower-middle-income neighborhoods generally could be purchased for less than buildings in other areas. So, you concentrated your search in these types of neighborhoods.

In Chapter 4, I suggested that you use your County Recorder's Office to get the names and addresses of owners of properties you felt had potential for profits on a syndication basis. I recommended that you then contact the owners to ask them if they had any interest in selling their properties. You did this, and came up with some interesting possibilities. Let's assume that one of the owners did, indeed, have an interest in moving his property. He just happened to be thinking about selling out and retiring when you called.

Contrary to the previous coffee shop example, you will be staying in this investment for a management fee and an ownership percentage. Your task in this analysis and structuring effort is the same as with the coffee shop venture, except this time the management fees and ownership percentage you are trying to justify will end up being for you.

In the analysis of this project, I will assume that you have a real estate salesman's license placed with a broker friend who gives you the total commissions you earn, or that you have a broker's license yourself. While it is not necessary to have a real estate license, it is an advantage when some of the deals involve real estate. I think this will be apparent to you as the analysis unfolds.

The property you found is a twenty-two-unit apartment building in reasonably good repair. Checking with the resident manager, you find that there are presently two vacancies. Some more discussion with the manager reveals that all units are generally full, however, and that units rent quickly in this area.

The owner agrees to pay you a 5 percent sales commission (instead of the 6 to 7 percent common in most transactions of this type) if you find a buyer for his property. This saves him at least 1 percent and all the aggravations of listing and showing the property to many different would-be buyers and agents. He will accept a 25 percent down payment on a $655,000 sale price. His asking price is 8.75 times the current gross income. (A "gross income multiplier" rule of thumb is used in obtaining a quick feeling for values of residential multiple-unit income properties.)

Based on your previous discussions with the real estate brokers, you know that buildings of this type generally sell for 8.5 to 9.0 times the gross revenue. As such, you feel that the owner's asking price is reasonable, but you also detect that he is flexible about price, terms, and conditions. After several discussions, the owner finally agrees to sell for a price of $600,500 (8.01 times the gross) with a down payment of $108,000 (18 percent of the purchase price, reasonably good leverage). (Incidentally, this is a very realistic price. Properties still can be purchased at these levels or less, particularly in certain parts of the country. Occasionally, purchases like this can be made even in the high value southern California area. Not too long ago, I bought three apartment buildings in Los

Angeles, California, at gross multipliers of 7.11, 6.95, and 6.92.)

Regarding the financing, there is a first loan secured by a mortgage from an insurance company. This loan is $320,000 at 9.75 percent interest, and it can be assumed. The owner agrees to take back his equity in a second mortgage for the $172,500 balance, at 10.5 percent interest only for seven years. Armed with these facts, and with the rent rolls and expenses for the last two years' operation, you are ready to begin your analysis.

NOTE: This entire exercise can be completed on one 8½x11-inch piece of paper, so it is a very compact analysis. In order more fully and clearly to indicate how it should be done, however, I am going to do it on a step-by-step basis for you over the next several pages.

Step One: Forecast Annual Operating Expenses and Income. Checking with your previous information sources and with others in the business, you verify that the expenses paid by the owner are about what they should be. Some variable expenses such as maintenance and replacement may prove to be higher for you in order to keep the apartments in better condition, so you plan to budget for more expense in these areas. (Replacement costs will be minimal, though, as most units are unfurnished.) Also, you plan to accomplish the property management supervision yourself, so you want to build in a nominal professional property management fee of 6 percent of the gross income.

You will break out your projected property tax expense separately. This way, all other expenses can be increased 10 percent annually without affecting the property tax number. (The 10 percent increase is used to realistically forecast each succeeding year's operating performance in the Annual Income Statement, in Step Four of this analysis.) The property tax expense will not increase more than slightly from its base of 1.0 percent of the purchase price (in California). To be conservative, however, you will use a flat 1.2 percent, or $7,200, for your annual tax expense projection. (Simply call your county tax assessor, if you are outside of California, to obtain an estimate of taxes for your area.)

With the foregoing in mind and armed with the seller's

current annual operating expense figures, you detail out your projected annual operating expenses as follow:

PROJECTED ANNUAL OPERATING EXPENSES

Property taxes (1.2 percent of price in California, approximately)	$7,200
Fixed expenses:	
Insurance	$ 800
Utilities (building lights, etc.)	1,740
Trash service	840
Gardener	600
Exterminator, miscellaneous	150
No pool or elevator	0
TOTAL:	$4,130
Variable expenses (as a percentage of projected annual operating income of $74,880)	
Vacancy allowance	– 2.0 percent
Maintenance	– 4.0 ″
Replacement	– 3.0 ″
Professional property management	– 6.0 ″
Resident manager	– 5.0 ″
Miscellaneous	– 3.5 ″
TOTAL:	23.5 percent

To make other parts of this analysis easier, you want to have both the Fixed Expenses and Variable Expenses as a percentage of the projected annual operating income. As the Variable Expenses are already in this form, you need only convert the Fixed Expenses, as follows:

Fixed Expenses as a percentage of the projected annual operating income:

$$\frac{\text{Fixed Expenses } \$\ 4{,}130}{\text{Gross Income } \$74{,}880} = 5.52 \text{ percent}$$

Now to annual operating income. The present income level is one of the things that got you excited about this property. After talking to the owner, the resident manager, and others in the area, you found that the present income level is under what the market will pay. One bedroom/one bath units are presently at $245.00 per month, and should be bringing about $275.00. Two bedroom/one bath units are at $325.00, and will bring $365.00. With two units vacant, you can raise the rents to new tenants for these units immediately. Others will be raised on an attrition basis (when they become vacant). A rent control ordinance in the city restricts annual increases to 7 percent; however, when a unit becomes vacant, the property owner may raise the rent to the new tenant to the market level (what the traffic will bear).

Even with rent control, you know that you can count on about 11 percent per year average increase in overall rental income. This has been verified with the property management firms, and with other owners and managers. Turnover is relatively frequent in this area, so the combination of 7 percent automatic plus new higher rents on vacated units should average this 11 percent. Accordingly, your gross rental income should look like this over the years (for Current Income, assume all units are full):

PROJECTED ANNUAL OPERATING INCOME

Current:	
12 one bdrm./one bath at $245.00/mo. times 12 months	$35,280
10 two bdrm./one bath at $325.00/mo. times 12 months	39,000
Laundry room net income	600
TOTAL CURRENT GROSS INCOME:	$ 74,880
End of 1st year of operation (111 percent of current)	$ 83,117
End of 2nd year of operation (111 percent of prev. year)	$ 92,260
End of 3rd year of operation (111 percent of prev. year)	$102,409
End of 4th year of operation (111 percent of prev. year)	$113,674

And ad infinitum.

Step Two: Determine Annual Debt Service. The first mortgage still has many years of its original thirty-year term to run. Monthly payments of $3,007.08 add up to $36,085 per year. The second mortgage to be held by the seller is interest only for seven years at 10.5 percent interest, or $18,112 per year. Annual debt service is a combination of these two figures, as follows:

First mortgage	$36,085	
Second mortgage	18,112	
	$54,197	Total Annual Debt Service

Step Three: Calculate Depreciation Benefits. Allowable depreciation deductions are a major benefit to owners of real property. Although it still can be done, acquiring income properties that start out paying you a positive cash flow is becoming difficult. As such, tax savings derived primarily from depreciation may be your only return on investment on a property until a positive flow of cash is realized.

The Economic Recovery Tax Act of 1981 provided a new method of depreciation, called the Accelerated Cost Recovery System ("ACRS"). Generally, the 1981 Act allowed depreciation of this class of property over a fifteen-year period. The new Tax Reform Act of 1984 has revised the minimum period for complete depreciation of this class of property to eighteen years, with deductions under ACRS greater in the earlier years of the property's life than in the later years. However, to avoid recapture (to the taxpayer) of excess depreciation (the excess of depreciation allowed over depreciation allowable if straight-line depreciation were used), we will use straight-line depreciation over eighteen years as our basis for this calculation. Our depreciation then becomes:

Building:	Purchase price	$600,500
	Less: land value (20 percent)	−120,000
	Less: furniture/fixtures	− 20,000
	Net Building Value:	$460,500

So, *annual* building depreciation allowed is:

$460,500 divided by 18 years = $25,583

Furniture/Fixtures: Depreciation allowed under ACRS is:

$20,000 value = 15 percent 1st year, or $3,000
22 percent 2nd year, or $4,400
21 percent 3rd year, or $4,200
21 percent 4th year, or $4,200
21 percent 5th year, or $4,200

Total Depreciation: In accordance with the above calculations, our combined building and furniture depreciation would be:

1st year: Building $25,583 + Furniture $3,000 = $28,583
2nd year: Building $25,583 + Furniture $4,400 = $29,983
3rd year: Building $25,583 + Furniture $4,200 = $29,783
4th year: Building $25,583 + Furniture $4,200 = $29,783
5th year: Building $25,583 + Furniture $4,200 = $29,783
6th year through 15th year: Bldg. only = $25,583

Step Four: Run Forecasted Annual Income Statement for intended Holding Period. You now have developed all the ingredients necessary to determine if this can be a profitable venture. You have:

1. Current annual fixed and variable expenses. Assuming a 10 percent average annual increase in costs, you can forecast each succeeding year's expenses.
2. Current annual gross income which you have forecasted out into the future at 11 percent increase per year.
3. The amount of total annual debt service.
4. Allowable annual depreciation deductions.

All these data now can be assembled into a very succinct picture of what you can expect from this venture. We will assume for simplicity that escrow will close about the end of the year. We will run our forecasted income statement for as many years as it appears that we receive tax sheltering benefits on our income.

Your analysis shows an attractive situation. There is negative cash flow only in the first year, and the amount is small at that. The second year shows $4,574 in positive flow, which builds to $20,464 in the fourth year of operation.

There also is substantial equity buildup (paydown of the first loan principal) each year. More important, you are bene-

FORECASTED INCOME STATEMENT

	At Escrow Close (End of Year)	End of 1st Year + 11 percent	End of 2nd Year + 11 percent	End of 3rd Year + 11 percent	End of 4th Year + 11 percent
Scheduled Gross Income	74,880	83,117	92,260	102,409	113,674
Less Operating Expenses					
Taxes (1.2 percent of purchase price)		7,200	7,200	7,200	7,200
Fixed expenses (5.52 percent inc.)	4,130	4,543	4,997	5,500	6,050
Variable expenses (23.5 percent inc.)	17,597	19,356	21,292	23,421	25,763
Debt service		54,197	54,197	54,197	54,197
Cash flow		(2,179)	4,574	12,091	20,464
Equity buildup (mortgage reduction)		4,850	5,364	5,880	6,444
Depreciation		(28,583)	(29,983)	(29,783)	(29,783)
Net income (loss)		(25,912)	(20,045)	(11,812)	(2,875)

fiting from the spendable (cash flow) and equity buildup each year on a tax-free basis. (Note the Net Loss, which is a paper loss only, for tax purposes each year. Since depreciation is a non-cash expense, you really are making money each year. This money is sheltered from income taxes by the depreciation, with enough deduction left over to shelter income from other sources, too.)

You can see that the net paper loss is down to $2,875 at the end of the fourth year, and that you will have a taxable income if you hold the property a fifth year. Obviously, then, you want to sell the property sometime during the fifth year of ownership in order to maximize tax benefits (i.e., continue to receive cash flow with no income tax liability).

All of this is great, but you do not have the money to purchase this property on your own. You know that by syndicating this property, there can be substantial fees in this for you (buying and selling commissions, management fees, organization fees, and a share of the profits). The deal standing by itself shows a profit. But, you do not know at this point if a syndication will work. A forecast of syndication monies required must be prepared. This, then, must be folded into this entire transaction to see if it can make sense for the investors as well as for you.

Step Five: Determine How Much Syndication Money Is Needed. This can be accomplished easily and quickly. You know that $108,000 is needed as a cash down payment to go to the seller. You also conducted a unit-by-unit inspection of the building. As a result, you feel that approximately $7,000 should be budgeted for minor painting and fix-up of deferred maintenance. The legal agreement between you and the investors can be finalized for about $2,500, and $300 should take care of an accountant's review of the financial data in the documentation. There will be a small amount of negative cash flow in the first year of operations although prorations of rents and rental deposits at close of escrow probably will more than offset this outflow. Just to be safe, though, you will budget for the approximate $2,000 negative cash flow shown in your Forecasted Income Statement.

These are the individual items you are aware of that must

be included in your budget of funds required. You also should establish a reserve for unforeseen contingencies. There will be some minor printing costs, and may be some minor escrow closing costs, too, In addition, your attorney and/or accountant may feel that a more detailed review of the tax implications of the project should be made and reflected in your investment documentation. Their more detailed review and the other minor costs mentioned should be well covered by a $10,000 reserve.

And now you. What do you want to make? Well, 3 percent of the purchase price of $600,500 as an administrative/organization fee is justified, so let's build in an $18,000 fee for yourself. (This is in addition to sales fees, management fees, and a share of the profits, all of which are quite substantial as you will see later.) This $18,000 will be paid to you at the close of escrow.

Our total budget for syndication money needed looks like this:

SYNDICATION USE OF PROCEEDS

Down payment	$108,000
Refurbishment	7,000
Legal/accounting	2,800
Administrative fee	18,000
Reserve for contingencies	10,000
TOTAL:	$145,800

NOTE: The legal fee cost projection ($2,500) should be adequate to cover the preparation of the legal agreement needed. It would be to your advantage to use an attorney experienced in these matters as he will have other similar agreements previously generated. He may be able to use an "off the shelf" agreement, modifying it for your particular situation. This would ensure staying within the cost projection.

Step Six: Determine If Project Will Support Investors and You. Your last step is to overlay your Step Four Forecasted Income Statement with the above information, and to forecast the end results. This analysis proceeds as follows:

ESTIMATED SALE AT THE END OF FOUR YEARS' OPERATION

Probable value at the end of four years (conservatively):
8.5 x Scheduled Gross Income

So, 8.5 x $113,674 = $966,229

Debt still owing at sale:	1st loan	$297,462
	2nd loan	172,500
TOTAL REMAINING DEBT:		$469,962

Net equity calculation:

Forecasted sale price	$966,229
Less: debt	−469,962
Gross equity:	$496,267
Less: 6 percent sale commission	− 57,974
Net equity:	$438,293

You would like to have a structural arrangement with the investors which gives you 30 percent of the profits subject to the investors recovering the entire amount of their capital ($145,800), plus a minimum of 10 percent per year return on their investment. You would give them all of the tax benefits and all of the positive cash flow during the holding period. Accordingly, the profit distribution would look like this:

PROJECTED INVESTOR PROFIT SCHEDULE

Net equity in building	$438,293
Spendable (net cash flow while held)	34,950
Tax savings: Tax loss during four years equals $60,644. Assume 50 percent tax bracket investor, so total actual tax savings equal one-half, or:	30,322
TOTAL RETURN:	$503,565
Less: Return of investor capital	−145,800
NET RETURN:	$357,765

Investor share = 70 percent. So, $357,765 x .70 = $250,436

Profit per year: $\frac{\$250,436}{\$145,800}$ = 171.8 percent divided by four years equals: 42.94 *percent per year*

No question: this obviously would be a very good deal for the investors. It far exceeds the minimum 10 percent per year return they must receive to allow you to share in the profit. As such, your profit share would be a very healthy $107,330 (the net return of $357,765 times your 30 percent ownership interest). But, you already have made substantial compensation from other aspects of this transaction, so the total compensation you could expect for yourself would be as follows:

YOUR COMPENSATION FROM THIS DEAL

$ 30,025	original 5 percent sales commission paid to you by seller
18,000	administrative fee at escrow close
23,488	6 percent professional property management fee (paid to you during building operation)
28,987	minimum earnings for you from 6 percent sales commission (assumes another sales agent brings in a buyer and you give up one-half the commission. If you find a buyer yourself, you would receive the entire 6 percent.)
107,330	your 30 percent share of the net return
$207,830	TOTAL COMPENSATION

After going through this analysis, I do not think there is the slightest doubt what your decision would be regarding the viability of this project. Quite obviously, this is a very good deal for both sides. It allows you to earn a substantial amount of income just from using this system one time; it gives a group of investors the chance to pool their money to earn almost 43 percent profit per year. This is something they probably could not do on their own.

At this point, you would want to solidify your arrangement with the owner of this apartment building so that he does not sell it to anyone else. We will get into this aspect (tying up the deal) in the next chapter. Before moving to Chapter 6, however, there are some brief but important points for you to think about, sort of a summary of some key thoughts dealing with the chapter.

Additional Points and Thoughts

Structuring Profit Sharing with Investors. Generally, the higher the project risk, the greater the percentage you must give to investors to entice them into investing. Where the risk is relatively low and the potential profit is substantial, you can justify a higher percentage for yourself. Also, it is fairer to subordinate your ownership percentage to the investors' recovering their investment *first* along with a minimum annual return (as in the previous example). In some types of projects, however, the current cash flow is high and the selling profit looks to be low. In these cases, you can sell the investors on letting you share in the current cash flow as long as their cash flow share is more than some minimum annual return to them.

Fee for Raising Funds. In general, a fee of approximately 10 percent of funds raised can be taken for raising the investor funds. In addition, a fee of from 2 to 3 percent of funds raised can be charged for analyzing and structuring, and for packaging the documentation.

An alternate formula would be to charge a flat fee of 12 or 13 percent to cover both of these aspects. This ties in with the 12 percent fee charged in the coffee/sandwich shop example. It also ties in with the $18,000 administrative fee charged in lieu of a fund-raising fee in the income property example (the $18,000 is approximately 12 percent of the $145,800 to be raised).

These are guidelines only. Your front end fees can be more if it appears they are fair and reasonable for the deal. For example, I have been receiving closer to 15 percent for packaging and fund-raising on the last four syndications I have helped put together. These general guidelines should be subject to any special rules and regulations which might govern such fees in your state. Although there are not any such specific regulations of fees in some states, you must check your own local laws. To be safe, you may want to use the public offering fee guidelines in your state as a basis for how you charge fees in your own syndication.

Governmental Regulations. You must be sure to check out all local and higher-level regulations concerning businesses or other projects you anticipate involving yourself with in your area. For example, whether or not rent control is in force for mobile home parks and apartment buildings can be a significant factor in your analysis of those types of income properties. Do not let rent control scare you, however. A deal still can be quite profitable even with rent controls.

Number of Investors Allowed to Come into the Deal. This will be discussed more fully in Chapters 8 and 11. Speaking very generally, however, thirty-five qualified persons or entities will probably be the maximum you should count on having in the project. This conforms to Securities and Exchange Commission guidelines which allow thirty-five investors in a transaction of this type (private). However, if your state restricts you to use a lower number for these private placements, then you should plan to conform to the state plan. You should see an attorney to pin this down in any case.

Depreciation and Other Tax Benefits. As you can see from the last example, depreciation can be a major selling point for doing the particular deal you are considering. It not only gives investors a tangible and attractive reason to invest (tax-free income from the deal plus sheltering of outside income from other sources), it figures in the overall return to them. This effectively boosts their return and allows you to justify a larger share of the profits for yourself. Investment tax credits (ITC) generally are more attractive as they allow a direct credit (reduction) against the final tax bill. However, the Tax Reform Act of 1984 provides options to use only portions of ITC and depreciation when used in conjunction with each other; that is, you cannot receive 100 percent ITC and depreciation at the same time. You should see a qualified CPA specializing in tax to be sure of what you represent. This can be advantageous for you, because the CPA can be a good source of qualified investors.

You must be careful to inform investors of the possibility of recapture, if applicable. Recapture requires that a taxpayer recover accelerated depreciation — in excess of that allowed for straight-line — as ordinary income on residential real property. (This would not affect the investors in the income property example, because we used straight-line depreciation only.) With nonresidential real property, however (office buildings, warehouses, etc.), an accelerated method of depreciation allowed by ACRS results in the investor being taxed on all depreciation taken — including the straight-line portion — as ordinary income, and this is not advantageous. An expert in tax accounting should be consulted before final structuring to protect against such disadvantageous results.

NOTE: Readers are made aware that discussions on depreciation are related specifically to federal tax laws. Depending on where you live, there may be difficult depreciation calculations required for your state income tax purposes.

Leverage. Very simply put, leverage is the use of a small amount of cash to control a large amount of value. It allows you to enter a market without a big nest egg; it also enables you to pyramid your return more quickly than if you used all cash for a deal.

For example, our investor group purchased the building in the previous example for 76 percent leverage ($600,500 purchase price minus the $145,800 in total funds used leaves $454,700 which, divided by the purchase price, equals approximately 76 percent). In other words, 76 percent of the total funds required for the project was put up by the first and second mortgage lenders. Let's assume that the rate of inflation was the same as our rent increase, or 11 percent, during the first year. Then, let's compare our minimum return with that in the case of paying all cash for the building.

If we paid all cash, the 11 percent inflation would make our building worth $66,055 more, so our return at the end of one year would be 11 percent as follows:

$$\frac{\$66{,}055}{\$600{,}500} \quad \frac{\text{value increase}}{\text{cash invested}} = 11 \text{ percent in one year}$$

But, the people in our project put up only $145,800 in cash, so their return at the same point would be four times more than by paying all cash, or 45.3 percent:

$$\frac{\$66{,}055 \quad \text{value increase}}{\$145{,}800 \quad \text{cash invested}} = 45.3 \text{ percent in one year}$$

If we paid only 10 percent down on the property plus the syndication costs, we would only have to put up approximately $97,050. This would jump our return up to 68 percent as follows:

$$\frac{\$66{,}055 \quad \text{value increase}}{\$97{,}050 \quad \text{cash invested}} = 68 \text{ percent in one year}$$

Now, let's use the same 10 percent down, and assume that you or I could buy this property on our own as an individual (without syndication costs). Our return jumps substantially, up to 96 percent:

$60,050	10 percent down payment
1,950	approximate closing costs
7,000	refurbishment allowance
$69,000	total cash investment now required, so:

$$\frac{\$66{,}055 \quad \text{value increase}}{\$69{,}000 \quad \text{cash invested}} = 96 \text{ percent in one year}$$

Remember, the building value increased only 11 percent, yet you actually could have made almost 100 percent in the space of only one year. When you consider cash flow, equity buildup, and tax savings on top of this, your rate of return can become astounding! And most of this return is due to the effects of leverage.

CHAPTER 6

Tie Up the Deal

YOU'VE COME A long way. A project has been found, and it has been analyzed and structured. The projected return to the investors looks great, and there is a lot of money in it for you. The decision is to go forward, and fast. But you do not want to do a lot of work and then have the deal dissolve before you can make any money. So what do you do? You tie up the deal.

The deal will be one of two types: you will be a packaging/fund-raising syndicator only, performing these functions for someone else for a fee, with no further responsibility; or, you will perform all the syndication functions yourself, staying involved throughout the life of the deal. Let's look at each type of situation.

Raising Money for Someone Else

Being involved with the entire deal throughout its life is more attractive for you; however, there will be times when you want to raise money for someone else because it can be a quick and easy way to earn substantial fees. Consequently, you should know how to deal with this situation when it arises.

This is the same type of situation as that explained in our coffee/sandwich shop example. Someone else has an idea, but needs your help in packaging the investment and raising the money. You have confirmed the attractiveness of the project with your analysis and structuring. Both of you want to move forward. An agreement is the next step.

Enter into a Contractual Agreement. A relatively brief (two to four pages) Memorandum of Understanding should be drawn up to solidify your understanding and agreement of the duties and responsibilities of each side. I generally develop my own agreements, which are based on previous ones prepared for me by an attorney. Although I feel reasonably comfortable with my documents because of my years of experience in the business, I still continue to use an attorney's services to bless my memorandum each time in order to be safe. As such, I definitely recommend that you engage an attorney to draft this important document for you initially. He should not have to spend more than two or three hours on it. The small amount of money you spend will come right back to you anyway through your packaging fees to your client.

Some minimum basic categories of information should be covered in this legal agreement. The total amount of funds to be raised and its breakdown is certainly one of them. This total would include your fund-raising fee of approximately 10 to 12 percent, and your structuring and packaging fee. You also should specify the net amount of funds to be delivered to your client.

You should delineate your specific responsibilities/services to be performed for these fees, such as data gathering and its verification, analyzing, structuring, preparing and finalizing the documentation, and raising the funds. Then, do the same for your client, so that it's clear what information he is responsible for providing to enable you to do your job.

You also should discuss how all costs will be handled. I indicate that I will bear all costs associated with the packaging and fund-raising except for legal work, accounting review for the tax and financial section, and printing/binding costs for the final document. I indicate that these costs will be budgeted as parts of the funds raised, so that the investors actually will be paying for them, not my client.

I feel it's a good idea to have agreement on how the venture will be broken up as far as potential number of investors, and the size of the investment units. Another important part is clarification of how investor referrals from your client will be handled. If he is to share in the fund-raising fee for any referrals, then this must be specified (e.g., how much, when he is to be paid).

It also is important to state exactly how your client's purchase of any of the investment units will be treated. For example, will any of your fee be waived on his purchase, and if so, how much? Also, if there is a possibility of his purchase of some units, you should pin down the exact number he may buy (so that you know exactly how much you have available for investors), and when he has to buy them before they are sold to investors. A fuzzy understanding in this area can cause difficulty and embarrassment later on.

If your client has to perform certain key tasks before all or some of your work can be done, these should be specified. Details such as leasing space, obtaining a franchise, and other similar events certainly must happen before you spend too much time on the project. Additionally, a section should bind the client to paying you all or some percentage of your packaging fee should the project not go forward because of his inability to accomplish these key tasks. The timing for completion of his tasks, and for the fund-raising as a whole, should be clarified, also.

Do not paint yourself into a corner on any provision about which you may not feel completely confident. For example, I never guarantee that I can raise the required funds; I agree to perform the fund-raising on a "best efforts" basis only, with no promise. And, I always build in some benchmarks to allow me to terminate the relationship should I feel uncomfortable about the client.

In summary, be sure to cover at least the following basic elements in your Memorandum of Understanding:

a. Breakdown of total funds to be raised, including your fees and the net amount to be turned over to your client
b. Description of your responsibilities and services, and description of verified information your client is to furnish to you
c. Discussion of how costs are to be handled
d. Number of investors and size of investment units
e. How investor referrals from your client will be handled, and how you'll control the client's purchase of investment units
f. Key tasks to be performed by your client and their timing
g. A section binding your client to paying you some percentage of your packaging fee should he keep the project from going forward because of his failure to perform
h. Benchmarks to allow termination of the agreement, if necessary

Follow Up on Tasks Being Accomplished by the Client. Your first need is to have a good contractual agreement with your client. Then, while you work on the packaging, you need to make sure that he is accomplishing tasks necessary for the project to move forward. For example, if he is having difficulty finding space for the store or restaurant, or in completing other aspects of this particular project, you may want to shelve your work until things are more certain.

It's also possible that you may not feel as good about the client now that you have found out more about him from others, and have spent more time with him directly. You will have an obligation to put your investors' funds in a fair, just, and equitable venture, and to make sure that all aspects of the deal make good business sense. Because of this, you may want to terminate your efforts. As such, you should have benchmarks throughout the memorandum that would allow a graceful termination of the relationship if they are not met. As an example, your review and approval of the client's previous track record could be one such benchmark.

You may have agreed to help your client acquire debt financing that will be used in conjunction with the investor funds to get his project moving. This will necessitate significant paperwork and effort on his part; consequently, you must make sure his work is prepared quickly and professionally if you are to have a good shot at the financing. (Incidentally, you should get a separate fee for this financing effort.)

In short, you must protect yourself from exposure to working for nothing. A proper, contractual agreement is a must for this protection. Making sure your client is reputable and is accomplishing all necessary tasks is also key. Make a general schedule of events that must occur for project success, then follow up constantly with yourself and with your client to ensure that scheduled milestones are being met. And don't become lulled into having a loose agreement because the deal is financially attractive to you and your client doesn't want to give you any "outs." It won't take you long to discover that the client needs you more than you need him. A little planning at the outset can save a lot of problems down the road.

Doing Your Own Deal

Directly doing your own deal negates the need for a Memorandum of Understanding such as the one just discussed; however, you still have to tie up the project so that you do not end up spinning your wheels. You have to tie up the property, the franchise rights, the leasehold interest, or whatever the product is that you eventually will be promoting. You will be performing all syndication functions in this situation.

When you are trying to lock up some product for your venture, you obviously want to end up with the best deal possible. There usually is some negotiating room, although sometimes the demand is so great that you just have to pay the going price. A good, national franchise is one example of this. If McDonald's has a price of $325,000 for one of its franchise equipment packages, then you probably will have to spend $325,000 in order to get it. On the other hand, if you are trying to purchase the right to syndicate a race horse or a boxer, or are attempting to buy some real property, then you do not want to leave any money on the table by accepting the seller's offering price. You want to negotiate.

Common sense and persuasive arguing always will help you cut a better deal. You want to bargain with a seller even if you have no competition. Your final price may not be rock bottom, but you may end up with more attractive terms and conditions by jockeying for a better position. Be sure to start your negotiating with a low offering price and little or no clarification of your motivations. You do not want to give the seller any indication that you sense a super deal or that you have your heart set on his product. Be a poker player; do not show your hand and keep a straight face.

Listen more than you talk. By listening carefully to the seller's comments and responses to your questions, you will pick up his wants, needs, and motivations. You may find that terms are much more important to him than price (and they are probably more important to you, too). You will be able to plan your bargaining strategy around your constantly increasing knowledge about the seller. This will help you get much closer to your desired purchase price and terms.

Solidify the Arrangement. Once you have negotiated the best possible deal, you must solidify it in writing to protect yourself from doing a lot of work for nothing. The instrument you use will depend upon the nature of the acquisition. If you are pinning down a leasehold interest (some space in a shopping center for an aerobics exercise business, for example), your document will be a Lease Contract. If you have negotiated a right to purchase some land should the seller decide to sell it in the next few months or so, then you may use a Right of First Refusal agreement to protect your future project. A Purchase Option Agreement would give you a certain time period within which to make up your mind about purchasing some item of personal or real property (and would preclude anyone else from purchasing the item during your option period). A Purchase Contract may be used if an outright purchase of the item of interest is to occur.

In any case, an attorney should be used to help you draw up the appropriate contractual document (or at least to "bless" it if you or a real estate agent have used a standard form or made up your own document). The attorney should build in adequate safeguards so that you can feel comfortable with your acquisition, or planned acquisition. For example, adequate time to perform is very important (see next section). Contingencies in a Purchase Contract for real estate are necessary to give you "outs" if something keeps you from going forward on your project. In a Lease Contract, partial or no rent while the landlord is making tenant improvements is to your advantage. In short, there are many areas of protection that are important to you, and an attorney can ensure that your contractual document includes them.

As mentioned before, the attorney's fees can be reimbursed out of the funds raised so that you can put the project together without using any of your own funds. In some cases, the attorney may even be interested in taking a small piece of your project in lieu of his fees. One way or another, you will find that you can safeguard yourself properly without using any of your own money, except possibly on a temporary basis. And, I cannot stress too strongly how important it is to have good legal representation at every point along the way.

Build in Adequate Time. Regardless of the type of instrument used, you will have a time period within which you must perform some task or tasks. Any of the situations described above should be structured, if possible, to enable you to retrieve your consideration (front money used to tie up the deal) should you decide against proceeding. You also need time to do the packaging and fund-raising.

Regarding your consideration, if you have opened a ninety-day escrow for the purchase of some real property, you should try to build in some escape clause to enable you to recover your deposit. This might be in order if further investigation or some other factor makes you decide against the project during the ninety days. (Recovery may be difficult in certain instances, however. In the case of a Purchase Option, you generally must forfeit your option deposit if you do not exercise the option before the end of the option period; thus, your deposit would be lost in this case.)

The time period you negotiate is very important for two reasons. One, it gives you an inexpensive extension to look at the project in more detail. A few hundred dollars for some additional time could save you thousands of dollars and a lot of hassle should additional analyses show the project to be a probable loser. Two, it allows you to package the investment properly and to raise the required funds. Because of these factors, you always should try to negotiate the longest period possible.

In the case of an income property purchase, try for a minimum of ninety days, and take 120 days or longer if you can get it. As a rule of thumb, I would never give myself less than sixty days for any project that I planned to syndicate. That is, from the time I tied up the project, I would want a minimum of sixty days before I had to come up with any additional funds.

As with raising money for someone else, the main objectives in tying up the deal are to protect yourself from doing significant needless work, and to protect the deal from other persons. The two most important things to remember in this endeavor are to use an attorney for your contractual documents, and to buy yourself the maximum amount of time possible.

CHAPTER 7

Packaging the Opportunity: Planning

YOU HAVE CREATED an investment opportunity. It has been analyzed and tied up. A lot of money can be made from this venture by yourself and by investors. You are ready to charge forward and do the deal.

To make this money, however, you need a sales and ownership document, something to present to prospective investors for their review, something for them to sign if they are interested and qualified. This document is a very important element of the syndication process. Without it, your chance of putting the deal together is next to zero. And, you will want a good package regardless of your role in the deal, i.e., whether you are the packaging/fund-raising syndicator only, or are performing all aspects of the syndication. This and the next two chapters are devoted to packaging, to explain in detail how to come up with this documentation. But first, we need to expand a little bit on our discussion in Chapter 3 about syndications, and about the "private" method of putting them together.

An Investment Syndicate: Three Main Elements

You know from Chapter 3 that syndication investors pool their money and let someone else manage it for them. This pooling of resources is an association for profit of two or more persons under central management. This association, or syndication, has three main elements: the syndicator, the investors, the deal.

The Syndicator. The syndicator (you) is the bridge between the investors and the deal. As the bridge, he binds the investors and the deal together into a workable relationship. After finding, analyzing, and tying up the project so that it can be acquired with the investment group's money, he forms the syndicate and manages the project to achieve the investment goals. (We already know from Chapter 3 that, on occasion, two syndicators may be involved — i.e., the packaging/fund-raising syndicator, and the organizing/managing syndicator.)

The Investors. The investors, the persons who are pooling their resources, are one leg of this bridge. They rely on the syndicator and his investigation as a basis for making their investment decision. They also rely on the syndicator to manage the investment capital in such a way as to return a profit on their investment.

The Deal. The deal, or project, is the other leg of the bridge. It is the foundation for the syndicate; it must provide the return of investment and profits that projections show it capable of generating. The project itself, terms and conditions, financing, its effect from economic conditions, and other aspects must all work in harmony for it to perform as anticipated.

Business Form Used in a Syndication

A business venture can take any of a variety of legal business forms. Some of these include general partnerships, trusts, corporations of various types, real estate investment trusts (REIT's), joint ventures, tenants-in-common agreements, and limited partnerships. Usually, however, it is the limited partnership structure that is utilized as the legal form in bringing together investment groups of individual investors. It generally is the most suitable, as well as economically attractive, vehicle for both sides. The Partnership Agreement is the legal document signed by all parties to evidence their rights and ownership in the limited partnership syndication project.

The limited partnership structure has become an increasingly popular investment vehicle in recent years. It is a type of business structure that has two sets of partners: limited and general. The investors are the limited partners and the syndicator is the general partner. It is a vehicle for passive investors (the limited partners) to use to contribute capital to a business venture and to share in the profits and benefits of the operation. The investors also can share directly in the tax benefits which can be quite significant.

The limited partnership structure provides a great deal of flexibility, and is generally well understood and accepted. It keeps the investors off title in real estate deals (a must). It gives the general partner flexibility in designing profit-sharing plans between himself and the limited partners. It keeps individual investors from interfering in the day-to-day business activities since the general partner has complete control over the functioning of the partnership business. Yet, it imposes enough legal obligations upon the general partner to help safeguard the investors' interests.

A limited partnership structure usually limits the liability or loss of the limited partners to the amount of their investment, yet it allows pass-through of tax benefits directly to them. It gives the investor trouble-free ownership in that the general partner does all the work and provides the centralized management. And, in the private offering context used in this book, the limited partnership is probably the least expensive of the business forms to use insofar as governmental, legal, and accounting fees are concerned.

Private Offerings

As you know from Chapter 3, it is advantageous to avoid having to register your syndication project as a public offering with federal or state regulatory agencies. Registration involves obtaining a permit from the state or from the Securities and Exchange Commission, or both, for your syndication. Legal fees can run an extra $25,000 or more. Accounting fees and application fees are high. It also is very time-consuming and inconvenient to obtain a permit. Your investment opportunity can evaporate long before you can wade through the bureaucratic jungle involved with permit acquisition.

There is a way out of the cumbersome procedure discussed above, however. Securities and Exchange Commission Rule 147 exempts intrastate offerings and sales from federal registration requirements. This allows you to use a private offering and not have to go through the costly public offering registration requirements. However, your particular state may have adopted rules and procedures concerning private offerings that may be similar to the federal procedures contained in Regulation D under the Securities Act of 1933. If this is the case, there could be some guidelines in addition to those in Rule 147 which you would have to meet to use a private offering. To be safe, you must review your state's laws with an experienced attorney to determine your state's particular requirements.

In California, the Corporations Code provides a "limited offering exemption." In essence, this exemption allows you to put together a private offering for your syndication project if you meet certain guidelines, such as full disclosure, no public advertising, a fair, just, and equitable deal, and a limited number of investors. More details on the specific guidelines for using a private offering in California — and some information about limited offering exemptions in other states — will be in Chapter 11.

For the sake of illustration and because my experience is in California, the rules and guidelines of that state are followed here. Also, the models utilized in this book are for California nonpublic offerings — private offerings — sold only to California residents. California is a good model, however, because it generally is looked upon as one of the more progressive states in the private placement syndication field.

In any case, I used legal advice and services when I first began to do syndication projects. I still rely on legal expertise to keep me in line with changing rules and regulations. The legal fee will come right back to you from the monies you raise, or the fee might even be waived in lieu of some participation in the project. Another advantage of working with an experienced attorney at this point is the overall understanding you will receive in this area of federal and state exemption guidelines. If this discussion seems a little confusing, don't be too concerned. You'll quickly be familiar with this area through your attorney's comments, and through actually doing your first syndication with his guidance.

In Chapter 11 on how to obtain funds from other people, we will get into the specific guidelines you must follow in the raising of these funds. At this point, however, we know that we will use a limited partnership designed as a private offering exempted from federal or state registration requirements. So, let's get into the details of generating our documentation.

Documenting the Investment Syndicate

You need some documentation to accomplish the following:

a. to have a sales tool for raising funds from investors,
b. to define the legal relationship between you and your investors,
c. to ensure that the investors are qualified for the investment.

This documentation is assembled into one package called the *Confidential Memorandum.* Approximately the first one-half of this Confidential Memorandum is structured to accomplish point a. above; that is, to provide a sales tool for you to use with each prospective investor. This first part contains the story, the message about the investment, and it may be written in layman's terms. It also contains the full disclosure of all pertinent aspects of the venture as required by federal and state security guidelines. These disclosures of all aspects of the deal keep you, the syndicator, out of difficulty while you operate the project and try to meet the investment objectives. This first part of the Confidential Memorandum also discusses most of the general aspects of the relationship between the syndicator, the project, and the investors.

The Confidential Memorandum has two major attachments to it which cover points b. and c. above. These attachments are as follows:

1. **Attachment I — Agreement of Limited Partnership.** This is the partnership agreement, a separate section of the Confidential Memorandum that sets forth the legal understanding and obligations of the syndicator and the investors. It describes the project, the size of the investment Units, and the sharing arrangement between the parties. It discusses the management responsibilities and restrictions, and sets forth procedures for meetings, amendments, and dissolution. It contains the signature pages, as well as a listing of all the partners that eventually come into the syndicate.
2. **Attachment II — Statement of Suitability and Subscription Agreement.** This Attachment is important because representations made in it by the prospective investor help you to qualify him, to determine how suitable he is for the investment. His representations reflect his understanding of the partnership business, and also his ability to analyze and to invest in the partnership. He warrants certain income levels, business experience, and his understanding that there are risks in the investment. He provides personal information needed to properly register his purchase of the ownership units in the partnership. Based upon his representation of net worth, income, and other

qualifications in this Attachment, you either may accept or reject him as an investor.

This Confidential Memorandum package is an extremely important part of your syndication effort. It not only solidifies the deal in writing, it is your sales tool for enabling an investor to clearly understand the project, and for persuading him to place his funds with you. This package is an extension of yourself. It gives each investor an insight into the person to whom they are entrusting their funds. As such, it should be well thought out, and should be organized and prepared in a professional manner.

Anyone can sniff out what looks like a good investment. And most anyone can, with a little help, analyze the various aspects of a potential investment. But very few persons can raise money just on their good looks and charm. They need a sales tool that will give the investor that little extra edge of confidence he needs to convince him to gamble his dollars on this deal.

Two Model Packages

Because of the importance of this Confidential Memorandum package, a good part of this book is dedicated to it. In fact, I have included two complete, sample packages for you at the back of the book. The first sample package is very comprehensive, and is contained in Appendix I. It is a full-length model of a Confidential Memorandum that could be used to put together a nationally franchised restaurant and ice cream parlor.

This particular model shows two of your friends as the general partners of a limited partnership which will be used as the legal structure for owning and operating the restaurant. It assumes you have performed the analyzing and complete packaging, and are raising the required funds for them on a fee basis only. (The content would be exactly the same if you were the general partner; however, you then would be entitled to all the fees and ownership now going to your friends.) This model includes the three basic documentation sections discussed above: the first part of the Confidential Memorandum, which is your sales tool written in layman's language (we'll refer to this part as the Investment Circular portion); the Attachment I Agreement of Limited Partnership; and, the Attachment II Statement of Suitability and Subscription Agreement.

This Appendix I model displays all the data, and uses all the specific language that I would use in an actual package. Using it as a detailed guide should enable you to come up with your own package very quickly. While it is for a restaurant/ice cream parlor and is for illustration purposes only, it readily can be adapted to syndicate any business or venture. Consequently, this model should save you hours of time and trouble.

The second model, Appendix II, is a "mini-package." This model is patterned after one I used to quickly (in three weeks) put together a raw land purchase investment in which $626,305 of OPM was raised. This Appendix II model has been modified to show the purchase, operation, and sale of a residential duplex because this type of deal can be done quickly and with very little in the way of OPM. You are the sole syndicator in this example (that is, you perform all of the syndication functions), and you receive all of the fees, profits, and benefits. A project similar to this one could be your first because of the ease in putting together this type of investment opportunity. This "mini-package" serves the same purpose as the full package. It is less than one-third as long, however, which enables you to move out very quickly when time is a critical factor.

There is only one way for you to clearly learn and understand this major factor of the syndication process. It is for you to "walk" through each section of the full model Confidential Memorandum package, to see how it goes together and why each section is there. So, this is exactly what we are going to do. (We will do this for the full package only; the mini-package parallels it and can be easily understood after going through the more comprehensive one.)

CHAPTER 8

Confidential Memorandum: Investment Circular Portion

THIS CHAPTER BREAKS out the Investment Circular portion of the Confidential Memorandum model package in Appendix I. Each section in the model is keyed to its corresponding explanation here in this chapter for ease of understanding.

The Investment Circular portion of the Confidential Memorandum, unlike the remainder of the package, includes photographs, schedules, maps, plans, and narrative information designed specifically to fully acquaint the potential investor with the investment. Any information that clearly demonstrates the syndicator's knowledge of the project should be included. The most productive and successful Investment Circulars are those that show that the syndicator has "done his homework." This showing of complete knowledge, along with full disclosure to the investor of all aspects of the deal, are what we are trying to accomplish with the Investment Circular portion of the package.

The Investment Circular Portion (Keyed to Confidential Memorandum Model in Appendix I)

Outline: Your First Step. Your very first step in the packaging of the syndicate documentation is to *outline* what you think you should cover in it. This outline will eventually become your Table of Contents. So, if you were going to put together a restaurant/ice cream parlor package, your outline would look as follows:

- Brief summary of project
- The offering (a section on total money needed, Unit size, procedure for investing, etc.)
- Investor qualifications (a section explaining basic qualifications an investor should meet in order to invest)
- Use of proceeds (exactly how the investors' funds will be utilized)
- Risk factors (what the basic investment risks are)
- Background summary of project and site negotiations (a narrative about how the project got started, and the status of finding a site for the business)
- Site locator map (where the location is in the city)
- Location (of the business) in the shopping center
- Representative photos (four 4x6-inch colored photos which give a good idea of what the completed business will or should look like)
- Sample's ice cream company: Background information
  - Mains and Remotes (describes large and small stores)
  - Company expansion, promotion plans
  - General franchise information
  - Franchisee obligations
  - Franchisor obligations
- Ice cream industry: Background information (optional)
- Franchise terms, conditions, renewal
- Project status, opening schedule
- Cash distributions to partners — principals' compensation
- The general partners and their experience
- Income tax risk factors

- Pro forma financial projections
  - Projected income statement: 1st 12 months
  - Projected income statement: 2nd 12 months
  - Projected income statement: 3rd 12 months
- Projected limited partner cash distribution schedule
- Representations

NOTE: The above would complete the Investment Circular portion of the package. The remaining two sections of your outline are:

- Attachment I — Complete Partnership Agreement
- Attachment II — Statement of Suitability/Subscription Agreement

This outline may change slightly as you develop the Investment Circular, but it gives you a good base from which to start. In actual practice, I first develop the financial section of the Circular in final form just to verify my previous analyses one more time. I also skip around to different sections, first completing those where I have all the information I need, then going on to others. We will walk through this package in chronological order, however, as this will give you a clearer perspective of what the document is trying to achieve.

(A) Title Page. Your attorney can tell you what wording to place on this page. In general, you want to indicate what type of document this is (i.e., "Confidential Memorandum"), what the partnership name is, some caveats about this being a private offering with no governmental agency review or approval, the speculative nature of this investment, etc. It should be dated, and you may want to number each copy for control purposes. (There also may be a numbering requirement in the private exemption guidelines in your state.)

(B) Table of Contents. This, of course, is the last page to be completed after the entire package is finished. It is your original outline modified to conform to the actual sections and page numbers used in the development of the package.

(C) Brief Summary of Project. This can be called Summary Statement, Outline of Project, Summary of Offering, or some other designation. Its main purpose is to tell the prospective investor in a minimum of words just what this project is all about. Most people will not take the time to read through an entire package like this. You hope they will at least open the book and glance at the first few pages. If they do, you want to catch their attention right up front, to hook them by summarizing the entire project in just a few, descriptive words. They will then be interested enough to continue reading on.

In two or three short paragraphs, you tell the prospect what the project is, what its objectives are with regard to benefits to him, and who the general partner is. The investor will read on if interested; if not, he probably will stop here. But if he does stop, his time and yours will be saved to some degree. You will know very quickly whether or not he is a good prospect when you check back with him.

(D) The Offering. The basic structure of the partnership is summarized here. The total capitalization amount is noted, as is the number of ownership Units. I always divide the total capitalization by 1,000 to give me the total ownership Units available. Using $1,000 Units allows me some flexibility in accepting multiple Unit or fractional Unit purchases, and is just easier for calculation purposes.

The investors (limited partners) own 100 percent of the partnership business and assets subject to some minimum standards. In this case, it is return of an amount equivalent to 100 percent of their capital invested. (At this point, the investors have broken even, having recovered an amount equal to their original investment.) Once this milestone is reached, then the general partners are entitled to 35 percent of the distribution of cash and capital.

The second paragraph of this section gets into the minimum purchase amount. In California, thirty-five investors can be taken into a private offering investment syndicate safely, given all private offering guidelines are met. So, I divided $395,500 by thirty-five to give me the $11,300 minimum purchase amount. Some persons will purchase more than the minimum, so I have indicated that some smaller purchase increments may be available. Note also that this offering is nonassessable; that is, no investor is required to put in any additional funds should the partnership require them. (If additional funds were required to stave off a financial emergency, however, most investors would contribute an additional small amount. Those who did not would have their partnership interest diluted proportionately.)

A brief procedure for purchasing Units is described. Finally, a short clarification about how the funds will be collected and used is given. Note that the funds may be used when one-half the offering has been subscribed and paid for. This can be very important to you if progress payments, a lease deposit, or other cash requirements exist before all funds are collected. Do not use the money, however, if there is the slightest doubt about raising the balance of the funds. In fact, I do not endorse this concept unless you have completed several syndications and are experienced in raising investment funds.

(E) Investor Qualifications. This section is designed to help protect the general partners from taking nonqualified investors into the partnership. An investor looking at this package will know what minimum suitability standards are required for investment after reading this section. These standards are mentioned again in the Attachment II Statement of Suitability and Subscription Agreement, along with additional questions about the investor's financial status. These strict requirements also protect investors, because they quickly can get a feel for their suitability as partners in the project.

(F) Use of Proceeds. This is a schedule, or breakdown, of how the investors' funds will be utilized. Although this presentation should be self-explanatory, some comments are in order for clarification purposes.

This project involves all cash; there is no debt financing. If a loan were involved, however, you would show the complete project cost, minus the amount of the loan, thus showing the amount of partnership funds required. (The mini-package model does have a loan involved in its structure for comparison purposes.)

The Principals' Project Management Reimbursement fee of $5,000 is arrived at arbitrarily. It is an up-front fee a syndicator can receive. It could be $10,000, $15,000, or any reasonable amount. The $5,000 used in this example probably would be higher in actual practice. (Some states set a limit on fees, so you would want to check with your attorney before locking in on a certain fee.)

As the funds are collected, they are held in an interest-bearing account or money market fund which you control. As some funds are on deposit for several weeks, a few hundred or thousand dollars build up from this interest as additional funds for the partnership. (Although rare, I sometimes give investors the interest their funds earn from the time they put them up to the actual formation of the syndicate, if it looks as if fund-raising will take an unusually long time.) These funds become a partnership asset and provide some additional hedge against unforeseen costs, although I do not show this asset in the Use of Proceeds.

Regarding your fund-raising fee in this instance, you can see the Financial Packaging fee and the Underwriting fee noted, $3,424 and $39,550 respectively. The total of these two fees ($42,974) is what you would receive for your efforts; not too bad for two or three months' work. It could be even better, however, if you were also the general partner.

(G) Risk Factors. Any investment has risks associated with it. As such, it is important that you note as many as you can think of in the front part of the Circular. You want to put the investor on notice right up front that the security of his funds is not guaranteed, nor can it be. The risk factors in this example are not necessarily the ones you would indicate for a different investment. For example, if loan funds (debt financing) were involved, then you should include a section on the risk of losing the partnership assets to the lender should the payments not be kept up. Your attorney can help you adequately cover this particular section.

(H) Background Summary of Project and Site Negotiations. This is one of those sections that shows the extent to which the general partner has gone in order to research and create the investment opportunity. It also gives the prospective investor a much better feeling for how the project evolved, and for what some of the considerations were. This is an important section to show that the general partner is conscientious, and that he has "done his homework."

(I) Site Locator Map. For those investors who want to know more specifically where the project is located, or who might want to visit the project site, a map of the general area is included. The project location is pinpointed on the map, preferably with fine-line red, felt-tipped pen to highlight the location for the investor.

(J) Restaurant's Location in Shopping Center. This pinpoints the exact location of the restaurant itself in the shopping center. Some of the investors will want to meet with the general partner at the site before they invest. This tells them exactly where the investment location will be. I outline the exact store location with the same fine-line red pen, again to highlight it for the investors.

(K) Representative Photos. The old saying "a picture is worth a thousand words" could not be more true concerning the Investment Circular. If your restaurant/ice cream parlor is not yet constructed, you obviously cannot show actual photos, but you can show photos of other similar stores.

I always hold this section down to two pages with two, 4x6-inch photos on each page. The pictures should be good quality, glossy, and colored. For your restaurant, you might want to have one photo of the exterior, and three of the interior. One of the three interior prints should be an attractive display of the food/ice cream products for which your franchise is famous.

(L) Background Information of Company. This section is important because it offers some detailed information about the parent company behind the franchise. Make it several pages long. It can help provide the investor with a good feeling about his investment. If the company is on an expansion program, these data can be helpful to show the company's aggressive, businesslike stature in the industry. The section also should give some data about the franchise itself, and about the obligations of the franchisor and franchisee.

(M) Background Information on the Industry. This section is optional, necessary only if a good article or study relative to the subject of your syndication is available. Regardless of the type of project in which you involve yourself, a section such as this can help sell your project to investors. Try to find an outside article or study that gives good, detailed background information on the industry as a whole.

If you are syndicating a race horse, then an article on how syndicated horses have performed on the track and in the bank might be helpful. If it's a single family dwelling, a long article from a well-known newspaper or news periodical that talks about inflation, the increase in prices, the need for rental housing, etc., may be appropriate. When I put together a loan package to finance fitness centers, I used a report from a large appraisal association that spoke about fitness centers in terms of how well they did as an investment. It helped me obtain several large loans.

An article or study should be used only if it is very positive. For example, an article that gives statistics and confirms that people will pay a high price for a quality ice cream might be useful here. If the article mentions our specific franchise, this, too, would be helpful. All of these "objective" outside data help to give investors a positive feeling, a reinforcement for what they are contemplating for their investment funds. Be sure, however, to obtain prior written approval from the author and/or publisher, if required, before you use the specific article.

(N) Individual Franchise: General Terms, Conditions, Renewal. More specific information on the franchise as to how it relates to this particular site is given here. The franchise cost and terms are discussed, particularly since the franchise fee is "wholesale" (significantly below what a franchise on the open market is worth at the time). Noncompetition protection for this area and for the city as a whole is pointed out, too. Another important factor is the potential "right of first refusal" for additional locations in the rest of the county. These all are important items, things that an investor wants to see since they should help safeguard his investment.

(O) Project Status, Planned Opening Schedule. Here the lease status is described, and again, there are some unusual attractions about it. The terms are very favorable, another plus for going ahead with the deal. Some background on other stores in the shopping center shows that the center should be a good draw overall for the restaurant. A general opening schedule and some of the details associated with it are discussed.

(P) Cash Distribution to Partners — Principals' Compensation. The sharing arrangement between the limited and general partners is described here. Some cash distribution projections are noted ("cash-on-cash" refers to cash return — exclusive of tax savings — as a percentage of funds invested) and the total general partner compensation is discussed. This is one of the most important parts of the Investment Circular because of the keen interest on the part of the investors in what all parties will be getting from the business.

(Q) The General Partners and Their Experience. The names and résumés are fictitious, but the format and content are exactly what I recommend that you use for this section. Hopefully, this information will lend a feeling of stability and qualification to the principals. Applicable business experience and formal education should be emphasized, although the business experience is more important than the education.

(R) Income Tax Risk Factors. Tax sections in private placement Investment Circulars range from the very short to the very long. The short ones (one or two paragraphs) leave the reader feeling that the principal has an inadequate understanding of the tax implications. The long versions (twenty, thirty, even forty pages or more) boggle the average person's mind and render the section quite meaningless for him.

I have found that my relatively brief, general tax discussion, such as the one shown here, is very effective with investors. On some occasions, I will cite expected deduction figures and percentages which give a bit more information. Generally, however, I use this basic wording, along with specific paragraphs relating to the particular deal, and keep the discussion general on purpose. I do admonish the investor in the last paragraph to use his own counsel for more details and clarification. I cannot keep up with all the changing rules and regulations, and do not pretend to; however, just enough information is provided to make the investor comfortable with my handling of this area.

This section should be fully discussed with your attorney and accountant to ensure that the tax aspect presentation is adequate. This approach should be acceptable if your state regulations are substantially similar to those in California. You also should be sure your syndication is put together in accordance with SEC Rule 147 guidelines.

(S) Pro Forma Financial Projections. The introduction to the Income Statements gives some background as to how they were generated. There also are several paragraphs of caveats, admonitions that none of these data can be guaranteed. These caveats are very important because the investor must understand that the financial projections are estimates only, and actual performance may not be as projected.

Regarding the financial schedules themselves (in this case Income Statements), I always have used the KISS method of presentation (Keep It Simple, Straightforward). Normally, I use only one Income Statement showing one to five years of performance. Sometimes, as with an apartment house investment, the schedule will be much more complex with depreciation and other information on the same page. On other occasions, one or two additional schedules may be called for as with this situation. But, I never have page after page of schedules which call for constant flipping from one page to another in order to obtain some semblance of understanding.

The investors are told that they should receive cash distributions equivalent to the amount of their original capital investment within three years. I want to show them the forecasted income for at least this long so that they can be comfortable with this cash distribution projection. For this reason, three twelve-month schedules are used.

Additionally, I normally show only one column of forecasted income and expense figures on an Income Statement. In this case, however, I have used two columns as I want the investors to have the benefit of seeing not only the average actual sales, but also the highest actual sales of the restaurants used as source data. At the bottom of each schedule, I indicate what basis I am using to increase my income and expense figures each year.

Even though I have used three Income Statements instead of one in this package, the "Financials" section is crisp and clean in appearance. Everyone from the very sophisticated to the relatively uninformed can grasp the story in each schedule. The data help to clarify, not confuse; yet, they offer enough in the way of format and content to make one feel that the general partners know what they are doing. At the same time, they stop well short of being a complicated, lengthy jungle of figures that needs cross-referencing and a doctorate degree to understand.

(T) Projected Limited Partner Cash Distribution Schedule. This is one of the most important presentations in the package. It shows each investor what he reasonably can expect from his investment, given that everything goes as planned. If you ask, you will find that the great majority of prospective investors automatically turn to this section just after reading the introductory statement; they want to know how much money they can make from this deal.

This schedule is a bit more complicated than most that I use, again because I want to show projections for two different types of sales levels. The first section (points A and B) shows the projected return during the original investment payout period for each sales level; the second section shows the projected return for each sales level after the payout period. The second section reflects the general partners now sharing in the profits. Some qualifying comments and other data are mentioned in the next paragraph. And again, a caveat about the vulnerability of the partnership to outside factors is given.

(U) Representations. This short section is another caveat to help protect both the investor and the promoters.

This completes the discussion of the Investment Circular portion of the Confidential Memorandum. It's the most important in a sales sense because it's the part the investors tend to study the most. The two attachments are just as important, however, because they bind together the investor, the syndicator, and the deal in a legal sense. We'll take a look at these attachments next.

CHAPTER 9

Confidential Memorandum: Agreement of Limited Partnership, and Statement of Suitability and Subscription Agreement

LET'S LOOK AT Attachment I to the Confidential Memorandum first. This is the Agreement of Limited Partnership. Parts of this legal agreement are based specifically on information in the Investment Circular just reviewed. Certainly, the overall intent and language in this Agreement are for the specific investment described in the Circular. A good portion of this document, however, is standard in nature, both in format and content. These standard parts would be found in an Agreement for most any type of venture.

Because of these factors and because this document is legal in nature, I will not go over each specific section as I did with the Circular. If you have any questions, you should have your attorney review the Agreement to your satisfaction, because he is the one most qualified to do so. There are some particularly important sections in the Agreement, however, that I want to highlight for you.

Attachment I, Agreement of Limited Partnership (Keyed to Attachment I Agreement in Appendix I Model)

(A′) Article 1.3 Purpose of Partnership Business. A seemingly innocuous paragraph, this can give you some trouble if you make the business purpose too narrow. In one deal where the business purpose was for a "tennis and swim club," we decided to expand by building lodging units on adjacent land owned by the partnership. Because of a dissident limited partner, we had to spend months and thousands of dollars to get everyone to consent to expanding the official business purpose to include the new development. Consequently, be sure to keep the business purpose general.

Here, the wording — "operate same for investment and benefit to the partnership" — probably is general enough to give some latitude in conducting the partnership business. It could be opened up even further by stating that the leased space can be used for *any* operation that benefits the partnership, in case a restaurant/ice cream parlor becomes uneconomical in the future.

(B′) Article 3.17. This provision is extremely important. The concept that only a slight majority is required to vote on certain aspects of the partnership is carried throughout the Agreement. For example, it is referenced in Article 12.6 regarding the general partner's right to withdraw from the partnership with only a majority vote. It is referred to again in Article 15.3 with respect to unauthorized activities of the general partner unless there is a majority vote. And the majority vote concept is cast in concrete, in general, in Article 16.3.

Unless advised to the contrary by your attorney, *never* require more than a "majority" approval for any partnership activities. The same partnership deal referenced above (in Article 1.3) required a 100 percent approval of the limited partners to do anything discussed in this section. Consequently, the one dissident limited partner was able to hold things up almost indefinitely. The poorly drafted wording requiring 100 percent concurrence in that case caused everyone problems, in both lost time and money.

(C') Article 4.3.2. From a sales standpoint, this is important for the investors to see. They are not required to contribute further sums to the partnership. (In reality, however, they may end up doing so *voluntarily* should the partnership run into temporary financial difficulties.)

(D') Article 9. Compensation to General Partners. This section is important for the general partner(s) because it spells out what compensation he/they will receive (above and beyond their ownership percentage compensation, which is in a later section). The front end fee is noted in detail, as is the management fee, which includes a provision for an annual 10 percent increase at the syndicator's discretion.

(E') Article 10.2. Although they must use good judgment, general partners are reimbursed for all expenses in connection with partnership activities (except as provided in 10.1); this means all costs related to organizing, marketing, and forming the partnership. Recovery of these costs is important because they usually represent a substantial percentage of the total capitalization of the partnership. The general partners also can charge the partnership for automobile, travel, and necessary entertainment expenses. While the content of this section is fairly comprehensive, reimbursable expenses are not limited to those included herein.

(F') Article 11. Allocation of Net Income, Net Loss, and Distributions. Sub-Article 11.1.1 clearly describes the sharing between the general and limited partners of the cash from the day-to-day operations of the business. In 11.1.2, the formula for sharing proceeds of a sale or refinance is set forth. These two sub-Articles concern the profit-sharing arrangement and are, thus, of prime importance to all parties.

The importance of 11.2 is in defining who will receive the tax benefits and liabilities. In 11.2.2, the general partners begin to share in the losses at a certain point, which should be defined in a clear manner. I have had difficulty with this 11.2 section before because there can be so many variables in tax accounting depending on profits, losses, special allocations, and distributions for any given year. Making this section completely clear would require many pages of examples of all the various possibilities. In any case, however, be sure to have an expert tax accountant work with the attorney on the wording in this section.

(G′) Article 14.3. Here, and again in 14.4 and 15.1.5, the investor sees the general partners' obligation to provide quarterly reports and tax reports/information. The quarterly reports enable the investor to see, at least four times per year, exactly what the status of his investment is. The tax reports show the investor what the partnership business did as a whole. They also include a specific report of his individual share of the income/losses, so that he can incorporate this information with other personal tax data on his annual federal (and state, if applicable) tax returns.

(H′) Article 15. Rights, Authority, Powers, Responsibilities, and Duties of the General Partners. The very wide latitude of rights and powers granted to the general partners is evident here. In this section also, however, are activities that the general partners are unauthorized to perform without majority approval from the limited partners. Consequently, this section is very important for both parties to see.

(I′) Article 16.1. This one-sentence provision is one of the most important of all provisions in the partnership agreement for the general partners. It clearly and firmly sets forth the concept that no limited partner may take any part in the operation of the partnership business — i.e., the general partners have complete control of all aspects of the partnership business.

(J′) Article 18. Certain Transactions. Of particular importance to the general partners, this provision gives them freedom to engage in other activities. Though they must devote as much time as necessary to ensure the proper functioning of this partnership, the general partners know they may engage in other activities/partnerships without any obligation to the partners of this partnership.

(K') Article 22. Miscellaneous. If you are a real estate licensee or if you have any other special licenses that could earn you a commission upon the sale or disposition of the partnership project, a paragraph to this effect should be added here. You would want to indicate that any commission earned would not be considered a partnership asset so that you could retain it for yourself.

For example, should your project be an apartment building, you normally would have to engage a real estate broker to sell it. If you are a broker, you can list it with yourself on the same basis as with an outside broker. When it sells, you can put at least one-half the commission dollars in your pocket this way. If you also directly find the buyer, you may be able to put the entire commission in your pocket.

(L') Exhibit "A." This Exhibit follows the partnership signature page. When all funds have been raised and the offering is closed, this Exhibit is filled in with each investor's name, address, and social security number, along with the number of Units purchased and the investor's total capital contribution. This master listing is used for recording and/or filing purposes, and for transmittal to each investor for his files (more on this in Chapter 12).

Attachment II, Statement of Suitability and Subscription Agreement (Keyed to Attachment II Statement in Appendix I Model)

This third part of the Confidential Memorandum package is as important as the first two, and even more important in certain respects. It is designed to protect the general partners from accepting nonqualified investors into the deal. It is a vehicle to help you do your "due diligence," your investigation into the prospective investor's background to ensure that he is suitable for the investment.

As you read through this Statement of Suitability and Subscription Agreement ("Statement"), you will note that certain specific and very important items are discussed. The Statement is worded in the investor first person. Consequently, he is making these representations of facts to you, saying that you can rely on his representations as a basis for judging him to be a suitably qualified investor. This way, you can be as certain as possible that he has a good understanding of the partnership business and the risks associated with it.

The signed original of this Statement, as well as the signed originals of the Exhibits to this Statement, all remain in your files. They are evidence that you checked into the investor's suitability, and that the investor acknowledged the conditions in the Statement.

(A") Paragraph (1) ties the Statement to the Confidential Memorandum and to the Agreement of Limited Partnership. It also is an acknowledgment by the investor that he has received and read — and that he understands — these documents.

(B") In Paragraph (2), the investor acknowledges the private nature of the offering, as well as certain other investment conditions.

(C") Paragraph (3) and all its subparagraphs pertain to your investigation of the investor and his confirmation of suitability for the investment. In (3) (g), the investor indicates a preexisting relationship with you, if any. If none, his representations in (3) (h) become more important, as they show a background that allows him to protect his own interests in connection with the investment. Note that the investor may rely upon a personal adviser per his representation in (3) (h) (2).

The investor Questionnaire mentioned in (3) (i) is attached to the Statement as Exhibit 1. It is quite comprehensive. As such, its completion by the prospective investor is further assurance to you that he is financially and otherwise qualified for this deal.

(D") Paragraph (4) discusses the fact that tax benefits and consequences cannot be guaranteed. In fact, nowhere in the entire package should you guarantee anything, nor should you guarantee anything verbally in any of your discussions. You only can estimate and project things based on the data at your disposal. You cannot *guarantee* anything.

(E") Paragraphs (5) and (6) are caveats about the risks associated with the investment. These two paragraphs are extremely important should the investment not work out as attractively as first thought. They are acknowledgments by the investor that he understands he could lose his money, or could have difficulty in liquidating his Units in the event of a financial emergency.

(F") Paragraph (7) simply states the name of any person receiving a commission or fee in connection with this investor's purchase of partnership Units.

The balance of the Statement concerns itself with the subscribing of Units, including certain personal information about the investor. The Statement must be signed by the investor. Along with the signed Exhibit (s) discussed below, the Statement is complete now for retention in your files.

(G") Exhibit 1. — Questionnaire. This deals primarily with the prospective investor's financial qualifications. It is a part of the Statement, providing information supplementary to that contained in the Statement.

(H") Exhibit 2. — Selection of Purchaser Representative Form. This Exhibit is required only if the investor feels unsure about his ability to evaluate the investment, and chooses to have someone advise him on it. This lets you know up front who the representative is so that you can supply any information needed by him in his evaluation. You must check into the representative's background to satisfy yourself that he has the training and experience necessary to review your project properly and advise someone on it.

CHAPTER 10

Package Presentation Comments

OUR PACKAGE OF three separate sections/documents just discussed is important from a legal viewpoint because it sets forth the nature of the venture, as well as the terms and conditions surrounding it. Full disclosure of all aspects is key. A well-prepared package should provide answers to most of the legal and investment questions that may arise during the life of the partnership.

The package is very important from a marketing viewpoint, too, as it is a direct reflection of you. It is a sales tool with which you will try to bring investors into the project. Consequently, it must be put together in a professional manner. It must give an impression of completeness, thorough knowledge, clarity, and fairness. It must be neat and must look like a lot of work and thought went into it. It must be presented properly.

Printing and Binding

The form into which you assemble your three documents is important for marketing reasons. If the venture is relatively small, an elaborate, fancy package will give the impression of wasteful spending. On the other hand, a brief, incomplete, and unprofessional package for any size venture — large or small — will not foster any type of confidence in the syndicator on the part of the investor. So, a middle ground must be reached, one that shows good judgment and professionalism without lavish presentation and spending. In other words, you want a package that is nice, but not too nice.

I have been very successful with either Xerox-type machine dry copies, or offset printed copies. For several hundred pages, the copy process is probably the least expensive. Once you move up into the thousands of pages, however, offset printing should be your most economical way to go. For example, I recently needed 500 copies each of four typewritten pages reproduced into two pages printed both front and back (a total of 2,000 pages). The copy process price was $127.20. I used the offset method, which cost $70.50. Both processes appear basically the same. As far as quality of paper, 20-pound plain white paper stock is fine.

As recently as early 1982, I made sure that both sides of a page in a Confidential Memorandum package were printed, just as they are with the Appendix I model. This resulted in a slim, neat package that also saved a little on mailing costs when I'd send one to an investor. Lately, however, "thicker is better" seems to be the trend. Although it's more psychological than practical, investors and general partners seem to feel that there is more substance to a deal if the Confidential Memorandum is thick. Consequently, I now put together a package that has printing only on one side of a page. In addition, I prepare the entire Investment Circular portion — except for the title page and financial section — with one and one-half spacing, instead of single spacing. This provides a more readable document. I also do not right justify the Investment Circular margins; this seems to keep it more personal and informal than if they were right justified.

The legal agreement portion of the Memorandum looks and is more formal, so I make sure that it is single spaced, and right justified. This different handling of the legal agreement and the Investment Circular gives a clear line of demarcation between them, which seems to make the document package appear shorter than it really is. (The Appendix I model is entirely single spaced and printed both sides strictly in the interest of space saving herein. I recommend using the foregoing suggestions in actual practice, however, in your preparation of the Confidential Memorandum package.) I also would advise you to use actual, colored 4x6-inch glossy prints for your photo display instead of Xerox-type photocopies. The actual colored print gives more impact to your display of whatever it is that you are trying to promote.

There are many different types of covers you can use, and many ways of binding the package and cover together. When I first started syndicating, I used the folders with three prongs inside. After three-hole punching the left side of the package, I could insert it into the folder with the prongs folded back to hold it. This gave me a cover and binding system all combined. It also allowed one to remove the signature pages and Statement of Suitability without tearing any pages.

Another method I used is the plastic slide binding system. Colored card stock is used for the back cover, and a pliable clear plastic for the front cover. The covers and package are fastened together with a plastic slide that goes over the left margin of the documents. This, too, gives flexibility in removing parts of the documents without having to tear out pages. A third method is to spiral bind the same covers to the package (with plastic spirals). One still can remove sections of the package although it is more difficult with this type of binding.

Any of these three binding systems can be used. I prefer another system, however, because I believe professional appearance is more important than flexibility. My preference is to use a good quality, plain color card stock (with a grained surface) for the back cover, and a pliable clear plastic front cover. These covers are fastened to the package with the Velo-Bind process. This process utilizes narrow, thin strips of plastic material along the left margin of the cover and package, top and bottom, to hold together the document set. Small pegs, hardly visible, pass through the papers and hold together the two plastic strips.

This Velo-Bind process is available for your use in many copy service centers. The strips generally can be matched to the back cover color, so a very nice appearance results. The only drawback is that signature pages must be torn out, or copied. I get around this, however, by filling in and sending the prospective investor a separate, unbound set of the appropriate signature pages and Statement of Suitability. I do this once I am fairly sure he will be coming into the venture. This allows him to retain a complete package. At the same time, the already filled-in papers along with a stamped, self-addressed return envelope seem to encourage their prompt signing and return, thus committing my investor to the deal.

Additional Points and Thoughts

Armed with the sales and ownership documentation, and knowing a little about its presentation, you now are ready to acquire other people's money for your deal. We will be moving right into this aspect of syndication after some key points are looked at below.

Appendix II Mini-Package Model. You can dispense with the covers and binding on this much smaller document since you will have good rapport with your prospective investors or you would not be using this abbreviated version. In fact, I recommend using this mini-package only if timing on the deal is critical, and only when you know all prospective investors well. Good dry-type copies stapled together in the upper left-hand corner can suffice when everyone understands that the urgency of grabbing this good deal dictates a quickly prepared, brief document set.

This mini-package is just as important as the more extensive document set, however. It still serves the same functions of describing the deal and binding together the general and limited partners.

Take in a Partner? The answer to this is an obvious "no" if you just are going to raise funds for someone else and will not end up being the general partner. But what about a venture wherein you are the general partner, the organizing/managing syndicator with all the attendant responsibilities? Well, I would advise just doing the deal on your own if it is fairly straightforward and small. For example, if you are syndicating a single family rental house, or duplex, and you need to raise $30,000 to $50,000, you should consider being the sole general partner.

In a larger, more complex deal, my recommendation is to do the deal with a partner, someone you know well and can trust. There should be enough in the way of fees and profits to make it worthwhile for both of you. And if there are problems with the venture later on, it is reassuring to have someone in it with whom you can share the extra work, worry, and possible expense.

A larger deal to me is one that requires $200,000 to $300,000 or more in investor funds, and has a lease or some recourse debt associated with it. A lender for a restaurant or for a fitness club could come back to you if the business cannot service the debt, whereas with a small residential rental, the lender may under appropriate state law look only to the property for his security. Incorporating and being a corporate general partner can eliminate much of the liability for you, too, but you should let your attorney counsel you on this aspect.

Caveats and Language. You probably noticed my use of caveats throughout the entire Confidential Memorandum model package. These caveats are warnings about certain risks, or explanations to prevent any misinterpretation of figures, statements, or other data in the documents. As I stated before, you cannot guarantee anything and you do not want the investor to mistakenly feel that he has some kind of guarantee. You also want to make it very clear to him that there are risks associated with any venture, including this one. As such, be sure to incorporate caveats throughout your Investment Circular and Statement of Suitability sections of the Confidential Memorandum.

In general, you should shy away from direct, positive statements in your documentation. Never say an investor "will" receive a certain return or tax benefit; say he "should" receive the return or benefit being discussed. Use "should," "could," "it is anticipated that," "the project may," and other words or phrases that do not imply a guarantee, or that a certain thing will happen.

Your use of language in this manner is somewhat loose, but you have to be loose because you really do not know exactly how this investment is going to end up. You will find that the average person gives more credence to these logical kinds of statements than to the flat "you will receive" or "the project will produce" kind of representation. People are not stupid; they know that no one can look out into the future and pin down something that specifically.

Attorneys-at-Law, Accountants. It may sound strange to you, but I constantly run into situations where I am asked by attorneys how to syndicate something, or how to take title to ownership shares, or other information relating to syndication in general. You will run into this, too, as you become more knowledgeable about limited partnerships and syndication of investments. But I have not deluded myself — and I hope you do not either — into thinking that I know more than the attorneys, or that I do not need one.

The only reason that I run into these situations is that very few attorneys specialize in limited partnerships or the details involved with putting together a syndication. They have so much law thrown at them in law school, then are constantly barraged with changes in the law, that they cannot possibly be experts in everything. Conversely, I do specialize in syndications and much of the law applicable to them, and probably do know more than many attorneys about certain aspects of this one, narrow field. So, in some cases, I (and you eventually) do appear to know more than some attorneys.

I do not keep up with the constantly changing security, real estate, and other laws that affect me greatly, however. Consequently, I never can be smug about my capabilities in the field of law. Additionally, I am not licensed to practice law and can get into serious difficulty by trying to develop my own contracts or other legal documents.

For these reasons, I continue to use good legal services each time I put together a syndication. I want my legal representative to keep me out of trouble, so I let the person with the training take care of the legal documents and details. This is not to say that I do not take advantage of using a partnership agreement, generated by an attorney, more than once. I do, in fact, use the last agreement for another deal by marking it up to make it appropriate for the current venture. But, before using it, I run it by an attorney to "bless it," to make sure there have been no changes in the law which might give me trouble down the road.

Although some basic information about private offerings in other states is mentioned in the next chapter, it would be impossible for me to cover each state's rules, requirements, and exceptions. I have chosen to give you detailed scenarios by sticking with one state: California. Because of this and because you are just starting out, you must obtain legal assistance when you put together your first syndication. I cannot emphasize this too strongly: see an attorney! And see an accountant if you are not completely up on tax law and accounting principles. Your attorney and accountant will see that you get off on the right foot insofar as rules and regulations applicable to the state in which you work (e.g., your attorney can tell you if any special certificates or licenses are required). It won't cost you anything, either, as their fees can be charged to and recovered from the investor funds raised for your first deal.

All of the examples in this book are just that: examples. They are for illustration purposes only and are not meant to be used as is. They are orderly presentations of data that can make it very easy for you to do your own syndicating by using them as guides; however, they need to be written to conform to your specific deal and to the regulations in your specific state. Your attorney and accountant also can help you with proper modification of these examples.

CHAPTER 11

Coming Up with Other People's Money

GETTING TOGETHER A group of people to invest in a particular deal is another important aspect of syndication. After your group is together and all funds are on deposit, it's a nice feeling to be collecting commissions, or to be paying yourself a fat fee, or both. But there can be no commissions or fees, nor can there be cash flow, profit-sharing, or other benefits without the group of investors. So, getting this group together is the very important last major step that must be taken before you can start pocketing your thousands of dollars.

My experience in raising millions of dollars from hundreds of investors will be passed on to you in this chapter. You will be given a complete recipe for coming up with investors, for selling yourself and the deal to them. In this selling process, there are some guidelines we must follow because we are making a private offering. We want to adhere to these guidelines so that there is no chance of someone coming back someday and saying that we really had a public, instead of private, offering. Accordingly, we need to take a brief look at these guidelines before getting into the actual fund-raising itself.

Private Offering Guidelines

We will look at the basic California guidelines for a private offering (referred to as "limited offering exemption" in California). We also will look at some basic information about private offerings in other states at the end of this section. You will find that the guidelines in many other states are no more restrictive than ours in California — and in some cases, less restrictive — but again, seeing an attorney to pin down the actual private offering limitation in your area is a must!

The following guidelines are taken from the California Corporations Code. Exact wording of the Code is not used here; rather, certain key provisions of the applicable Code section are highlighted and paraphrased to give you a basic understanding of the limitations within which you must conduct your fund-raising efforts. If you are in California, your attorney can expand on any of these points; if out of state, your attorney can relate these to the limited offering exemptions pertinent in your state. The following discussion is general in nature.

The applicable part of the California Corporations Code is Section 25102. Except for pension or profit-sharing trusts, this Section exempts (from public offering requirements) any offer or sale of any security in a transaction which meets each of the following five criteria:

1. Sales are not made to more than thirty-five persons, including persons not in California.
2. All purchasers have a preexisting personal or business relationship with the offeror. Or, by reason of their business or financial experience, purchasers could be reasonably assumed to have the capacity to protect their own interests in connection with the transaction.
3. Each purchaser represents that he is purchasing for his own account, and not for resale.
4. The offer and sale of the security is not accomplished by the publication of any advertisement.
5. A Notice of Transaction form is filed with the Commissioner of Corporations within thirty calendar days after

completion of the transaction (at the time the offering terminates).

The purpose of these limitations is to protect investors against abuse through fraud and unfairness in securities transactions.

With respect to point 1, the thirty-five-person rule, a husband and wife are counted as one person. Some purchasers are not counted at all. These are institutional investors, the issuer's officers, directors, or affiliates, professional advisers, and investors meeting a certain minimum net worth requirement.

Points 2 and 3 are self-explanatory. Regarding point 4, the advertisement restriction, the law is interested in how investors are located. They must be located through personal contact by the syndicator. The syndicator cannot advertise in magazines or newspapers, use word-of-mouth campaigns, run radio ads, put notices on bulletin boards, or have flyers passed out to trade union members or those in large employee associations. He can, however, take in a third party stranger when an existing friend or investor tells the third party about the opportunity. The syndicator still has to do a due diligence on the stranger, though, checking him out for financial and business qualifications just as he would do with a friend or business associate. In short, the syndicator must not seek funds from the general public.

The Notice of Transaction form required in California under point 5 above is brief and basic, a pre-printed form one page in length. You or your attorney can complete the form easily and send it to the Commissioner's office after you have raised the funds required.

In order to protect yourself and your investor partners adequately, just remember that the entire deal and your conduct must be fair, just, and equitable at all times. To place this philosophy into practice fully, be sure to disclose completely all the facts and risks surrounding the transaction that you can think of. Everything pertinent about yourself, the venture, security for the investment, and the associated risks must be revealed. The investor then has a solid basis upon which to make his decision about going into this particular deal. Without the full disclosure, the investor is not adequately protected. Remember, you have a fiduciary responsibility to the investor: you must uphold the trust and confidence he is placing in you regarding the use of his funds.

Private Offerings in Other States. Generally speaking, other states have private offering guidelines and rules, too, although not all describe their guidelines to the same extent as California. I believe it's safe to say that most, if not all, states adhere to the tenet expounded in the foregoing paragraph, i.e., the deal and your conduct must be fair, just, and equitable at all times. Beyond this, there can be some fairly significant differences.

For example, in the area of number of purchasers permitted, there presently is no set pattern. Although I do not have information on all fifty states, forty-five states break down as follows:

Number of Purchasers Permitted	Number of States by Category
5	1 (New Hampshire)
10	11
15	7 or 8
25	13
34	1 (Nevada)
35	12 or 13
Total	45

The variable number of states noted opposite 15 and 35 purchasers is due to Texas allowing one or the other, depending upon its detailed rules. Some of the larger states allow thirty-five purchasers (California, Illinois, Michigan, etc.), but so do some of the smaller states (Arizona, Iowa, Mississippi, etc.).

The great majority of states allow certain "not counted" purchasers, have limitations on advertising, limit the amount of commissions, and have some filing requirement. Most also have other specific limitations and conditions detailed in their private offering guidelines.

Again, be sure to obtain the specific guidelines in your particular state from an attorney when first starting out. He also can let you know if your deal must be registered with the Internal Revenue Service under the new tax shelter registration requirement of the Deficit Reduction Act of 1984. This requirement can affect all syndicators, regardless of where they have their base of operations.

Finding and Closing Investors

The question asked of me most frequently is, "How do you find your investors?" Unless they already have done some syndicating, people generally show awed respect for this seemingly impossible task. In fact, it is not as mysterious or as difficult as they imagine, although it does require some organization and concentration. The one rule we know from our foregoing discussion is that it must be a personal contact.

Step One: Develop a First-Stage List. Whether this venture is your first or your fiftieth is of no consequence; you would start out the same way in either case. You obviously are not a hermit or a completely introverted person because you are reading this book. As such, you have friends, relatives, clients, possibly some close business or work associates. Put their names down on a list. These are the people you would like to see make money on this venture the most, would you not? Sure you would. You should have no trouble assembling twenty-five to fifty qualified names. And these people just happen to be the ones you know the best.

Set up your list in the same format as in the example that follows. Using this format gives you one central place to record telephone numbers, date of contact, follow-up dates, and other individual investor information during the fund-raising phase. By the time your syndication is put together, you'll have a very comprehensive list with many names and telephone numbers. (And most important, when you begin fund-raising for your next syndication, this marked-up list becomes the logical starting point for you at that time.)

USE THIS SAMPLE LIST AS A CENTRAL PLACE FOR RECORDING INVESTOR INFORMATION DURING FUND-RAISING EFFORTS

Date of Contact	*Investor Name & Mailing Address*	*Telephone*	*Follow-Up*	*Purch./ Passed*
7/5/84	John Bakerston 1232 Traynor Elmtown 9xxxx	938-1212-O 639-4500-H	O.K. Send pkg. today. F-up on 7/11.	
7/5/84	Burt Johnson 8799 South-mere Elmtown 9xxxx	639-3101-O 639-3099-H	Not inter. No $ 'til early '85. Call then.	Passed
7/5/84	Joe Hendrix (AM Company) -need address-	983-2445-O	Very inter. Take pkg. to him tomorrow 8:30 a.m.	
7/5/84	Jane Bauer (Pres. Vernon, Inc.) 590 Overlook Port Georges 9xxxx	983-2790-O 654-1200-H	Likes it. Put emphasis on early payback in cov. ltr. Mail today.	
7/5/84	Ken Almanor 10 Kent, Su. 4A Elmtown 9xxxx	639-7322-O 639-4076-H	Very inter. Will see in 30 min. (ok — is in for 2 Units)	2 Units

Step Two: Contact Those on This List. Although you eventually should try to meet with the prospective investor, your initial communication can be by telephone. After opening pleasantries, let your friend or relative know that you are involved in something that is "unique," or that "offers an unusual opportunity," or that "looks to be extremely profitable for me, and I can get you in on it if it makes sense to you, too." In other words, you want to hook your contact right up front; you want to use some catchword or phrase that piques his interest so that, hopefully, he will ask you to tell him more. And in most cases, he *will* ask for more information because this can be that special opportunity, that chance for him to get in on something good.

If your prospect does ask for more details, give him the highlights of the venture in terms of what it can do for *him* — i.e., his potential return on investment, tax benefits, cash flow (if any) during the holding period, excitement of owning a piece of the deal, etc. Keep in mind that you must always place yourself in your investor's mind as much as possible. You want to give him the aspects that would mean something to *him,* not a lot of words on how great a job you did in coming up with this particular opportunity.

Throughout all of this, though, be forthright and honest. Don't mislead your prospect. If the great returns are fraught with abnormal risk, then say so. If virtually no risk is present, tell him that risk is always a factor although it appears to be minimized in this deal. Even though you want to hook your contact's interest immediately, you cannot do so by misrepresentation.

This initial contact gives you the chance to screen out quickly and easily those in this first group who have no interest at all. Many persons you know will tell you to send the package to them, knowing full well that they are not going to put any dollars into your deal. Telling you to send the package gets them "off the hook" gracefully, because they easily can say the deal just was not for them when you call back later on. In the meantime, unfortunately, you have spent a lot of time; you have let your hopes build up about someone who never was a bona fide prospect in the first place.

I try not to give people the chance to waste my time. When I sense a hesitation or negative vibes, I tell them straight out that I am reluctant to take their time and mine if they are not sincerely interested in reviewing the package. This gives them the opening they are looking for. Usually, they will admit then that they just do not have an interest, which is fine. I really do not want to spin my wheels for lip service.

Step Three: Get the Confidential Memorandum Package in Their Hands. Ideally, you will meet with prospective investors for a few minutes to hand them the package along with a brief (one page or less) cover letter. Your letter highlights the main points (the venture, the income and tax benefits, timing, investment amount, etc.). These all are extracted from the package; they just are highlighted here.

The package and cover letter go in the mail if a personal meeting is not possible. Always mail the package First Class; it will get to the prospects sooner, and time is money to you.

The cover letter is a highly effective sales tool. Many of your prospects will not open the investment package; it just will sit and collect dust until you call back. But, when you hand the package to the prospect or he pulls it out of the envelope, the cover letter will be looking at him in either case. At the very least, most people will scan the three or four paragraphs, the highlighted facts and figures. This will embed these data in their minds a second time (the first pass was on the telephone). Unless your prospect is completely not interested and you just did not pick up this attitude over the telephone, he will be pulled into the document right then, or he will get into it at a later time. He now is hooked into giving it some of his attention.

If I just had spoken to a prospective investor on the telephone about the twenty-two-unit apartment building discussed in Chapter 5, I would use a cover letter substantially similar to the example on page 118.

Be sure to use letterhead, or to type your address and telephone number at the top of this letter, so that the investor knows how to reach you. Note that I leave off the colon after the salutation. I do this to add a personal touch, although I

July 5, 1984

John Bakerston
1232 Traynor
Elmtown, California 9xxxx

Dear John

Good to talk to you today. The 22-unit garden apartment complex in Los Angeles that we discussed has an assumable, low-interest loan. Even with today's high interest financing, apartment buildings usually can be good, fairly predictable real estate investments; however, when coupled with this low interest financing, an expected 42.94% per year return on investment results. This projected return includes:

a. cash-on-cash current distributions of approximately 5.99% average per year over the four-year planned holding period;

b. excess tax losses in early years to offset other ordinary income, plus capital gain tax rates upon the sale of the property;

c. substantial net profits through the mortgage debt reduction and appreciation of the property.

Referencing page xx in the Confidential Memorandum, you'll notice that approximately $10,222--after return of your $4,166 invested capital--is projected to be the net profit per share. This profit is based on what is felt to be a conservative sales price forecast. If a higher price could be obtained, a higher return could be available; however, all of this is based on future events and cannot be guaranteed.

Because of the potential cash flow, tax benefits, and expected market value appreciation, we feel this will be fully subscribed soon, John. Accordingly, I'll need to know in the next few days if you would like to share in the ownership of this building. Talk to you soon.

Best regards,

Rick

Richard H. Beguelin

Attachment

use a colon when writing to those I do not know well. I also reference important data and the page number from the Confidential Memorandum in the body of the letter. This is to encourage the prospect to get into the Memorandum right then.

I have found this type of cover letter to be very effective for me (rather than a short, handwritten note, or no note at all). Consequently, I suggest that you consider using such a letter in your investor communications.

Step Four: Develop a Second-Stage List and Get the Package to Those on This List. After completely going through the first list, you will know how many of those persons are good prospects. If you do not feel that you can fund your project solely with these people, you can begin to put together a second-stage list while you still are sending out packages to the first-stage people. This second list requires some deeper thought; names will not automatically flow off the top of your head as they did when thinking about the initial set of names. You will be amazed, however, at what will result by sitting for an hour with a piece of paper and a pencil, and just thinking. (The names you come up with can be added on to the first-stage listing of people so that all persons contacted will end up on the same master listing.)

This second list will begin to form with names of additional friends, business or work associates, and possibly some relatives again, but, it generally will not have the close persons in these categories that came out of the first-stage effort. You just did not think of these people on the first pass through your mind because they are not your closest contacts. Nevertheless, they constitute persons whom you know or with whom you have a business relationship, so they are appropriate prospects.

Additionally, list various categories of businesses, professions, and organizations, and use these to stimulate your thinking about people you may know in these categories. For example, note down teachers, accountants, attorneys, your church members, service clubs, any social groups to which you belong, etc. The accountants and attorneys are especially good because they have many clients whom they can recommend. And, if they go into the project on their own, they may not add to the investor count because they are considered "advisers."

Soon you will find that you have another twenty-five to fifty names with which to work. Your "close ratio" will not be as effective with these persons because you do not know them quite as well as the people in the first group. Nevertheless, you will see some of these people coming into your venture. You also will see several persons whom you did not even know when you began the fund-raising effort end up being investors. These people will hear about the deal from other investors already in it. Or, they may be referrals from some of your contacts who do not have the funds themselves, but who think it makes sense for their friends. The point is that soon you will have another prospect group with which to work that is as large as the first group of prospects.

Your selling efforts with this second group are exactly the same in terms of contact, getting the package and cover letter to them, and follow-up. You may find that you will be selling yourself more than selling the deal to some in this group as they will not know you quite as well as those first-stage prospects. In those cases where you and the prospect do not know each other at all (investor and adviser referrals), you may end up working *less* to get them committed. Many times, these referrals make up their minds more quickly than those who know you much better.

Step Five: Develop a Third-Stage Listing and Make Contact with These People. You may not need to go this far; you should have funded your venture with the investor prospects from the first two groups of persons. However, if you still need additional investors, the same concentration with pencil and paper as used before will produce more prospects for your deal.

Go through all the categories noted above to ferret out new names missed previously. Then, go through the Yellow Pages in your local telephone book, being careful to note the names of all the businesses with which you have some familiarity. Again, your memory will be jogged with the names of salespeople, doctors you have been to, business owners you know, and others with whom you have a personal or business relationship. Contact any real estate or security brokers/representatives whom you know as they have many clients and can act in an advisory capacity to these clients. (You may have to share some small portion of your fund-raising fee with these referral sources, but the exposure to their clients can be well worth it.)

You will find a third list developing, and will want to get packages to those that seem genuinely interested in your project. These people may be even harder to close for the reasons noted above, but you will bring a few of them into the deal.

NOTE: There may be a limit to the number of investors you may contact in your state. Be sure to have your attorney counsel you on this point.

Along with names on each of these lists, you will be using other names noted down that you thought of during this fund-raising period. People you meet at service clubs, parties, and other social gatherings can become prospects. You can query them at the time if the opportunity arises, or you can make a note of their names for later contact. Your friends can be sources of prospects, too. While you do not want to enlist them as formal "finders" of prospects as this would constitute a word-of-mouth campaign, their knowledge of your deal can result in some of their friends being interested in your venture.

Step Six: Close Your Prospects into the Deal. You will, of course, be signing people up and collecting their funds throughout this whole time period. As you are doing so, you must make sure that they qualify for the deal. Much of your due diligence can be done over the telephone or in your personal meeting with the prospect. Don't be afraid to tell him that he just does not qualify (too little income/net worth, lack of understanding, etc.). It is much better to lose him now as an investor than to get him in and have him pressed financially if the deal does not work out as planned. Also, he may be a future prospect and will hold you in high regard for being firm with him on this deal.

If the prospect is qualified, however, have him complete and sign the Statement of Suitability and its Exhibit(s). This Statement, the signed Partnership Agreement signature pages, and his check constitute the documents you need to have him firmly in the deal. I suggest that you always fill in the documents for the prospect (except for the Statement Exhibit 1 Questionnaire, of course, which requires specific details you cannot fill in). Have them reviewed and signed in a physical meeting, or send them (including Exhibit 1) to the prospect along with a stamped, self-addressed return envelope. He will be impressed by your professionalism, and more important, will fill in Exhibit 1, and sign and return the documents more quickly, committing him to the deal.

Flexibility Equals Success

As far as selling techniques are concerned, I generally use a soft sell approach. Always sincere, I convey a feeling of low pressure in my presentation, professional but with a slight folksiness coming across. Most people appreciate this approach over a hard-hitting, hard sell effort. Some people will need a little push, however, which you can sense as the sales effort proceeds. Others who are on the fence need a negative push or sell, a "maybe this just is not for you" approach which has worked very well for me. (This category of person starts feeling that he is going to miss out on something good when you turn on the negative sell.) And then, a few people will need a strong, no-nonsense talking to about how this product fits them perfectly (assuming, of course, that it does), and how sorry they may be if they let it go by. The main key to success is for you to adapt your personality to fit the personality of your prospect. Do not be rigid; remember, flexibility equals success.

Your first syndication will be the hardest to put together. Each one after the first will become easier in terms of getting investors. You will see a pyramiding effect; as your base of investors builds up, new ones will come in rapidly and progressively, enlarging step-by-step your qualified investor list. The size of your ventures can increase, which means more fees and profits for you. Your net worth will build and and very soon you may be independently wealthy. You must walk before you run, however, so do not become discouraged if this first venture takes a little longer than you thought it would. The quality time and effort you devote to it will be well spent.

Additional Points and Thoughts

Purchaser Status List. Set up a handwritten log or list of purchasers as they sign up for your deal. This will enable you to track exactly where you are at all times in terms of how much of the offering remains open. (This is a separate list, different from your prospective investor list wherein you noted dates of contact, when you sent packages, follow-up dates, etc.) This purchaser status list should contain the minimum following columnar data:

1. Date sold (committed)
2. Name(s) of purchaser(s)
3. Amount purchased
4. Documents received:
    a. Payment check — yes or no
    b. Signature pages — yes or no
    c. Statement of Suitability — yes or no
5. Dollars due (if any)
6. Cumulative purchases

Always attempt to obtain payment in full; however, if a deposit (at least 10 percent) is necessary to preserve the transaction until all funds are available to the investor, the balance due can be noted in column 5 mentioned above. Regardless of the amount of actual monies collected, update the Cumulative Purchases column with the total investors' commitment amount so you know how much of the offering is gone at all times.

This list serves two primary purposes:

1. It keeps you from overselling the deal, then having to give back the person's money (not great for customer relations when the investor thought he finally had bought into his once-in-a-lifetime deal); and
2. It is a great sales tool. Some persons want to know who else already has invested, which they can see when you show them this list. Almost invariably they will know or will know of someone on the list, which is a positive influence on them. Toward the end of the offering, the list also can be a positive factor in telling prospects that there are "only one or two investment Units left, so you had better make your decision quickly."

File Folder for Each Investor. In conjunction with filling in the purchaser status list, be sure to set up a separate file folder for each investor at the same time. You want to make sure that each folder contains all three of the documents mentioned above in 4a, b, and c. (A copy of the check should go in this folder. The original check, of course, will be deposited.)

It is very important now to check again on the signatures required. Be sure that proper signatures are on the Partnership Agreement signature pages. And make sure that the Statement of Suitability and Exhibit 1 are properly filled in and signed. These documents are confirmation of your due diligence to ensure that your investor is qualified. (Although not required in California, you may have a requirement in your state for the investor signatures to be notarized, and for the Partnership Agreement — including investor signature pages — to be recorded with your County Recorder. If so, you would check at this time to be certain that all signatures have been notarized properly.)

Collecting Funds. I always open a bank money market fund account or other relatively safe, liquid savings account in which I deposit funds collected. This maximizes the interest earned on monies deposited. I usually do not represent to investors that their dollars will earn interest for them *until* all offering funds are on deposit (and maybe not even then, depending on the type of deal). This earned interest gives the partnership some added cushion in the way of total capitalization when it is formed and operating. Occasionally, I will give investors the interest earned on their funds if it appears that fund-raising will be a lengthy process. Also, an investor sometimes will insist on some interest return if he comes in early. In those rare cases, I will reimburse him some nominal interest amount, on a pre-agreed basis, when the offering closes.

Commencement Date for Minimum Return. The model offering package in Appendix I does not provide for a minimum annual return to the investors before the general partners are entitled to take anything for themselves. (Instead, it provides for a 100 percent return, with no time restriction, before the general partners receive any portion of the cash flow.) Many of my offerings do call for this minimum annual percentage return on the investors' capital, however, so the beginning date for commencement of this minimum percentage becomes very important. I insert the beginning date in the Cash Distribution to Partners section in the Investment Circular, and again in Article 11.1.1 of the Partnership Agreement. In all cases, I state this date to be ". . . when the project commences to do business," or ". . . when the partnership project opens its doors for business." This commencement date can be significantly different from the date that the investor gave you his funds; consequently, it must be pinned down and be clearly understood by all parties.

Screening Investors. Try to use some objective judgment in taking investors into your venture. Some people just should not invest because of temperament, suspicion, lack of sophistication, or any number of other reasons.

You certainly do not want a person who begrudges you a fee or profit for your risk, effort, and imagination. You should stay clear of very elderly people (in their seventies or older) because their motivations are much different; they do not have a lot of time to see if this investment is going to perform as projected. A suspicious person who tries to catch you in what you say, a financially weak person without staying power, a "know-it-all," a nitpicker, or an argumentative person are people to steer clear of.

You want people who are goal and result oriented, who have the ability to think and communicate, and who have had a prior relationship with you, if possible. The prior relationship does not guarantee anything, but at least you will have a feeling for the type of person with whom you are dealing. Most important, you do not want to let any one person buy more than 20 to 30 percent of the offering. As your Partnership Agreement will provide for a majority vote to make certain decisions, this protects you against one bad apple being able to control the entire partnership.

Out of all the several hundred investors with whom I have dealt, only one has caused me any difficulty. And guess what? I (and my co-partners at the time) let him buy 80 percent of the partnership interests. It did not matter that the deal was the best one we had put together. The investor was receiving high, tax sheltered cash flow, and the partnership property was appreciating significantly in market value. However, this very wealthy man was used to telling people what to do; he was not of the proper temperament to be a passive investor in a limited partnership. Consequently, he forced a sale of the property which cost all of us — him included — a lot in cash flow and profits.

In his case, several mistakes were made. The investor was a dictatorial, argumentative person. He tried to negotiate downward our front end fees and our percentage ownership of the profits. And, he was allowed to purchase 80 percent of the ownership. We allowed him to participate in spite of all these warnings because his large investment would make it easy for us to commit all the funds required. It was a mistake.

No matter how diligently you attempt to screen out potential troublemakers, you never can be sure that none of the limited partners will be a thorn in your side. Chances are, however, that you will not have any difficulty if you take some pains at the outset to shy away from questionable persons. The old saying "an ounce of prevention is worth a pound of cure" is very applicable in working with investors.

A Show of Success. A man with whom I was a partner for a while kept telling me to buy an expensive car with some of the high income I was earning. He said my performance and success would increase significantly by doing so. After holding out for several months, I finally sold my older model car and bought a new one that happened to be the most expensive American model one could purchase at the time.

My car usually was parked in front of my office or was in my driveway when I was home. Almost immediately, friends and neighbors (some of whom I had never met) began stopping by my office or home "just to say hello." Invariably, they would ask what I did for a living, which was a perfect opening for me to tell them about the deal I was just putting together. Many of these people ended up becoming investors.

The point here is that I suddenly became a very "smart" person in the eyes of others. It was almost like announcing that I had a genius-level IQ, even though most of the people crediting me with these brains had more than I did. My expensive car meant that I was successful, and people associate success with brains. A lot of people suddenly wanted to have some of my success rub off on them. As my partner had said, my performance and success did increase significantly.

You and I both know that material things and "show" do not make a person any better or smarter than anyone else. But, most people in our society are impressed by these things, right or wrong. You do not need to be gaudy, but upgrading your car, office, and home when you can afford it can make you more successful in this business. The new image acts like flypaper; it attracts. And what it attracts are investors.

Selling Yourself. You soon will discover that most investors really are putting money into *you* more than into the investment. The investment must look good and reasonable, and the package needs to look good, too. But in the final analysis, no one will put his funds into the deal unless he feels very good about you. Accordingly, your reputation, your appearance, and the way you operate become very important aspects of this business.

I already have told you how to analyze deals and how to develop a good, professional package. Some tips on contacting investors and selling them on the deal have been given, too. The other major part of being successful is you, and how you conduct yourself. Always be honest and fully disclose things to the investor. Never give an answer you may not be sure of; tell the investor you will get the answer and get back to him. Do not act better than anyone else. Be responsive to investor questions and keep him informed as to the venture's progress. Be a good human being. Remember, the investor really is buying you.

CHAPTER 12

Forming the Partnership and Closing the Investment Transaction

THIS IS ONE of the most enjoyable parts of the syndication process because it contains your payday. Your front end fee from the partnership and any real estate commissions or other fees earned come to you during this time period. Another major benefit is the self-satisfaction you can expect from watching the partnership and the investment opportunity merge together into a completed transaction. The realization that you made this opportunity happen can be very rewarding, and should not be minimized in the overall scope of things. It's the feeling of enjoying one's work, after all, that makes life much more satisfying.

If you are working only as a packager/fund-raiser, your work is almost finished once the partnership funds have been raised and are on deposit. You only need to turn over all signature pages, suitability documentation, and funds to your client, collect your fees, and be on your way. However, if you are fulfilling all of the syndication functions, four main tasks need to be completed before you can settle into the investment management mode:

1. paying yourself;
2. sending a Notice of Transaction form to your state securities department (if required in your state);

3. forming the partnership; and
4. closing the investment transaction.

I accomplish these tasks in this exact order (except for 3 and 4, which, on occasion, sometimes reverse themselves).

Paying Yourself

Yes, you literally write yourself a check, or checks, which is one of the very nice things about raising the funds and being the organizing/managing syndicator (or one of them), too. Quite obviously, this payout should not be accomplished until all partnership Units have been sold, *all* funds have been collected and are on deposit, and you know the partnership asset will be acquired. Once this is done, however, there is no reason why you cannot pay yourself.

Using the model Memorandum (Investment Circular) in Appendix I for reference, the Use of Proceeds and the Principals' Compensation sections define what fees/charges you can pay yourself in addition to reimbursement for out-of-pocket costs. In that example, I assumed that I (or you) was raising funds for others, and would, therefore, receive only a packaging fee, and a fund-raising fee. Had I also been the organizing/managing syndicator, however, I would have withdrawn four checks from the savings account I used for the collection of monies raised. These four checks would have been for the following purposes:

a. Printing, binding, photos, etc.	actual amount
b. Financial packaging, structuring, etc.	$ 3,424
c. Underwriting cost (fund-raising)	$39,550
d. Project management reimbursement fee	$ 5,000

In other deals, I might also work in an organization fee of several thousand dollars for the considerable front end work involved, or just take a larger project management reimbursement fee (as it is called in the model). Real estate, consulting, or other commissions or fees would come from whatever source(s) you described in the Investment Circular to the limited partners. If an apartment building was being purchased by the partnership, for example, and I was licensed to transact real estate business, I would receive a commission at the close of the purchase escrow. This normally would be paid by the seller of the property, not by the partnership.

From an accounting/audit trail viewpoint, you should identify clearly on the checkbook stub the nature of the checks drawn. Or, if no checking account is yet available, you should note exactly what the checks are for in the savings account passbook itself. Further, I recommend that you prepare a brief, handwritten accounting statement entitled simply "Reconciliation." Its purpose is to summarize, in one place, exactly what details, if any, make up the individual checks you receive. Applicable receipts should be attached to the statement. For example, the one check for out-of-pocket expenses should itemize the photos, printing, binding, and other expenses being recovered. As yet, I have not been questioned by an investor or anyone else about my "payday" checks. If ever I am, however, the detail as well as the applicable receipts are in my files.

Notice of Transaction Form

This form was discussed earlier in Chapter 11. In California, the form is a brief, pre-printed one-page document that you can easily fill in yourself. Your attorney can do this for you if you would rather not be concerned with it. In any case, calendar this task to be handled about two weeks after you terminate the offering to ensure that it is completed well in advance of the 30-day time limit (in California).

Forming the Partnership

In the Additional Points and Thoughts section of Chapter 11, we discussed the careful review of each of the documents collected, and the establishment of file folders for each investor.

After all funds are collected, we once again want to check carefully that all signature pages are properly signed, and that they and the Statement of Suitability are on file. At this point, there are some specific steps to follow to ensure appropriate forming of the partnership and good investor relations.

1. Establish a Partnership Checking Account. Although you have a money market or some other type of savings account, you will need an account out of which you can write checks for various partnership expenses. Set up such an account as soon as possible in a bank convenient to the partnership's place of business, which may be your office or home. The three-on-a-page checks are good as you can note substantial information on the large check stubs. If there is not a lot of checking activity in your partnership, the stubs could end up being accounting source data for your bookkeeper or accountant at year end, thus saving you time and money for bookkeeping.

2. Fictitious Business Name Statement. Filing of this statement with the County Clerk in your area (if required) satisfies certain legal and other requirements which your attorney can explain to you. It also puts the public on notice as to your "doing business as" (dba) name for the limited partnership. This is a very minor task, but one you should be sure to accomplish depending upon advice from your counsel.

3. Partnership Agreement Signature Pages. Assemble all signed signature pages in one stack. You, as the organizing/managing syndicator, and your partner(s), if any, then should sign all of these pages as the general partner(s). After making a copy (for each investor) of each completely signed page, these copies and the originals will go back into the investors' file folders until the first report goes out to them.

4. Filing (Forming) the Partnership. Either you or your attorney can handle this task. In order to officially form a limited partnership in California, the general partners must sign and file a one-page Certificate of Limited Partnership Form LP-1, along with a $70.00 filing fee, in the office of the Secretary of

State. This Certificate will be duly certified by the Secretary of State, and is conclusive evidence of the formation of the limited partnership.

It's possible in your state that there may be a requirement to record the Partnership Agreement with your County Recorder, or there may be some other requirement. Check with your attorney to verify that the Partnership Agreement need be recorded, or otherwise processed, in your particular state.

5. Mailing Documentation to the Investors. If the raising of funds takes several weeks, it is a good idea to send out a brief progress report to the investors who came in early to let them know that the offering will be closing "soon." In other words, keep them informed. Beyond this first brief note you may have sent out, the next mailing will constitute your first complete report to the investors since acquiring their funds.

After the Certificate of Limited Partnership has been filed, it is important to write a comprehensive status report to the investors. The report should bring the investors up-to-date on the project, and should be sent to them along with the following:

a. A copy of their Partnership Agreement signature page which, of course, will show your signature on the page, also.
b. A copy of the Exhibit "A" listing of all limited partners which displays names, addresses, and amounts of capital contribution for each.
c. A copy of the escrow closing statement (if any), or any other pertinent data.

A file folder of this and subsequent investor reports should be maintained so that all general correspondence to investors is assembled in one central place. A copy of the Exhibit "A" list stapled to the inside cover of the file folder serves as your mailing list. This Exhibit "A" list should be kept current for mailing purposes, as well as to satisfy a California requirement to maintain such a list on a current basis.

Closing the Investment Transaction

Depending upon the investment itself, there may be nothing to do insofar as ensuring that the partnership investment asset is intact. For example, in the Appendix I model, the leasehold interest had already been acquired. No real estate was being purchased, so there was no escrow to close. The only extra effort required here would be to assign the ice cream franchise and the leasehold interest rights to the limited partnership.

Other non–real estate ventures may or may not require some closing action. Some may have Option Agreements that must be exercised to acquire a partnership asset. Others may involve contracts for services or certain rights. Whatever the case happens to be when an agreement is involved, the partnership should be given the rights in the agreement, if possible. It is the partnership funds, after all, which are being used to acquire or pursue the investment.

Real Estate. For purchase of real property, the general partner must be in control for the benefit of the partnership. Typically, a Purchase Agreement, Option Agreement, or escrow instruction is involved, and the transaction is in the general partner's name or provides for an "assignee" of the general partner. When it is time for an option to be exercised or an escrow to be closed, always end up taking title in the partnership's name, not in each investor's name as a tenant-in-common, nor in your name as the general partner. You still will have complete control of the asset as the general partner, but you want the partnership to be the legal owner.

Since there may be certain investors who will not feel secure unless they see their name as grantee on a deed, why not take title in the individual investors' names as tenants-in-common? Well, one obvious reason is that you, as the general partner of the partnership, will have to go around and collect everyone's signature every time the property owners must sign something. This would be cumbersome, but there are much more devastating reasons for not doing it this way.

One partner could declare bankruptcy or be sued, which would result in the property being tied up in bankruptcy or civil court. A civil judgment could result in a lien against the property. Death of a partner could tie up the property again, this time in probate court. Other legal problems on the part of one partner could cloud the title. And if all but one partner want to sell the asset to benefit from the property appreciation, the one unwilling partner could prevent the sale, because it could not occur without his signature. Your attorney can give you other reasons never to place a group of investors directly on title, but you probably get the message from the few reasons expressed here.

When a real estate transaction culminates, the escrow company will prepare an escrow closing statement that lists all the costs and credits associated with the transaction. This statement should be sent to the limited partners as described previously in this chapter. At the close, any real estate commission due you from the seller will be paid out of escrow. Additionally, you may have advanced a deposit to tie up the property. After closing, you should reimburse yourself for the deposit or other out-of-pocket costs from the partnership checking account.

In summary, you'll like this part of syndication the best because it includes a big payday for you. You also should experience some real self-satisfaction as you see the deal go together. Now you're ready to manage the partnership, and to pick up some additional earnings from the syndication process.

CHAPTER 13

Managing the Partnership

AFTER THE PARTNERSHIP has been formed, the centralized management aspect of the limited partnership structure goes into full effect. The investor has contributed his investment dollars, and the investment asset has been acquired by the partnership. As the general partner, you will stay involved in the partnership activities throughout its life; you will manage the partnership business and make all the business decisions. Only when the partnership asset is sold or refinanced will the investor possibly be actively involved again. (In most cases, the investor must approve or disapprove the sale or refinance proposal submitted to him by the general partner.)

This passive investment and usual limited liability are attractions to an investor. He is relying on the sound judgment and experience of another person to manage his money, and to relieve him of all the hassles normally involved with an active investment. The general partner can be wrong about the investment to begin with, or he can do a poor job managing the investment. But, no matter what may happen, the investor's economic risk usually does not go beyond the amount of his investment; he is limited as to what he can lose (although this is not the case in certain unique situations). On the other hand, there is no limit to what he may reap from the investment in terms of financial benefits.

Managing the Partnership Assets

The general partner has 100 percent control of the operation of the partnership. He now is involved in the day-to-day operations as opposed to the organizing/formation activity. His duties and responsibilities are far-ranging and diverse. He can commit to contractual matters, order services and supplies, and bind the partnership in any way deemed advisable to carry out the purposes of the partnership business.

Article 15 of the Partnership Agreement in the Appendix I model expands on the powers and duties of the general partner. It also specifies what he cannot do without approval of the limited partners. Generally, the exclusion of major business decisions is relatively narrow (for example selling the assets or assigning them to creditors). Although many exclusions appear in this section, most are commonsense acts a general partner would not want to perform anyway, except under unique circumstances. Most agreements do not exclude the general partner from any outside business activity; however, in all cases, the general partner must act in the highest good faith to the limited partners and may not obtain any unfair advantage over them. The general partner bears a fiduciary relationship to the limited partners by law. If there is any question regarding what the general partner may reasonably do, he should ask his attorney for immediate clarification. A fair, just, and equitable approach to the limited partners will always keep a general partner in good stead.

Management Contract. If the partnership asset requires active management (i.e., more than just watching money sitting in a savings account), the general partner should have a management contract if he is to be paid a fee for this management. The contract can be relatively brief, but it should spell out the functions and responsibilities of the manager in return for the fee to be paid. The general partner can sign the contract as the manager, and as the general partner of the partnership. This contract should be signed and in the partnership files before filing of the Certificate of Limited Partnership.

If the general partner chooses to have an outside (third party) firm perform the management, the contract becomes even more critical. In this case, the general partner will not receive a fee, but will be responsible for watching over the outside management firm. A good contract will enable him to protect his partnership vis-à-vis the management firm, thereby aiding him in living up to his fiduciary responsibility to the partners.

Management Fee. If the general partner is performing the day-to-day active management himself, he is entitled to a fee for this effort. Paying this fee is sound business judgment for the partnership. It will have someone with incentive to ensure income stability; the partnership business will be more economically self-contained; and, a good status quo is more apt to be maintained with a general partner as manager.

In a real estate income property investment, the management effort results in a "property management fee" to the general partner. This usually is based on a percentage of the monthly gross revenue earned by the income property. Generally, this fee runs from 5 percent to as much as 10 to 12 percent of the gross income, and it is paid monthly. (I suggest a nominal 6 percent fee for the general partner.)

In a non–real estate investment, the management effort generally results in compensation based upon a percentage of some figure (gross income, net income, etc.), or upon a monthly salary. If a salary, it is reasonable to build in an annual increase in the salary so that the management income keeps pace with expected inflation. Our Appendix I model is a good illustration of this. There, the general partners are to receive a beginning salary of $2,000 per month with built-in escalators of 10 percent per year.

The management fee, whether a percentage or a salary, is *not* subject to any minimum return to the limited partners. In other words, this compensation belongs to the general partner without regard to how much money the limited partners may or may not receive. This is an important concept. As long as you as the general partner are doing the best job possible, your income for your services is protected without regard to how well the partnership does as a whole. If the partnership is doing poorly, you may not receive your built-in share of the profits if your share is subordinated behind a minimum return to the limited partners; however, you will receive your management fee as long as there are funds with which to cover this compensation.

Partnership Reporting/Investor Relations. Contrary to day-to-day asset management services for which a fee is justified, no fee is justified for general partner duties associated with normal investor reporting and relations. Keeping the investors informed of partnership asset performance is an expected general partner duty and, in fact, is very important to the general partner's current and future career goals. Although it is a simple and easily overlooked task, a regular, brief status report does more good for the investor's sense of well-being than just about anything else a general partner can do.

Whether or not required by the Partnership Agreement, the general partner should prepare and send out quarterly status reports to the investors. The reports should contain the following:

1. A one- or two-page detailed summary of the status of the partnership business. Management problems, economic effects, or anything else of a general interest should be covered. Even if the information is gloomy, the investor has a right to know how his investment is doing, and it is better for him and for the general partner to air problems now instead of later.
2. A summary profit and loss statement for the quarter. (Some passive investments may not have enough activity to call for such a statement.)
3. A distribution check (if applicable to the deal and if there is cash available for distribution).

The report can be typed on white bond and sent in a plain white envelope; there is no need for custom letterhead and envelopes. The report should be sent no later than thirty days after the close of the quarter.

At the close of the partnership's fiscal year (usually set up on a regular calendar year basis), the general partner must arrange for a partnership tax return which will include a Schedule K-1 form for each limited partner. This is the form which is used by each limited partner to report his gains and/or losses from the partnership on his individual tax return. The general partner should arrange with the accounting firm to have the tax return and all K-1's available no later than sixty days after the end of the tax year.

You may want to hold an annual meeting of the limited partners. You can review the previous year's performance and problems, and can present general plans for the coming year. This is an excellent way to keep the investors informed. It also is a good way to use them for brainstorming any partnership problems that can benefit from having several minds applied to them. If you decide to have a meeting, be sure to arrange a time and place convenient to most of the partners. Also, be sure to mail each of them adequate notice of the meeting.

A Lot of Mileage. The most important point about partnership management and partner relations is this: A very little amount of time and effort spent to keep your investors informed buys you a lot of mileage. Do not assume that they know what is going on. Do not keep problems from them (except for minor day-to-day operating problems). Always be responsive if a partner asks for special information or for a little bit more than you think you ought to be responsible for. These existing partners are your best source of investors for new deals. If they have been made to feel important and informed, they will go into the next deal with you as long as they have the money.

Selling the Partnership Assets

Selling the assets represents another task, but also creates another source of income for you. A commission, consulting fee, or other fee can be taken depending upon the nature of the asset, and depending on whether you are licensed in real estate or are performing the service for a fee. In a reasonably successful venture, selling the assets will also enable you to share in what could be significant profits.

Liquidation of the assets is sometimes necessary because of poor performance, but generally, it is accomplished because the assets have appreciated in value or all tax benefits are used up. In any case, there are some standard steps that are required to effect a sale or lease.

Step One: Searching for a Buyer. If the asset is an apartment building or other similar income property, it can be listed with you (if you are licensed), or with an outside real estate company. Even if you are licensed, you may want to work with an outside company on a split commission basis to increase your exposure to prospective purchasers. If the asset is not an income property of some kind but is a business or possibly some unusual asset, you may be able to find a business opportunity broker who can help advertise and sell the item. Regardless of the nature of the asset, you will have to "get the word out" through some type of advertising in order to attract potential buyers.

Working to sell an asset can cause problems. For example, with a tennis, fitness, or other membership club, people may stop buying memberships if they find the club is for sale or lease. Other business ventures — even apartment buildings — can suffer revenue and/or employee problems when word of an impending change gets out. So, instead of publicly listing the asset for sale, you may have to search more quietly for a buyer. Make a list of all potentially interested parties, then contact them through letter or telephone. Eventually, you should find a buyer or lessor for the partnership asset.

Step Two: Negotiating the Transaction. You, as the general partner, will be the one who does the negotiating with the potential buyer. The best interests of the partnership must be considered at all times, yet you will have to be flexible to effect a sale. Usually, several meetings and phone calls stretching out from a few weeks to a few months are required. This work is what entitles you to a commission or fee. It is not an overnight task to sell or lease a partnership asset unless it is very small in terms of value and is in demand (e.g., a profitable rental property). I never feel greedy about taking a fee for this effort, and the fee can be quite substantial.

Step Three: Transaction Approval. After negotiating a mutually acceptable deal with a buyer, a tentative agreement is prepared. This agreement should include a good faith deposit from the buyer. At this point, you must obtain the approval of the limited partners per the requirements of the Partnership Agreement. (In your written deal with the buyer, you will, of course, have the partners' approval as a contingency).

This tentative Purchase Agreement should be condensed for the limited partners. It should embody the main details for their review, and highlight the financial aspects and benefits. In addition, there should be three or four schedules added that summarize the partnership results from inception to this sale, including payout terms if an installment sale is involved. Complete limited partner return on investment figures — incorporating tax dollars saved — should be detailed along with figures showing that you are entitled to a portion of the profits (if applicable). Be sure to include your commission or fee in these schedules as a partnership expense before calculating the return of cash and promissory notes to the limited and general partners.

A consent form (a simple paragraph stating, in general, what is being consented to) is sent to the partners along with the condensed transaction details and a stamped, self-addressed return envelope. Normally, you will want a majority consent and will want it within a few days so that you know you can go forward with the buyer. Providing the return envelope always expedites return of the consent form; it can mean the difference between having all consent forms returned over a one-month period or within a week.

Step Four: Closing the Deal. If real property is involved, an escrow company or "escrow situation" should be used. If no real property is involved, there still should be an escrow situation (a third party holding the cash consideration and notes payable/other securities concerned). Once the buyer's cash is in and all documents are properly signed and recorded, escrow can close.

Step Five: Payout of Commission/Fee and Sale Proceeds. Again, it's time to pay yourself. Right off the top, your commission or fee can be taken. If you are selling a $400,000 or $500,000 asset, this can mean $20,000 to $30,000 for you, more if the asset is larger. Then, there is your share of the profits. If your share is subordinated behind a return of capital, or a minimum per-year return, you may have to give all cash proceeds to the limited partners and take your share from promissory note payments. Regardless, you can count on your share now or in the future. And this sum can be substantial, too. Remember the examples of some of my deals in Chapters 1 and 2? Some of my profit shares were around $60,000 or more, and my share of the office building example was about $115,000.

As soon as possible (within two or three days), you should send out checks and a summary statement to each limited partner. I also include a brief payout schedule if a promissory note from an installment sale is part of the sale transaction. The limited partners then know approximately how much will be coming into the partnership each quarter and about how much they can expect to receive as a result.

Step Six: Collecting the Partnership Payoffs. Someone has to make sure that all payments due from the buyer are received and "warehoused" until a quarterly distribution is appropriate. That someone is you (or your secretary/associate if one is present). Do not look at this as a chore, because it is advantageous to you.

First, you will be controlling receipt and application of monies which may include some of yours (your profit share). Second, you reasonably can charge a fee, or a percentage of the gross receipts, for your collection service. And third, it keeps you in contact with a group of investors who should be happy because they are receiving cash payments from a profitable venture. You will have more deals coming up, and what better people to sell on investing again than your satisfied former investors. The time involved in the collection and distribution process is normally miniscule, too.

If the collection process requires very little time and effort (for example, just the collecting of a check and disbursing of investor checks once each quarter), you may want to charge just a service fee per check plus a charge for coordinating the tax report preparation. On the other hand, there may be some underlying debt on which your partnership still is making payments, along with monitoring of a leasehold, equipment, or other partnership activities. In this case, you would be justified in taking 2 or 3 percent of the gross monthly receipts as a management fee for the work involved. You must look at each situation individually, depending on the tasks required. The bottom line again is to be fair, just, and equitable in your dealings with the limited partners.

CHAPTER 14

Increasing Your Fees, Income, and Net Worth

BY NOW, you should be able to take what you have learned and put together a complete syndication. Following the road map and illustrations laid out for you in this book should help make your syndication a successful one. Success means you will be putting substantial dollars in your pocket. The various case studies and examples used should leave no doubt as to the amount of fees and profits available to you through the syndication process. As large as these fees and profits are, however, there are ways to make them even larger, and to help build your net worth faster.

Increasing Your Fees and Income

Real Estate License. I have mentioned several times that you can increase your income by becoming licensed to sell real estate. There are usually two levels of licenses in each state: (1) the salesman's license; and (2) the broker's license. Either one of these will do, although it is worthwhile to work toward your broker's license eventually. (The salesman's license requires you to have a sponsoring broker who will share, to some extent, in your commissions; the broker's license gives you the chance to operate independently and, thus, to keep 100 percent of the commissions you earn.)

The time involved to obtain the salesman's license is not excessive, requiring as little as thirty to forty days of study on close to a full-time basis to be ready for the exam. In the alternative, you can take a class about two or three times a week and be ready for the exam in sixty to ninety days. Check with your state Real Estate Board or Commission for specific requirements, and with a real estate school in your area for course of study, timing, etc. Even if you never go further and do not begin to do syndications, the practical knowledge you will acquire through the learning process will prove to be invaluable for you.

In dollars and cents, the license can make a huge difference. If you are putting together a deal, you always can charge an organization fee or a fund-raising fee. But with the real estate license, additional fees can be obtained when the deal includes real property. For example, if you are raising $300,000 in OPM to purchase an apartment building selling for $1,500,000, the difference in what you can earn is staggering.

	With No License	*With Broker's License*
Organizing/fund-raising fee (10 percent)	$ 30,000	$ 30,000
One-half 6 percent real estate commission on purchase	0	45,000
Property management fee (for three years)	28,000	28,000
Your percentage ownership (25 percent of $400,000 sale profit)	100,000	100,000
One-half 6 percent real estate commission on building sale (sale price of $1,900,000)	0	57,000
TOTALS:	$158,000	$260,000

The money you lose by not having a real estate license is a *minimum* $102,000! (You might receive another $57,000 if you directly find a buyer, thereby enabling you to take the entire 6 percent commission. In addition, some areas traditionally work on a higher commission. Seven percent or more is not uncommon, so your commission could be even higher yet.) If you only put together two deals a year like this one, you would lose out on $90,000 on the front end and a minimum of $114,000 on the sale of the property.

Quite obviously, a few evenings of part-time study are well worth the monies you will leave on the table without a real estate license. The transaction does not have to be an apartment building, either. Many of your deals will involve leasing space, buying land on which to build something, or raising money for someone else who has you negotiate the real property aspects for him. In short, the number one way to increase your earning potential if you are going to be a syndicator is to obtain your real estate license.

Contractor's License. The idea is the same here as we just discussed above. This license is more difficult to obtain, but add it to the real estate license and the bucks can tumble in. If you wanted to syndicate a deal to buy a $400,000 piece of vacant land on which to build a $2,000,000 office building, the fees and profits might look like this:

	With No Licenses	*With Contractor's and Broker's Licenses*
Organizing/fund-raising fee (10 percent of $450,000 of OPM raised)	$ 45,000	$ 45,000
One-half 6 percent real estate commission for land purchase	0	12,000
General contractor fee (5 percent of building cost)	0	100,000

(continued on next page)

	With No Licenses	*With Contractor's and Broker's Licenses*
Building management fee (for three years)	51,000	51,000
Your percentage ownership (20 percent of $800,000 sale profit)	160,000	160,000
One-half 6 percent real estate commission on building sale (sale price of $3,200,000)	0	96,000
TOTALS:	$256,000	$464,000

This time, you leave a minimum $208,000 on the table. Not having a contractor's license costs you $100,000 of this loss. Needless to say, if you do not visualize building any projects, then the contractor's license may not make sense for you. However, many syndicators do build structures as part of their syndications. In these cases, the difference between a license and no license is substantial in terms of lost dollars.

Finder's Fee. After you have completed a few syndications, you will be receiving calls from people — some of whom you may know and some of whom you may not know — who are looking for something. They may want you to find a project for them to syndicate, or may want you to use your contacts to get them something, or may have any number of other requests. These requests come in to me repeatedly. There may not be any real estate or fund-raising involved, yet you will be providing a service for them.

I have picked up several finder's fees for various services performed in these instances. Generally, no license is required, but you definitely should have some type of agreement with the person, in writing, that sets forth the terms and conditions of your services, and payment for these services. These fees are a very real source of additional funds, some of the "fallout" of the business.

Packaging. Many people have an idea for making money through a syndication, yet have no idea how to develop the documentation for doing it. There is no reason why you should not run a small ad from time to time promoting your packaging expertise. You will have slack times between syndications, and can devote some of this time to putting together a package for a healthy fee. Not only is it a good source of additional cash, but it invariably brings in new investors. Sometimes, it also results in a syndication for you to put together for additional fees and profits.

Using Your Investor List. Other people in the syndication business will contact you, asking for help in raising funds for their deal. If you are too busy or just not interested, you still can "rent" them some of your investors for a percentage of the amount invested by your people. You perform some initial contact work with certain of your investors, then let the other syndicator do the real selling and closing work.

I do not like to do this except on rare occasions. The other syndicator may have deals that appeal more to your investor, thereby resulting in a potential loss of the investor from your ranks. Additionally, if the deal goes sour, your investor could unfairly blame you.

Consulting Fees. Consulting work can be a very nice income source. There are persons who want to know how to put together a syndicate, how to acquire a loan, some details about a certain business with which you are familiar, etc. You should charge at least $100 to $150 per hour for your time, plus all out-of-pocket expenses and some travel time. This service can be advertised along with your packaging promotions and ads.

Seminar Speaking. I achieved considerable expertise in the racquetball/fitness club field during the time I syndicated eight such centers throughout southern California. As a result of this experience, I began to speak for a company that put on "how to" seminars on these clubs throughout the western United States.

My presentation at each seminar was brief, a description in simple terms of how I acquired the land, and how I raised the loan and equity funds to develop each club. I simply related to the audience what I had been doing all along. For each brief speech, I received several hundred dollars plus all my travel and living expenses. These seminars proved to be excellent diversions from my normal activities, and also netted me many investors and long-term friendships.

Newsletters. A simple one- to four-page newsletter containing interesting information on finances and general investments can be a real winner. Giving brief case histories of what others have accomplished with their investments, as well as examples of potential investments not available to the general public, can earn you extra monies. Anything new and exciting in the syndication field can be included, too.

Your existing investors are naturals for this monthly newsletter, but so are others who are interested in making more money. General advertising, direct mail, and word of mouth can acquire new subscribers. Needless to say, this will help you in building additional income for yourself. You must be sure not to advertise any specific investment — or investment opportunities — in this newsletter if you plan to syndicate something as this would be in violation of private offering guidelines. Once you do have something to syndicate, however, you can contact your subscribers on a one-on-one basis. Consequently, you should end up with more investors through this medium.

College Classes. You will become expert in the field of syndication after you have a few of them under your belt. If there is a college or university near you, approach the administration about conducting an evening or extension class on syndication. Or, discuss a more general class on investing with emphasis to be placed on syndication as a vehicle for getting an investment off the ground. In addition to financial compensation for giving the class, you can expect to pick up a good percentage of your students — now or in the future — as new investors.

Equity in Your Work. Always try to end up with equity in the project on which you are working. When you are the general partner in a syndicate, you almost always will have an ownership position. But, sometimes you will not be a general partner; you will put together a syndicate just for a fund-raising fee. In this latter instance, try to negotiate an ownership position in addition to your fee, if possible.

When you do negotiate such an arrangement, make sure it's either a limited partner percentage, or a piece of the general partner's share through an arrangement with the general partner. Then, you also will share in the mortgage reduction, market value appreciation, or other net worth–increasing aspect of the deal.

Increasing Your Net Worth

Once you begin to put together deals, you should increase your personal income substantially. With more money coming in, you will have more opportunity for increasing your net worth. Do not forget, too, that all this income is generated without using any of your own money; this income is generated through other people's money.

Pay Number One First. That's right; take care of yourself first! For as long as you can remember, you have been told that you should take 10 percent of your gross earnings each month and put these funds away for the future. Well, I'm going to tell you this again because it is absolutely true: putting away 10 percent of your earnings and then adding any extra from time to time will speed you on your way to achieving a "high cash flow–no financial worry" life-style. It's all right to invest these monies. In fact, that is exactly what you want to do: invest these funds. But, never, never spend these dollars on the depreciable trappings of life, or on normal day-to-day living expenses. These funds are for building into more funds, and more assets, so that some day you can live off the interest and/or cash flow without ever touching the principal amount.

It is difficult for the average person to do this because he needs every penny from his paycheck just to make ends meet. But remember, you are not the average person. You picked up this book, read it, and you will be making big money by following its precepts. You will not need all the money you make just to make ends meet, but you still can fall into the trap of seeing your expenses rise to meet your income. Don't do it. Pay yourself *first* each month, before the bills or anything else. And put in more than 10 percent when you can. Then, watch the compounding effect mushroom these savings and investments into a net worth that will far exceed anything you ever imagined possible.

Emphasize Residential Income Property Investments in Your Net Worth Building Program. I do not mean to imply here in any way that real property income investments are the only place to be, or even the best place to be. There are other places to invest, some of which can be better than real estate. In fact, I have had some of these myself. They include wise (or lucky) stock market investments; stock in privately held corporations; and ownership in a chain of fitness clubs. While highly speculative, other ventures such as different types of franchises, securities options, mining, oil and gas, and movie syndications can be windfall investments, too.

What I do want to get across is that residential income property investments for you are a good place to concentrate when starting out with limited funds, or even when you are at the point where you are beginning to pyramid some of your holdings. Why? Because as an individual, you do not have the protection of a relatively low investment in a limited partnership with twenty or thirty people. Instead, you are in the deal alone, or possibly with one or two other individuals. Consequently, you are concerned with the highest possible returns and the lowest possible risk. Residential income properties still can help you meet these objectives. Here is why.

A. Control. With oil and gas, movies, the stock market, and most other investments, you are at the mercy of someone else. This is particularly true with the stock market where unforeseen national and world events can and do cause the market to fluctuate radically, sometimes on a daily basis. Even when the market is fairly stable, you never will know when one of the big investment funds will sell thousands of shares of stock of the same company in which you own shares, probably causing the price (and thus, value) to drop significantly. While you cannot have 100 percent control over the market for residential income properties, your management and handling of your own investment can give you a certain measure of control over the value of your property.

B. Need for Housing. Housing is a basic necessity. More and more people coming into the housing market each year create a constant and increasing demand. Aggravating this situation is the slowdown in construction over the last few years of new, multiple-residential housing units (apartments). In addition, more people are being forced into renting instead of buying because of higher prices for homes. This constant upward pressure for rental units eliminates much of the risk associated with most other investment vehicles.

C. Inflation (Appreciation). Normal appreciation of value due to cost of living increases plus added appreciation from improvements you make to your property almost guarantee at least a "paper" return on your investment each year. In years just past, normal inflation rates have reached into the double digits. Even now, normal inflation coupled with added appreciation from improvements should guarantee you several percentage points per year in value increase.

D. Leverage. We discussed this in Chapter 5. Even with down payments of as high as 20 to 30 percent, which is typical today, it would be difficult for you not to achieve a paper return of at least 15 to 20 percent per year just from leverage aspects.

E. Cash Flow. It is difficult today to purchase residential income properties, with good leverage, that begin giving off positive cash flow immediately, or even in two or three years; prices for these properties have increased significantly in the last several years, particularly on the West Coast. By searching diligently, however, you can still find good deals that can give off cash flow initially, or in a relatively short time. Clearly, cash flow is an attractive aspect of having this type of investment; it can provide you with spendable income while you are holding it.

F. Equity Buildup. This factor increases your overall return on investment. Your gross income (rental income) makes the payments on your mortgage loan for you, and some of this payment goes to reduce the loan principal balance. This mortgage reduction can amount to several thousand dollars each year. Depending upon the amount of your initial investment, equity buildup can give you another 10 or 20 percent or more return on your investment each year.

G. Tax Shelter. Because of depreciation and other allowable deductions, your income property cash flow is normally sheltered by these deductions from income taxes. In fact, these deductions can be much greater than your cash flow; consequently, your income property can shelter income from other sources, too. The higher the tax bracket you fall in, the greater this tax shelter can mean to you, but it works for you in any bracket.

When all the above factors are combined, your rate of return on your investment can be anywhere from a low of 10 to 15 percent to well over 100 percent per year. Additionally, even after you have sold your properties, you probably will be receiving healthy payments at a good rate of interest for several years from a mortgage or trust deed you take back for some of your equity. Because of these factors, it is a good idea to make sure that some of your syndications include residential income properties. I still receive monthly checks from apartment house syndications even though the properties were sold three or four years ago.

Pyramid Your Investments. Once you have a duplex or an apartment building and have owned it for a while, do not spend the principal or the profit when you sell or trade it. Use these funds to trade or buy into a larger income property. Then, as the compounding effects take over, your net worth will increase more rapidly each year because you will be earning profits on top of profits.

If you use some of this investment capital and the resulting profits for living expenses or for desired luxuries during the early years of your net worth building program, the results can be disastrous. There will be no compounding of profits; in fact, you may slip backwards and never build up enough net worth to be able to quit working. On the other hand, if you give your investments the benefit of compounding for several years, taking out large sums later on will not make a noticeable dent in your net worth. The message is clear: Pay yourself first, and let these funds compound into a fortune before you start taking out sums for everyday living and luxuries.

In my opinion, it is important to keep a good share of your net worth in income properties, so that the depreciation and other tax benefits will keep your income taxes to a minimum. But, you also should plan to diversify your investments. Do not put all your available funds into real estate, or into any one other investment vehicle. Build up some of your portfolio in stocks and high-rated tax-free municipal bonds. Place most of the stock funds into blue chip companies and utilities for security. Some can be placed into more speculative securities, but the bulk should be in the safer ones. Stocks, along with real estate, can give you long-term capital gain tax benefits, which also reduce your income tax liability.

Attempt to find some secure, discounted trust deeds or mortgages which, after the discount, will provide 20 or 30 percent or even higher annual yields. These instruments become available frequently when people need cash. Some of them have plenty of equity to collateralize themselves; others have junior trust deeds/mortgages for added protection.

Keep your eyes open for acquaintances who have a good business idea, but who are short of capital. From time to time, you may be able to put some funds into this type of deal, buy enough control for safety, and make windfall profits for your trouble. Always keep some funds liquid, for emergencies, and for taking advantage of exceptional deals that do come along more often than you think they might. Keep your cash in a money market fund or a certificate of deposit, or in some high yield instrument to maximize interest. Make sure that wherever they are, you can get to the funds by withdrawing them, or by borrowing against them.

In summary, always work to expand your net worth once you have begun to build it up. Being a syndicator can give you enough money to live very comfortably, and enough extra funds to start you on your net worth building program. Living comfortably with extra money to play with is one of the nice things about this system of using other people's money. And now you have the tools with which to become a successful syndicator.

CHAPTER 15

The Winning Combination

A COUPLE OF days after I finished this book, I was sitting at my desk in my home office looking out the window. It was an overcast day with a light rain spattering gently on the lemon and avocado trees below my house. Some sun rays were just breaking through the rain clouds over the Pacific Ocean, painting a beautiful view out of my window.

I was analyzing a spreadsheet of figures, trying to determine if I should take the packaging/fund-raising job just offered to me by two local friends who were expanding their business. Seeing the striking picture before me out of my window made me stop and reflect on what it was that I really had in my grasp.

Here I am, I thought, on a cold, rainy day, sitting in the warmth of my house overlooking the ocean, contemplating whether or not I should accept this offer to put $60,000 to $70,000 in my pocket within a two- to three-month period. I am my own boss, no one to report to, no regimentation of a company to adhere to, no company politics to deal with. I am never bored; each deal that comes along is wildly different from the one before it. I always have a challenge; I am never stifled by company policy.

Security? Yes, I have the ultimate in job security. I never have to worry about layoffs or about how I am going to make my next dollar. When I need — or want — to make some more money, I only need to look around me and soon I will have something to syndicate.

I do not have to work. I work only when I want to, and because I want to. And I have the flexibility to work two or three days a week, or just two or three months a year. There is time, ample time, to enjoy life with my wife and sons. We can spend time at our second home in the Sierras, take South Pacific island trips, or just play some tennis and lounge around here locally. In short, I do not need a company, a boss, a time card, the "security" of a job. I have job security, the ultimate job security: the ability to make money whenever I choose!

Okay, I do have a good life, no question about it. But I was not born into this kind of life. My parents were somewhat on the poor end of life's spectrum. My father had two jobs when I was a kid. Once, I even had to loan him money from my part-time school job to replace an old washing machine that finally gave up. There was no money to help me through school either, so I had to roughneck on a rotary drilling rig in the oil fields to earn enough to allow me to just barely squeeze through on my own.

I did not even find this kind of life on my own after I married, had children, worked hard for years for a big company. Plus, I ran into other setbacks when my first wife and I divorced only a very few years ago, split the assets in half, and wiped out the savings account. Not the best way to build up a solid net worth; not the best way to set yourself up financially so that you can quit working while you are still young.

So how, then, did I get to this enviable position in such a brief time, in only eight short years? One word: SYNDICATION. I put together some deals without using my own money; I used other people's money. I made front end fees, and back end fees and profits. And, I began to pyramid the 10 percent or more that I paid myself each year into a larger and larger net worth: into the capital amount that now pays me over $120,000 a year without touching the capital, without working one day or one hour.

About the income I mentioned throughout this book: $197,553 in the example in Chapter 1; up to $3 million from my ongoing tennis club involvement; hundreds of thousands of dollars in the "fallout" examples. You can believe them.

They already have happened, or are happening, to me. No, I do not think you will make these amounts of money on your first or second syndication. I didn't. But my income started building to these levels fast.

These figures are reasonable goals for you. They are reasonable because they are attainable. And who knows what is on the horizon. Real estate is still around and always will be. We are moving with great speed into high technology products and services that will open up all kinds of syndication capital needs in this field. New sports, leisure time, and service businesses pop up all the time. As ever, there are endless possibilities and opportunities out there for anyone to jump on who has a little drive and initiative.

You quite possibly can do better than I have. Believe me, I have not worked nearly as hard as I could have, so I know that I could have done much better. Regardless of how well you do, however, you more than likely will do much better than you are now. But the greatest thing you will have is total job security! No more worries about money. You will be able to do a deal whenever you want, which is a nice benefit from the field of syndication.

At this point, you have the road map, the tools necessary to achieve big success as a syndicator. How or whether you apply these tools is up to you. There is no set formula for how to apply yourself to take advantage of this opportunity. But, there are some ingredients which I feel make it almost impossible to fail if you mix them in with the road map in this book. Together, they can make a winning combination.

Desire. You already have this quality because you have read this book. Obviously, you want to improve your life. You want to do better; you NEED to do better. You need to do better because something inside is pushing you forward, driving you on. And now, through this book, you have the practical foundation upon which you can build a solid net worth and achieve your desire to succeed.

Persistence. To me, this is one of the most important qualities a person can have to ensure success in anything he may try. No matter what you try, you will come up against roadblocks, problems, discouragements. It is very easy to give up, to back off, to try something else. Most of the people I know are this way. I think it is human nature to quit trying when the going gets rough. But, that is exactly when you do not want to quit; you want to forge ahead, because those that do are the winners, the doers, the people who find success.

You must have persistence. If you believe in something, stick with it until you make it happen. If you want a piece of property, keep badgering the owner, keep coming up with alternative proposals until you finally strike a deal. If you are having a little trouble raising money, keep coming up with new lists of names, keep calling the people, and try using different sales pitches until you find one that clicks. In other words, do not give up! Be persistent! Make it happen!

Positive Mental Attitude. If you think that you will make it, then you will. If you do not think that you can make it, then you will fail even if you could have made it. It's as simple as that. Hard work and persistence coupled with a negative attitude will buy you a lot of nothing.

Maintain a positive attitude. KNOW that you can do anything. You will not be uptight anymore, and you will get better results. To others, your attitude will come across as one of power, one of mastery of your life. Investors will be much easier to sell to because of the confidence you display; they will be more confident in you. Activities that come hard for others will fall into place for you because you KNOW that you can make them happen.

Do Not Reinvent the Wheel. Examples of doing deals abound. You also have a good, detailed model of a Confidential Memorandum package — including the Investment Circular portion, and the Partnership Agreement and Statement of Suitability attachments — right here in this book. Do not agonize over your own masterpiece; rather, mark up this model of a complete package to get yourself off the ground on syndication Number One. Then, improve on your package as you do each subsequent deal. But use this model as a base: It works.

Some more advice: Do not figure you are going to do your

own legal and accounting work. Again, use what is already available as a base, then run it by an attorney and an accountant for their comments and blessings. They are experts in their fields. Use their knowledge to keep you from getting into any difficulty. This is especially important for your first syndication.

Brain and Body. Here is some free advice I am going to throw in for you. Whether you take it to heart or not is up to you. But, because this advice I am going to give to you has made such a radical improvement in my business success and quality of life, I sincerely hope you do take it to heart.

As you embark on this new career, as you work through one syndication and then another, do not forget to work on yourself. You can increase your ability to function more effectively by working on your brain and body along with your deals. Let your brain and body grow right along with your assets because if you do, your assets should multiply even faster. And, you will enjoy life much more.

Over the years, there have been numerous articles about brain power, about exercising your brain. Lately, more and more articles appear as researchers verify that the brain needs exercise, too. These articles indicate that through physical and mental exercise, your brain size can actually increase. The tens of billions of brain cell connective glia cells can increase the size of the brain and its mental capacity if one does things to stimulate it. Constantly reading, analyzing, and exercising your brain in general can help this to happen.

On the other hand, no hobbies, no reading, no mental stimulation, no exercising of the brain will render it less alert, with diminished power. At best, it will stagnate. Constant living in a narrow routine gives tunnel vision, a narrowed viewpoint of the world as a whole. But, as you broaden your horizons, as you pack more and varied experiences into your life, you will want to learn more, and more learning will be easier for you. Your mental capacity will be growing, not stagnating. Getting into the syndication business can help your brain to grow, and exercising your brain can aid you in becoming a successful syndicator.

The body: I do not have to tell you about the benefits of rigorous exercise. Articles abound on the subject in all types of magazines and books. Maybe this rigorous exercise is not for you. But, if you can convince yourself to try it for a few weeks, you probably will be amazed at the results. I know; I have followed a rigorous exercise program since early 1968.

The physical benefits of rigorous exercise are too numerous to name them all, and because I am not a doctor, I could not do them justice anyway. There are some specific benefits, however, that I feel *can* aid significantly in your attainment of success. One is more energy. You will find that you can do the same work within the lower half of your capacity; you can produce twice as much without ever approaching your limit. You will tire less, be able to stay at your work longer, and find that you always seem to have a reserve of energy inside you.

As your body becomes stronger through rigorous exercise, there will be a vast increase in the quantity of blood vessels carrying blood to the different parts of your body. One of these parts that benefit is your brain. You will have a greater supply of blood going to your brain; more exercise for your brain, more mental capacity for you. You will be ahead of the person — in terms of brain power — who is sedentary. And, more good health in general should come your way.

Working on your body helps your mental processes, too. You will feel better mentally, which is a terrific payoff of your exercise program. You will know that you have one up on the sedentary guy sitting across from you. You will have much more self-confidence.

One of the benefits that I enjoy the most is the tension release that hard exercise provides. When I have frustrations in my work or in my personal affairs (and we all do), my form of rigorous exercise — a good thirty- to forty-five-minute run — works to cleanse my mind, body, and emotions. I feel refreshed, can think more clearly, and can put these frustrations in their proper perspective. My positive attitude returns in full force, and I am ready to handle both the business and personal tasks effectively.

Maybe it's tennis, bicycling, swimming, or something else for you. But I sincerely hope that it is something. Exercise is the cheapest form of therapy and assurance of success that I know. It works, and I encourage you to combine it with your new syndication efforts.

Being a syndicator is a good life; it's financially and personally rewarding. You can be a syndicator wherever you live right now, or wherever you may want to live. I know that if you want the rewards of this profession strongly enough, then you will be able to make it happen right now. It's a lot of work, and a real challenge. But then, where else can you find such large rewards without using a penny of your own money? Syndication is the best way I can imagine to make a good living. And it's yours for the taking.

All you have to do is to keep up your level of motivation, and be determined to succeed. Keep thinking about the financial security that can be yours, about the time you can have to devote to your family.

Let these things be your motivation, your target, your pot of gold at the end of the rainbow. Then be determined to achieve these goals. Do not dwell on past mistakes. We all have made some. Just set your mind to these admirable, attainable goals and drive forward with determination. Along with this motivation and determination, you will be armed with the knowledge in this book; together, they can ensure that you attain your goals.

Appendixes

Appendix I

MODEL FULL-LENGTH PACKAGE

A COMPLETE MODEL Confidential Memorandum package is displayed in the following pages. This Confidential Memorandum package contains the three sections discussed in Chapters 7 through 9: the Investment Circular portion; the Attachment I Partnership Agreement; and, the Attachment II Statement of Suitability. Sections of information in this model are keyed to corresponding explanations in the text for ease of understanding.

This is a model of a complete package that could be used to syndicate a hypothetical, nationally franchised restaurant and high-quality ice cream parlor. In this particular model, two of your "friends" are the general partners (organizing/managing syndicators). It assumes you have done the complete packaging and are raising the required funds on a fee basis only. You are a packaging/fund-raising syndicator in this example. Names and places used are fictitious; however, this model displays all the data and specific language that could be used in an actual document.

This package is meant to be used as a comprehensive guide. You can modify the Investment Circular portion slightly to match up with the particular investment opportunity you envision, then use it as a working document. Using the model in this manner should save you hours of time and effort. Be sure, however, to have an attorney review your documents for adequacy of information, and for adherence to state and federal regulations that may be applicable.

Appendix I

(A) CONFIDENTIAL MEMORANDUM

SAMPLE'S ELMTOWN, a

California Limited Partnership

Restaurant/Ice Cream Parlor

THE LIMITED PARTNERSHIP UNITS DESCRIBED HEREIN ARE BEING SOLD UNDER THE EXEMPTION FOR "NON-PUBLIC OFFERINGS AND SALES" PURSUANT TO THE LAWS OF THE STATE OF CALIFORNIA. THESE UNITS HAVE NOT BEEN QUALIFIED WITH ANY GOVERNMENTAL REGULATORY AGENCY IN THE STATE OF CALIFORNIA OR ANY OTHER STATE. NO REGULATORY AGENCY IN THE STATE OF CALIFORNIA HAS PASSED UPON THE ACCURACY OR ADEQUACY OF THIS MEMORANDUM. ANY REPRESENTATION TO THE CONTRARY IS A CRIMINAL OFFENSE. THESE UNITS HAVE NOT BEEN APPROVED OR DISAPPROVED BY THE SECURITIES AND EXCHANGE COMMISSION NOR HAS SAID COMMISSION PASSED UPON THE ACCURACY OR ADEQUACY OF THIS MEMORANDUM. ANY REPRESENTATION TO THE CONTRARY IS A CRIMINAL OFFENSE. THESE UNITS ARE BEING SOLD PURSUANT TO AN EXEMPTION FROM REGISTRATION UNDER THE SECURITIES ACT OF 1933. THE GENERAL PARTNERS DO NOT ANTICIPATE THAT THIS OFFERING WILL BE REGISTERED OR QUALIFIED WITH OR BY ANY FEDERAL, STATE OR LOCAL GOVERNMENT COMMISSION OR AGENCY.

NO DEALER, SALESMAN OR ANY OTHER PERSON ACTING IN ANY CAPACITY WHATSOEVER WITH RESPECT TO THIS OFFERING HAS ANY AUTHORITY TO GIVE ANY INFORMATION OR TO MAKE ANY REPRESENTATIONS OR WARRANTIES, EITHER EXPRESSED OR IMPLIED, OTHER THAN THOSE WHICH MAY BE CONTAINED IN THIS CONFIDENTIAL MEMORANDUM, AND, IF GIVEN OR MADE, SUCH INFORMATION, REPRESENTATIONS OR WARRANTIES MUST NOT BE RELIED UPON AS HAVING BEEN AUTHORIZED BY THE GENERAL PARTNERS OR THE PARTNERSHIP.

THE UNITS OFFERED HEREBY MAY BE CONSIDERED TO BE SPECULATIVE, AND THERE IS NO ASSURANCE THAT THE PARTNERSHIP WILL REALIZE A PROFIT FROM ITS OPERATIONS OR UPON THE RESALE OF ITS ASSETS.

THIS FORM IS FOR ILLUSTRATION PURPOSES ONLY. IT MAY NOT MEET ALL RULES, REGULATIONS, AND PROCEDURES OF YOUR STATE, NOR HAS IT BEEN EDITED FOR SUCH PURPOSES BY THE AUTHOR.

IT IS POSSIBLE THAT AN INVESTOR MAY LOSE ALL OR PART OF HIS/HER INVESTMENT WITHOUT ANY RETURN OR WITHOUT AN ADEQUATE RETURN. THE PARTNERSHIP HAS NO OPERATING HISTORY NOR IS THERE ANY PUBLIC MARKET FOR THE SALE OR TRANSFER OF THE PARTNERSHIP UNITS AS DESCRIBED IN THE LIMITED PARTNERSHIP AGREEMENT.

THE OFFER AND SALE OF THESE UNITS ARE LIMITED TO PERSONS WHO MEET CERTAIN MINIMUM FINANCIAL REQUIREMENTS AND THIS MEMORANDUM DOES NOT CONSTITUTE AN OFFER TO SELL OR A SOLICITATION OF AN OFFER TO BUY EXCEPT TO THOSE PERSONS MEETING SUCH REQUIREMENTS AND WHO ARE SATISFACTORY TO THE GENERAL PARTNERS IN THEIR ABSOLUTE DISCRETION. THE INFORMATION HEREIN IS PROPRIETARY TO THE GENERAL PARTNERS. ANY REPRODUCTION OR DISTRIBUTION OF THIS DOCUMENT, IN WHOLE OR IN PART, OR THE DIVULGENCE OF ANY OF ITS CONTENTS WITHOUT THE PRIOR WRITTEN CONSENT OF THE GENERAL PARTNERS IS PROHIBITED.

THE DATE OF THIS CONFIDENTIAL MEMORANDUM IS JULY 1, 1984.

(B) TABLE OF CONTENTS

Attachments

(C) BRIEF SUMMARY OF PROJECT

This Memorandum describes an offer to qualified persons to purchase ownership interests (Units) in Sample's Elmtown, a limited partnership entity which will own and operate a large Sample's restaurant and ice cream parlor. The restaurant will have a parlor decor and will offer a variety of attractive foods along with the renowned Sample's high quality ice cream products. Approximately 2,888 square feet of floor space will be divided between a 90-seat sales parlor, the ice cream bar, the ice cream manufacturing center, and storage/service areas. A key, desirable corner location--in the new shopping center at the intersection of Main Street, Armistice Road, and the Veteran Freeway in Elmtown--has been promoted by the Sample's Ice Cream Company and acquired by the General Partners.

The primary objectives of the Partnership are to provide the partners with (1) rapid return of capital invested (within 21 to 31 months per projections), (2) continuing and annually increasing cash distributions from business operations, and (3) certain tax benefits attributable to the ownership of leasehold improvements and operation of a business.

The General Partners of Sample's Elmtown are Brent E. Stace and Patrick Marris. They have investigated the project for over two years and have acquired a franchise for this Elmtown store, the first Sample's to arrive in this area of the state. Both General Partners will be actively involved in the day-to-day operations of the business.

(D) THE OFFERING

The Partnership is being organized pursuant to the Agreement Of Limited Partnership which is Attachment I to this Memorandum. This Offering consists of three hundred ninety-five and one-half (395.5) ownership Units at ONE THOUSAND DOLLARS ($1,000) per Unit for a total of THREE HUNDRED NINETY-FIVE THOUSAND FIVE HUNDRED DOLLARS ($395,500). These Units represent a full 100% ownership of the Partnership business and assets, and entitle the Limited Partners to receive all cash available for distribution from the business operations until an amount equivalent to 100% of their capital invested has been returned to them, in cash. Thereafter, although they will have had their initial investment returned, they will continue to receive 65% of all the cash available for distribution throughout the life of the Partnership.

In order to conform to state and federal security laws, the General Partners will limit the number of Limited Partners subscribing to the Offering. Consequently, each partner will be required to purchase a minimum of 11.3 Units, or Eleven Thousand Three Hundred Dollars ($11,300), unless the majority of the Offering is subscribed by only a few persons. In this case, some smaller ownership increments may be accepted; however, prospective investors should plan for the minimum purchase of 11.3 Units. Partners will not be obligated to contribute additional capital to the capital of the Partnership.

In order to purchase Units, a partner must submit to the General Partners a signed copy of the Statement Of Suitability And Subscription Agreement, a signed Partnership Agreement signature page, and a tender of Eleven Thousand Three Hundred Dollars ($11,300) for a minimum 11.3 Unit purchase. A prospective participant may purchase any number of additional Units up to a cumulative total of 75 Units; however, purchase of more than the minimum Units will require a higher net worth. The General Partners may refuse or reject any subscription for purchase of Units for any reason, including disapproval of qualification standards.

All proceeds from this Offering will be deposited into Sample's Elmtown account. Funds may be utilized when one-half of the Units have been subscribed and paid for. The proceeds from the sale of Units will be utilized as described in the section entitled USE OF PROCEEDS.

(E) INVESTOR QUALIFICATIONS

This transaction involves a certain degree of risk. As such, it is suitable only for persons who understand the risks involved, who have substantial financial resources, and who can afford to lose their entire investment. An investment in Units is available only to prospective investors who are residents of, and who are currently residing in, the State of California, and who meet the "Requirements" which are set forth below.

Requirements

The requirements for each investor are as follow:

1. The investor is acquiring the Units for investment and not with a view to resale or distribution;

2. The investor can bear the economic risk of losing the entire investment;

3. The investor has a net worth sufficient to bear the risk of losing the entire investment (generally, a net worth

of at least ten times the amount of his investment);

4. The investor must sign, date and complete in full the Statement Of Suitability And Subscription Agreement (Attachment II to this Memorandum);

5. The investor has adequate means of providing for his current needs and personal contingencies and has no need for liquidity in his investment in the Units;

6. The investor has substantial knowledge and experience in making investment decisions of this type, or is relying on his own purchaser representative in evaluating the merits and risks of this investment and in making this investment decision;

7. The Partnership can accept a total of 35 investors who are referred to in the California rules as "Counted" investors without regard to any requirements. Therefore, the Partnership may accept contributions from up to 35 of such "Counted" investors who come within the general requirements;

8. The Partnership can accept any number of investors without regard to the 35 rule when such investors are not "Counted" investors, provided that such investors are classified "Not Counted" or "Excluded Purchaser" investors in California. Such an investor in one of these classes must meet one or more of the following conditions:

   a. Purchase $150,000 or more of the securities being offered, provided: (i) such purchaser, or his professional adviser, has the capacity to protect his own interests in the transaction as noted in Section 25102(f)(2) of the California Corporations Code; and (ii) the investment does not exceed 10 percent of his net worth; or

   b. He has an individual net worth (or joint net worth with spouse) at the time of purchase of $1,000,000, or his individual income (or joint income with spouse) exceeded $200,000 in the current year, given that (i) the purchaser, or his professional adviser, is capable of protecting his own interests in the transaction as noted in Section 25102(f)(2), California Corporations Code; or (ii) the investment does not exceed 10 percent of his net worth.

These requirements will be reviewed to determine the suitability of prospective purchasers. The General Partners will have the right to refuse a subscription for Units if in their sole discretion they believe that the prospective purchaser does not meet the applicable suitability requirements or the Units are otherwise an unsuitable investment for the purchaser.

(F) USE OF PROCEEDS

Complete Project Cost:	$395,500

Planned Allocation Of Funds

Leasehold Improvements, Gen. Constr. (including all plumbing, electr., HVAC, etc.)	$150,000
Interior Equipment & Decor Construction:	
Kitchen Equipment	37,345
Ice Cream Machine/Equipment	38,741
Millwork & Decor	24,119
Furniture & Accessories	7,959
Booths & Tables	14,112
Franchise Fee	20,000
Three-week Training Program	3,800
Principals' Project Management Reimbursement	5,000
Legal & Accounting (estimated)	1,900
Lease Deposit, Licenses, Utilities Deposits	4,300
Opening Inventory	18,800
Initial Insurance, Preopening Advertising, Printing, Forms, Miscellaneous	5,900
Financial Packaging, Placement Structure, & Development	3,424
Underwriting Capitalization Cost	39,550
Beginning Working Capital	20,550
Total Equity Capitalization:	$395,500

(G) RISK FACTORS

Investment in Units of the Partnership involves risk and is suitable only for persons of financial means who have no need for liquidity of their investment. It should be recognized that the risk factors set forth below are those which, at the date of this Memorandum, seem to the Partnership the most likely to be significant. Prospective purchasers of Units should realize, however, that factors other than those set forth below may ultimately affect the investment offered pursuant to this Memorandum in a manner and to a degree which cannot be foreseen at this time.

Partnership To Be Newly Formed--No Operating History. Although the General Partners have spent considerable time researching this project, this Partnership will be newly formed and therefore has no operating history.

Return On Investment. No assurance can be given that a purchaser of Units will realize a substantial return on his investment, or any return at all, or that he will not lose his investment. For this reason, each prospective investor should read this Memorandum and all Attachments thereto carefully, and should consult with his own personal attorney, accountant, or business adviser prior to making any investment decision.

Speculative Nature Of Business. Notwithstanding the nationwide popularity and success of Sample's outlets and its foods and quality ice cream products, it is impossible to accurately project the demand for this type of establishment in Elmtown. The restaurant and ice cream market is very competitive and subject to constant change. Being competitive in this area is a key to the success of the Partnership business. Regarding similar ice cream competition, there is presently a Baskin-Robbins 31 Flavors shop in the West Points area, and a Clarrigans slated for the shopping center being developed on Parsifal Avenue. This part of the coastal area is well populated and has a solid business and residential base from which to draw, as well as a good vacation and recreational base. However, notwithstanding no like competition in the immediate geographic area, any future competing facilities could offer amenities exceeding those to be offered by the Partnership business.

Limited Use Improvements. The Project involves improvement of the interior of a building complex which will be limited in use, being designed and built specifically for the restaurant and ice cream manufacturing and sales business. Should the business be less profitable than anticipated, it may be difficult to sublease the premises or to convert the area to an alternative use.

Economic Factors. The business in which the Partnership will engage is very competitive. Notwithstanding the fact that the high quality, best tasting ice cream brands have continued to see large sales increases each year and are forecasted to see continued growth, the Partnership business is vulnerable to adverse changes in general and local economic conditions and to other factors which may be beyond the power of the Partnership to control. Additionally, there is no assurance that the Partnership assets will continue to increase in value or that the Partnership will realize a profit in the event of a sale of the Partnership assets and business. Even under the most favorable economic conditions, there is no guarantee that the business can be operated continually at a profit or that the Partnership assets and business can be sold on terms and conditions favorable to the Partnership.

Restriction On Capital. No Limited Partner may withdraw his

capital contribution without the consent of the General Partners and all of the Limited Partners, nor shall the Partnership be required to return any portion of the capital contribution of any Limited Partner at any time prior to dissolution of the Partnership.

Limited Transferability. Prospective investors should be fully aware of the long-term nature of an investment in the Partnership. Each investor will be required to represent that he is purchasing Units for his own account for investment purposes and not with a view to resale or distribution. The Units will not be registered under the Securities Act of 1933, or, with certain exceptions, under state securities laws by reason of specific exemptions under the provisions of such securities laws, which depend, in part, upon the investment intent of each investor. While the Units are transferable, no transfer of a Unit may be made if the transfer violates federal or state securities laws, or if it affects the status of the Partnership for federal income tax purposes either by termination of the Partnership or causing it to be classified as a corporation or association taxable as a corporation.

Liquidity Of Investment. The ownership Units offered hereby cannot be transferred except in accordance with Article 12 in the Agreement Of Limited Partnership, and it is not anticipated that a public market will develop for the purchase and sale of Units. Consequently, holders of Units may not be able to liquidate their investment at a reasonable price in the event of a personal financial emergency and the Units should only be considered as a long-term investment.

Reliance On Management. All decisions with respect to the management of the Partnership will be made exclusively by the General Partners. The Limited Partners will have no right or power to participate in the management of the Partnership. Accordingly, no person should purchase any Units unless he is willing to entrust all management aspects of the Partnership to the General Partners.

No Certainty Of Distributions. The Partnership intends to make quarterly distributions of all cash from operations which is available for distribution. However, there is no assurance that there will be any distributions. Distributions, if any, shall at all times be subject to the payment of Partnership expenses and the maintenance of reserves, and may be restricted or suspended when the General Partners determine in their absolute discretion that to do so is in the best interests of the Partnership.

Financial Projections. The financial projections included herein were prepared by the General Partners, and are based on assumptions and hypotheses made by the General Partners regarding future events. Projections are only a prediction of future events and should not be relied upon to indicate the actual results which may be attained. Accordingly, there is no assurance that actual events will correspond with these assumptions. Actual results for any period may or may not approximate such statements.

Tax Factors. Although it is anticipated that purchasers of Units will receive certain tax benefits, no assurance can be given that any deduction or other benefit that may be claimed will be allowed by the Internal Revenue Service, nor is there any guarantee that the Internal Revenue Code, or the Treasury regulations promulgated thereunder, will not be amended in such a manner as to deprive the Partnership and its partners of any tax benefits that they might receive. (See INCOME TAX RISK FACTORS.) Each prospective partner should consult his own legal counsel and/or accountant as to legal, tax, and related matters concerning an investment in Units of the Partnership.

Management Fiduciary Relationship. Except for certain matters described in the Agreement Of Limited Partnership , the Limited Partners will not have the right to participate in the decisions made by the General Partners. However, by law, the General Partners bear a fiduciary relationship to the Limited Partners. In all proceedings connected with the conduct of the business and affairs of the Partnership, the General Partners are bound to act in the highest good faith to the Limited Partners and may not obtain any advantage over them by misrepresentation, concealment, threat or adverse pressure of any kind. Pursuant to such duty and in addition to the obligations of the General Partners as set forth in the Agreement Of Limited Partnership, the General Partners must account to the Partnership for any benefits or profits derived by the General Partners directly or indirectly without the consent of the Limited Partners from any transaction connected with the Partnership business. Each Limited Partner or his duly authorized representative may inspect the Partnership books and records at any reasonable time during normal business hours.

(H) BACKGROUND SUMMARY OF PROJECT AND SITE NEGOTIATIONS

In early 1982, the General Partners discussed the idea of opening a high quality ice cream parlor in the City of Elmtown. Research revealed that small, independent retail ice cream operations were satisfactory, but that a well established, quality franchise could be very successful. Additional investigation showed that there was one ice cream store franchise that stood out among the rest in terms of high quality products, public recognition, and success: Sample's Ice Cream Company.

Preliminary contact was made with Sample's executives and the General Partners were surprised to learn that the franchise rights were available for all of Elmtown County with the exception of Johnston Village and the Somm Valley. The General Partners then travelled to Sample's home office in Houston, Texas for further research and negotiations which resulted in an agreement for the rights to purchase a franchise for the City of Elmtown. Sample's also indicated it would give the General Partners the first right of refusal for all other open areas within Elmtown County.

Several months were spent investigating potential sites for a store. Sample's was consulted frequently since it has very stringent requirements that must be met before it will authorize acquisition of a site. For example, major concerns and considerations were: traffic count; demographics of the area, including overall population and whether the residents were of a transient or permanent type; visual exposure to surface streets and freeway routes; volume of walk-by traffic; and concentration of office buildings in the area. Several sites were, in fact, turned down by Sample's as inappropriate for its standards.

The General Partners learned of the proposed Armistice Plaza development and contacted the leasing agents early in the Plaza's planning stages. The potential of this particular location was obvious. Centrally located within the City with surrounding land for a high concentration of professional office as well as light industrial development, a high traffic flow by and through the center was assured. The high walk-by traffic would also be assured and enhanced by the incorporation into the center of a Penney's and Good Catalog Store, as well as a Chuck E. Cheese's entertainment center. Sample's Director of Real Estate flew to Elmtown to personally review the site and enthusiastically endorsed it as very appropriate for a large Sample's store.

Since the General Partners began negotiations early in the Plaza planning stages, they received first selection of store locations within the development. The location selected and agreed to by Sample's is the southwest corner of the development fronting on Armistice Road. This will afford a high degree of visibility from many vantage points including the Veteran Freeway, Main Street traffic travelling east, and the entire Armistice Road area around the center. Construction of the extension of Armistice Road to Holbey Park Drive has been completed and Armistice Road will now be one of the primary travel routes from the Carsen and Port Georges beach areas to Elmtown. Both Sample's executives and the General Partners agree that this site should be conducive to a successful operation.

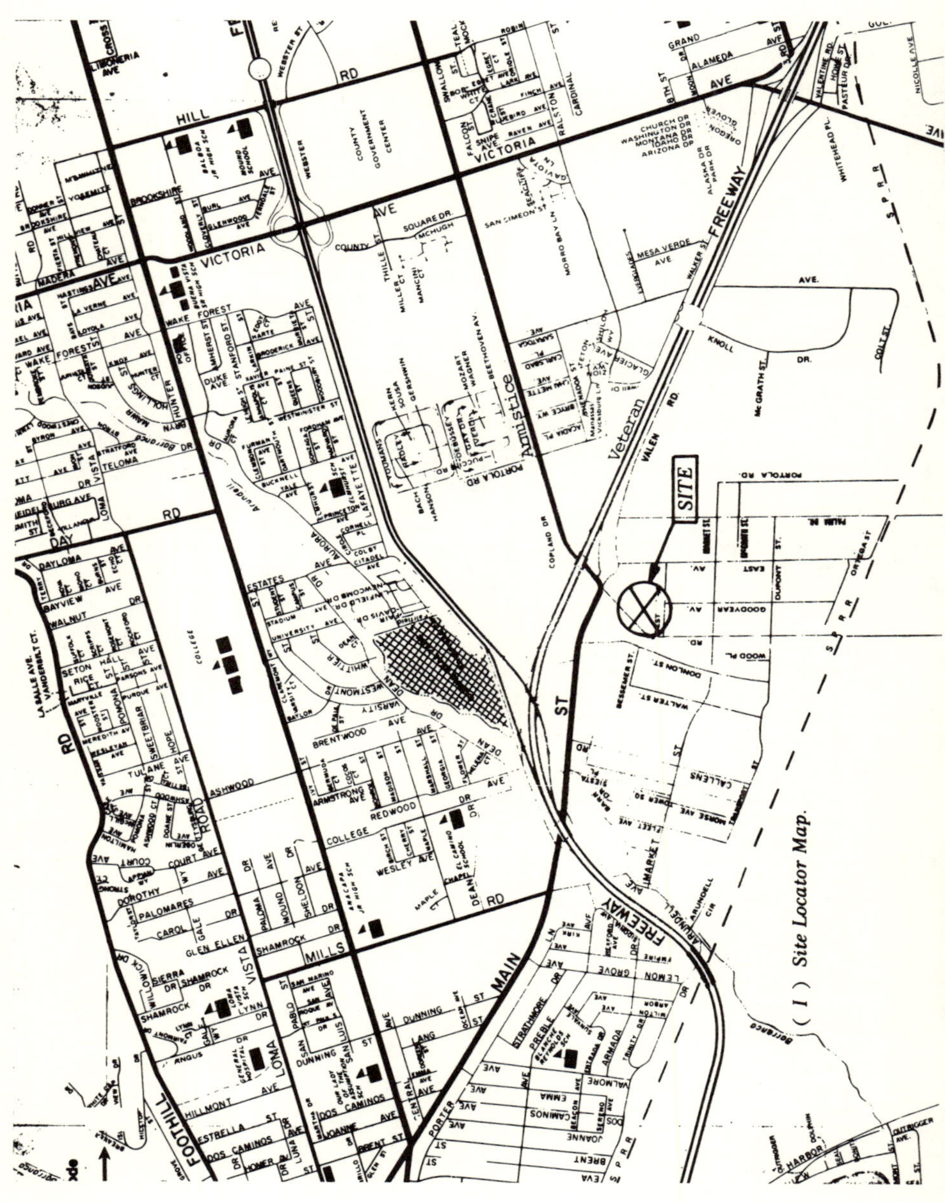

(I) Site Locator Map.

Appendix I

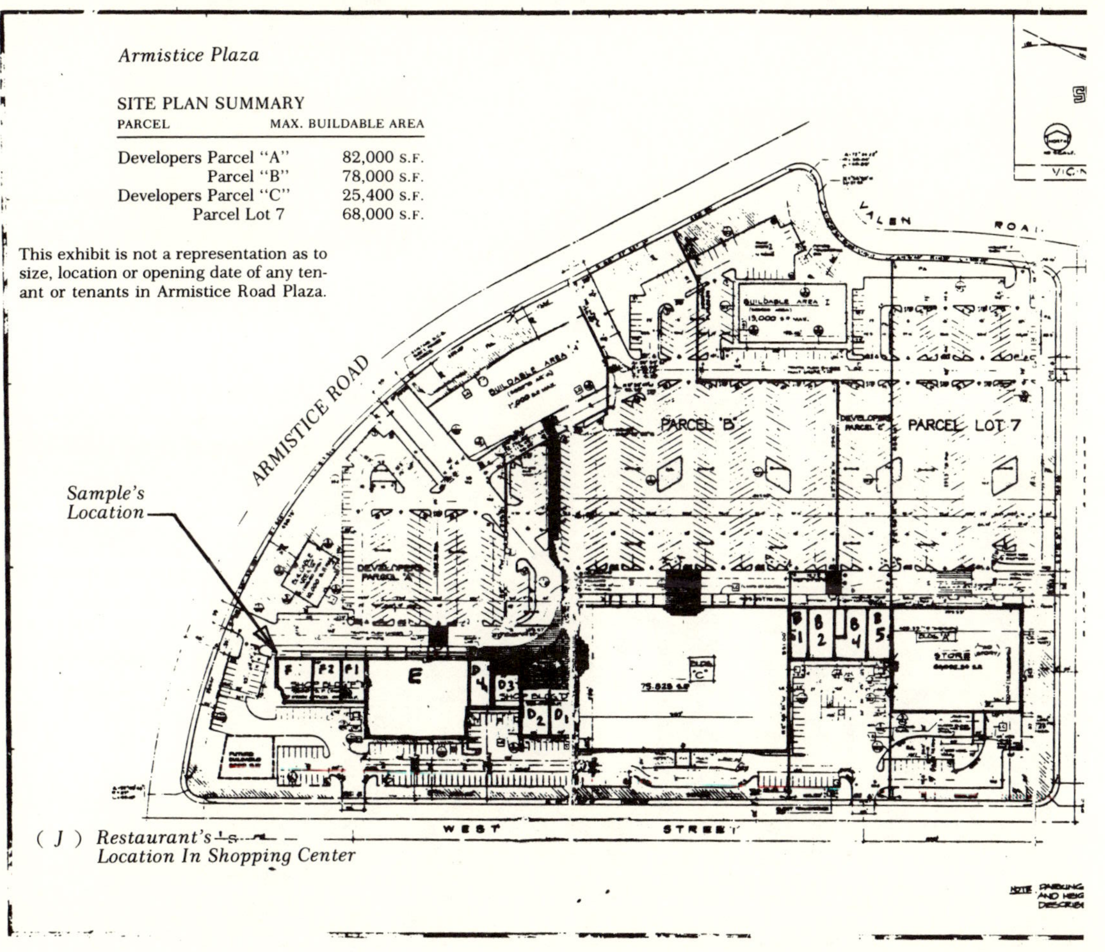
Armistice Plaza
SITE PLAN SUMMARY
PARCEL
MAX. BUILDABLE AREA
Developers Parcel "A" 82,000 S.F.
Parcel "B" 78,000 S.F.
Developers Parcel "C" 25,400 S.F.
Parcel Lot 7 68,000 S.F.
This exhibit is not a representation as to size, location or opening date of any tenant or tenants in Armistice Road Plaza.
Sample's Location
(J) *Restaurant's Location In Shopping Center*
ARMISTICE ROAD
WEST STREET
VALEN ROAD
PARCEL 'B'
PARCEL LOT 7
E

(K) REPRESENTATIVE PHOTOS

IF APPROPRIATE, USE ONE OR TWO PAGES HERE IN YOUR ACTUAL INVESTMENT CIRCULAR FOR REPRESENTATIVE, 4" BY 6" PHOTOS.

PHOTOS MAY BE ATTACHED IN ANY OF SEVERAL WAYS AVAILABLE: E.G., TRANSPARENT TAPE, TWO-SIDED TAPE, SPRAY ADHESIVE, RUBBER CEMENT.

(L) BACKGROUND INFORMATION OF COMPANY

Organization And Operation

Sample's has become the quality name in ice cream around the world. The concept that has made Sample's the leader in its field began in 1942, when Dorien Sample opened his first small ice cream shop at Jones and Baker in San Diego, California, along the streetcar run from the central city to the Harbor area, San Diego's most popular tourist haunt. This San Diego landmark has been a popular tourist stop ever since, with thousands of tourists mentioning Sample's as one of their favorite delights when talking about the many attractions of the City.

Dorien Sample's goal was simple: to manufacture and sell ice cream that would be first in quality, richness, and flavor. He backed this up with good service in an attractive, pleasing setting, and saw his formula for success mushroom into a highly successful, internationally known business. Today, Mr. Sample still maintains an active role in the business. He personally supervises flavor control of the 160 secret ice cream recipes, and he oversees the development of each new flavor for the Company.

The Sample's Ice Cream Company presently has a total of 450 stores operating internationally, and the Company is expanding. It opened 40 stores in 1983 and is in the process of opening another 40 stores during 1984. The present total includes 316 in the United States with 134 locations outside the U.S. in Canada, Spain, Mexico, Japan, England, France, and Germany.

The Sample's franchise system began in 1958 when Mr. Sample licensed the Company to use the Sample's trade names, trade secrets, recipes, and methods of operation. The license permits the Company to franchise shoppes world-wide except for the City of San Diego. The Company never has granted franchises for any business other than ice cream stores, preferring to maintain its excellence in the high quality ice cream industry. Sample's Ice Cream Company is a California corporation with corporate offices located in Houston, Texas.

Sample's ice cream shoppes cater to the general public, and are located in regional malls, shopping centers and other high traffic retail locations. They compete with local, regional, and other national retail ice cream establishments catering to the food and dessert market. However, Sample's provides a "best of the line" product and atmosphere not available from any of its competitors. Shoppes are divided into two categories: large stores, known as "Mains,"which manufacture ice cream on the premises and frequently offer a limited hot food menu; and small shoppes, known as "Remotes," which sell only ice cream manufactured off the premises, and ice cream-related novelties. Along with selling franchises for the operation of Sample's ice cream shoppes to qualified applicants, it owns and operates 115 company stores.

Mains And Remotes

Sample's Mains are large shoppes that produce and sell ice cream and related products, as well as sell a quality food line consisting of hot and cold sandwiches, soups, and salads. Mains have a high quality, pleasing decor and, depending upon the size of the facility, may seat from 30 to over 175 persons. The Company licenses Main franchisees to manufacture ice cream on-site in the store according to the Company's treasured, secret recipes and specifications. Fountain and food items are for on-site and/or off-site consumption.

Sample's Remotes are generally small shoppes of 750 square feet or less, with no ice cream manufacturing capability or permanent seating capacity. These "dipping stations" cater to a carry-out trade, and are located in areas of heavy pedestrian traffic. The menu is strictly limited to fountain and ice cream products appropriate for carry-out. Ice cream is not manufactured in Remotes, but rather is purchased by Remote franchisees from other approved Sample's manufacturers who prepare ice cream and related products in Mains to Company specifications.

Individual Sample's Mains are capable of making 160 different ice cream flavors. Each store across the country must carry a minimum of 45 of the flavors at one time. The ice cream is made fresh in a brightly lit, windowed manufacturing area where customers are invited to watch the unique Sample's process of "turning" the ice cream rather than whipping it. This process is the old-fashioned way of making ice cream. Sample's is proud to be one of only two of the large companies in the field to make ice cream in this manner.

The shiny ice cream machine which pours out this "home-made" creamy ice cream is a modern stainless steel version of the old-fashioned hand crank freezer. Sample's uses it to produce the turning action which gives the finished product a firm, rich consistency, free from any ice crystals. By making only 25 to 50 quarts at a time using Sample's special ice cream butterfat mix and the finest possible ingredients, Sample's produces an ice cream that is 22% richer than most quality ice creams. It is so rich, in fact, that a single dip cone actually weighs over a quarter of a pound. In itself, it is a complete food with high nutritional value.

One of the reasons for Sample's popularity is its ice cream fountain menu; it's one of the largest and most colorful in the industry. This taste-tempting menu offers sundaes, sodas, and all sorts of ice cream specialities. The most popular of these deliciously rich concoctions on the menu is the "Creamy Fudge Banana Split." It features vanilla ice cream layered over banana slices and topped with generous portions of creamy, hot fudge and whipped cream, sprinkles of nuts, and cherries. Sodas are served in all favorite flavors, and special concoctions are made on request. A unique "Kids Section" on the menu provides junior-sized malts, shakes, and sundaes, as well as a cardboard "cookie house." All items are available for take-out. Hand packed by weight, pints and quarts are a full one pound and two pounds, respectively. Some of Sample's special toppings and all of its ice cream cakes and pies are packaged for take-out, too.

Sample's presentation of its delicious ice creams and foods is outstanding, and all are served in a setting that makes a visit to the store a pleasurable experience for all ages. The motif includes real oak tables and an old-fashioned soda fountain with a classic marble top. Wood paneling throughout the shoppes is custom made and finished. Old-fashioned Tiffany-type lamps and wooden overhead fans hang from a special acoustical ceiling. Borders of tiny lights trim perimeters of large, hand-worked mirrors that give the entire store an elegant, yet warm, nostalgic touch.

Sample's is unique in the fast-paced food industry world because of its ambience and friendly service. When you enter a Sample's, you can return to the nostalgic era of things that are real, fundamental, warm. The product is genuine and of high quality; the service is friendly and courteous. Waiters and waitresses are trained to be concerned with the customer having a fun time, as well as good food and ice cream. They are carefully selected to provide an all-American freshness and uncompromised good service. A relaxing, old-fashioned feeling greets each customer so that he can relive the good times of a bygone era in today's world of high-speed living.

Company Expansion, Promotion Plans

The 450 Sample's stores noted above are made up of 321 Mains and 129 Remotes which is indicative of the Company's continuing emphasis on the larger ice cream and food centers. The 40 stores planned for opening in 1984 will tend to follow this basic ratio of stores already in operation. In early 1983, James D. White, 42, assumed the presidency of Sample's Ice Cream Company. Prior to accepting this position, Mr.

White was Executive Vice President of Foods International and the President of the Foods International Franchisee Association. Mr. White is well known throughout the food-service industry and, prior to joining Foods, he spent five years as Executive Vice President of Marketing for Burgers, Incorporated. While with Burgers, Inc., he was responsible for introducing the first fish sandwich to the fast food industry and the "be somebody" advertising and marketing campaign.

When Mr. White joined Sample's, he stated, "I'm very pleased to join the undisputed leader in the high quality ice cream industry. I believe the Company is positioned perfectly for the expanding market of the 80's with a high-quality product and an excellent marketing concept. Those seeking a franchise in the food-service business should have Sample's in the number one position on their lists, and my main job will be to see that Sample's has that distinction. Those joining Sample's franchise community now will be getting in on the largest growth period our Company has ever seen because we are taking advantage of the newest shopping areas, the latest developments in national and international markets, and our unsurpassed quality reputation."

To back up its agressive expansion plans, Sample's 1984 goals also include an increased advertising program. The highlight of this program will be an advertising promotion to coincide with the opening of the movie "Family Times." Sample's has negotiated the right to nationally promote its ice cream and food products in conjunction with what is projected to be the largest family movie event of our times. In addition, Sample's is taking over sponsorship of the highly rated TV dramatic series, "Eagles Lair." These new concentrations in the mass entertainment market are expected to take gross franchise and Company sales well over the $2 billion mark for the current year.

General Franchise Information

Sample's Ice Cream Company operates Company shoppes, and also offers to qualified applicants franchises to operate Sample's ice cream shoppes. These shoppes engage in the retailing/wholesaling of ice cream and food products, and are either the large Mains, or the smaller Remotes, as described above.

Sample's franchise fee for its Mains presently is $35,000, and for its Remotes, $25,000. This franchise fee paid by each franchisee goes directly to the Company which allocates it primarily to (1) costs incurred in the evaluation of potential franchisees, and in the marketing and sale of the franchise; (2) reimbursement for a portion of the Company's initial and continuing costs for the Sample's franchise information documentation, operations manuals, suggested shoppe designs, and shoppe specifications; (3) the Company's expenses in consulting with the franchisee on site selection, lease terms, financing alternatives, design, construction, and the equipping and opening of the shoppe; (4) the Company's costs to staff its training school, and to train franchisees; (5) the Company's general and administrative expenses; and (6) the cost of compliance with governmental franchising regulations, and federal, state and local taxes.

The Company, at its expense, arranges for a representative to be present at a Main for 10 days before the opening, and for such additional time after the opening as in the Company's judgment is required, usually a total of about four to seven days. This representative will advise on all last minute opening details, will supervise and advise in establishing satisfactory operating procedures, and will aid in the training of shoppe personnel. Within each category of shoppe, these fees are the same for all new Sample's shoppe franchises regardless of the size of the proposed outlet, its location, whether or not it manufactures ice cream, or the degree to which the franchisee uses the services of the Company.

The franchisee is financially solely responsible for the design and construction of his shoppe, and the Company assumes no responsibility therefor, unless contracted for by the franchisee. However, the Company provides a suggested store layout applicable to each particular site. It also suggests typical equipment and decor specifications to both Main and Remote franchisees for use in the design and construction of their shoppes. The Company also will consult with franchisees regarding the design of their specific shoppes, the selection of contractors, and related construction details. All plans and specifications prepared for shoppes must be approved by the Company prior to the commencement of construction. All changes to the final plans and specifications similarly must be approved. The Company has been and is receptive to franchisee suggestions, however, even when such suggestions may deviate from accepted standards.

Occasionally, the Sample's Company will agree to grant a franchisee the exclusive right to open several Mains and Remotes in a relatively large area, and to accept deposits from no one else for the area. The General Partners have expressed the desire to open subsequent stores, after the first store is established, and the Company has indicated it will grant them the right of first refusal for additional franchises throughout Elmtown County, excluding Somm Valley and Johnston Village. Each store is a separate franchise and, thereby, would require an additional franchise fee.

Should the General Partners pursue opening other Sample's outlets in Elmtown County on a limited partnership basis similar to that of this first Sample's shoppe, each partner herein will have a right of first refusal to participate in the ownership of each said outlet based on the ownership structure then applicable. Any subsequent outlets may purchase ice cream on a wholesale basis from Sample's Elmtown which would be an approved Sample's manufacturer. Sample's Elmtown and any subsequent outlets as described in this paragraph will be separate legal entities and, as such, each may deal with the other on a normal arm's length basis.

As heretofore mentioned, the franchise agreement specifies that the Company must approve the plans and specifications for shoppes prior to the commencement of construction. For an additional fee, Sample's will handle construction of the new shoppe from beginning to end on a contract administration basis. The General Partners have researched this option and have found it to be the most efficient and cost effective means for completing the project. This has been provided for in the development budget.

The franchisee is obligated to pay the Sample's Company a monthly royalty of 5½% of gross sales on all products sold at the shoppe, whether for on-site or off-site consumption. As part of the franchise agreement, all franchisees automatically become members of the Sample's Advertising Association. Members of the Association pay 3% of their gross sales into the Association which allocates these funds for advertising and promotional purposes. Of this 3% of gross sales, 1% is spent for support of the Association and for national advertising benefiting all franchisees, while the other 2% is allocated for local advertising, promotional activity, and public relations activity for the local benefit of each individual member. This Association, and the total marketing program produced by it, are both essential to the successful operation of each individual store. The fundamentals of the Sample's system--common products, trademarks, decor, symbols, logos, and slogans--are the only way that the consumer has of knowing that he can rely on the same high quality being consistent from shoppe to shoppe.

Franchisee Obligation To Purchase Or Lease From Sample's

Because of the attractive, uniform appearance, and consistently high quality of product and service from all Sample's shoppes, the Sample's franchise system has achieved a high position of acceptance and recognition by the consuming public, as well as by investors in its franchises. Preserving the public'c ability to rely on this consistency of high quality and service is key to the continued success of the Company, its franchise system, and the franchisees' market. Because of this, the Company has established minimum, basic guidelines for the manufacture, purchase, and handling of ice cream and ice cream related products.

By agreement, Main franchisees must use the specific freezer and related accessories specified by the Company to manufacture the Sample's ice cream product. In addition, the butterfat mix used in the preparation of Sample's ice cream must be purchased from manufacturers to whom the formula has been disclosed. (The butterfat mix and the recipes and processes for manufacture are considered unique and constitute trade secrets. The franchisee's right to purchase and use the mix, recipes, and processes is granted pursuant to the franchise agreement.) The franchisee is required to follow the recipes and processes closely to prevent ice crystals from forming, to maintain consistency of product, etc. The Company does not receive any income from the sale of the freezer or the butterfat mix; it derives its income solely from each individual franchisee's royalty percentage.

The Company--unlike many franchisors--does not offer supplies or food products for sale to franchisees. It feels that this possibly could put income into the Company at the expense of each franchisee losing the ability to negotiate lower prices from third party suppliers. For this reason, it has arranged with various suppliers to carry requisite items. Franchisees may buy supplies or equipment from any of these approved sources, so long as the supplies and equipment meet the Company's standards. Any items used in and on ice cream must be approved by the Company to ensure compliance with the Company's standards and requirements prior to use.

Franchisor Obligation/Assistance To Franchisee

Sample's has many obligations to perform to assist in the success of its franchisees. Most of these obligations and services are detailed in the foregoing section, "General Franchise Information." Additionally, the franchisees have the right to use the Sample's name, goodwill and trade secrets, the Sample's way of doing business, and Sample's operations and related manuals and training materials once their shoppes are opened. The Company also designs, develops, and provides sales promotion materials, advertises nationally on behalf of all franchisees, and aids each franchisee with his local advertising budgets as described above.

Each franchisee is aided greatly by Company manuals that set forth basic knowledge needed by the franchisee to operate his shoppe smoothly and efficiently. This large library of data includes information related to the preparation, presentation, and serving of ice cream, fountain and all food products. It also provides instructions for accounting, advertising and sales promotion, employee hiring and training, ordering, inventory control, and other related matters. The Company also provides assistance in the way of representatives to consult with the franchisee on continuing store operations and introduction of new products and services.

A powerful training program also is provided by the Company. In fact, each franchisee is required to take this training prior to the opening of his shoppe. The program includes in-depth classroom instruction, as well as practical on-the-job training in actual operating Sample's stores. The instructional expenses are absorbed by the Company so that the franchisee pays only the personal expenses, including travel, lodging and any salary of the trainee or trainees, for this three-week course. In addition, the Company sends out periodic bulletins to all franchisees. These bulletins provide current information regarding store operations, new innovations, suggestions by a franchisee that can benefit all shoppes, and helpful tips.

(M) BACKGROUND INFORMATION ON THE INDUSTRY

--OPTIONAL--

This section is OPTIONAL. It should be used only if a good, outside "objective" article or study relative to your syndication project is available.

An article/study that gives statistics and confirms that people will pay a high price for a quality ice cream would be useful here. This "objective" outside data can help to give investors more confidence in the investment which they are contemplating. Be sure to obtain written approval, if necessary, from the author and/or publisher before you use such an article.

N) INDIVIDUAL FRANCHISE: GENERAL TERMS, CONDITIONS, RENEWAL

On December 12, 1982, the General Partners entered into an agreement for the purchase of a Sample's franchise for the City of Elmtown. Since that time, they have been involved actively in site selection, marketing research, and lease negotiations in order to locate the best possible site for their franchise. This has been accomplished with the leasehold acquisition in the Armistice Plaza location.

Since 1982, the franchise cost has increased from $20,000 to $35,000, for a net cash increase of $15,000. However, the General Partners have the advantage of the lower amount due to their signing of a contract prior to the increase. They will pass this savings through to the Partnership, transferring their franchise to the Partnership at cost.

The franchise term is 20 years and is renewable for two additional periods of 10 years each. The franchisee must notify the Company in writing of his intention to renew his franchise at least six months prior to the scheduled expiration of the franchise term. No additional franchise fee will be charged on renewal, but the terms of the Franchise Agreement, including percentage royalty fee, will be the same as are being offered to new franchisees at the time of the renewal, except for the term of the Agreement.

During the initial term of the franchise, Main franchisees are granted a non-competition radius around their Sample's Mains. Non-competition radii are normally described in terms of a radius around the shoppe by means of reference to a map made a part of the Franchise Agreement as an exhibit. For Armistice Plaza, the non-competition radius is expected to preclude another Sample's from opening in the City of Elmtown (unless it is another store developed by the General Partners). Sample's also agrees not to establish a Company-owned Sample's Main or Remote, and not to grant to other persons a franchise for the use of the licensed trademark within this area. Sample's has also stated that it will grant the General Partners a "first right of refusal" for additional shoppes in other Elmtown County areas, including Carsen, Lighter, Franken Oaks, and Oberton.

One of the franchise terms is very advantageous to the Partnership in the event of a sale of the business. The Franchise Agreement gives the Company a right of first refusal on sale or transfer of the franchisee's interests. Thus, the Company has the right, but is not required, to purchase the franchisee's business on the same terms and conditions as are offered to a third party. The franchisee must give the Company written notice of the proposed sale or transfer and set forth all of the pertinent terms thereof. The Company has 30 days after receipt of the notice within which to exercise its right of first refusal to purchase the shoppe on these terms. If there are changes in the terms, the new terms must be offered to the Company.

(O) PROJECT STATUS, PLANNED OPENING SCHEDULE

The General Partners' expectation of a Sample's Ice Cream Main in the City of Elmtown is close to being achieved. Lease negotiations concerning a shoppe location in the Armistice Plaza were begun in February, 1984. The lease document has addressed Sample's basic requirements of a 20-year lease by approving a 15-year base period with a five-year option. The lease terms and conditions can be renegotiated if the General Partners renew their Franchise Agreement for an additional 10 or 20 years.

The lease terms are very favorable to the Partnership. The payments are below the market and fixed for the first three years (a lessor concession to having Sample's in the shopping center), increased slightly and level (no cost of living increase) for the next four and one-half years, then level again for the second seven and one-half year period, but at a slightly higher rate. Specifically, the lease package includes rental for the 2,888 square foot shoppe at $.95 per square foot for the first three years and $1.00 per square foot for the next four and one-half years, or 5% of the gross revenue, whichever is higher. After seven and one-half years, rent will be at $1.25 per square foot versus the same percentage. A common area cost sharing charge is projected in the income statements. Due to the General Partners' early negotiations, the lessor will include some plumbing and electrical features at no added cost.

Penney's, the largest store in the Armistice Plaza project (approximately 77,000 square feet), is presently under construction with a planned opening date of July 20, 1984. The developers are hopeful of a Grand Opening for all the "in-line stores" of the center shortly after the official opening of Penney's. Pouring of foundation and other construction work on the "in-line stores" are currently in progress.

The General Partners have arranged with Sample's for coordination of the total construction package. Once the foundation and shell for the shoppe are completed, all architectural, engineering service, and construction management services will be provided by Sample's. In addition, representatives from Sample's architectural and construction division will come to Elmtown for periodic inspections of the general contractor's progress to ensure conformance to Sample's construction standards.

The General Partners have planned for a fall opening of the shoppe. Prior to this time, the Houston training class will be attended. The bulk of the late summer and early fall period is scheduled for completion of the store interior, setting of equipment in place, and recruiting, hiring, and training of all employees.

(P) CASH DISTRIBUTION TO PARTNERS--PRINCIPALS' COMPENSATION

It is anticipated that the Partnership will begin quarterly distributions of cash to the purchasers of Units for the first quarter of 1985, based on present schedules. Due to non-cash deductions from income such as leasehold improvement and equipment depreciation, and deduction and amortization of certain expenses, it is anticipated that the cash distributions will have some shelter from income tax liability for some period of time.

Referencing the income statements and cash distribution schedules in the FINANCIALS section, anticipated cash-on-cash distributions to the Limited Partners should range between a low of 39% and a high of 57% per year of invested dollars during the first two to three years after opening, until an amount equivalent to invested capital is returned. As per the Partnership Agreement, any cash available for distribution from operations shall be distributed in its entirety to the Limited Partners until an amount equal to their original capital is received by them. Thereafter, the General Partners shall receive thirty-five percent (35%) and the Limited Partners shall receive sixty-five percent (65%) of the remaining cash available for distribution. Accordingly, the General Partners' interest is completely subordinated behind the Limited Partners first recouping an amount equal to the original amount invested.

After return of dollars equivalent to initial invested dollars per the foregoing, anticipated cash-on-cash distributions to the Limited Partners should continue to range between a minimum of 31% and 47% per year of original dollars invested. This return is expected to continue throughout the operating term of the franchise. These returns could be looked at as a 100% per year return as no Limited Partner would have any of his original capital still at risk; i.e., all funds invested would have been returned. No projections for cash distributions beyond 15 years have been generated although the business is expected to continue for many years beyond this point. All of these figures are estimated, however, and cannot be guaranteed.

The Partnership may eventually sell the business. While the principals have no way of accurately forecasting when or if a sale might occur, or for what sum, there should be some additional benefit in terms of appreciation of the leasehold interest and of the value of the franchise and business itself. As previously noted, Sample's Company does have a right of first refusal to purchase the business which would appear to be an advantage to the Partnership.

With respect to distribution of capital from a sale, liquidation, refinance, or other disposition of the property and business, the General Partners, collectively, shall receive thirty-five percent (35%) and the Limited Partners, collectively, shall receive sixty-five percent (65%) of the distribution of capital subject to the Limited Partners having first received a cash sum from all sources equal to one hundred percent (100%) of their original investment.

In addition to the foregoing, the total General Partner's compensation is restricted to the following:

(1) Per the Franchise Agreement, the General Partners are responsible for the shoppe's operation and they will be spending a substantial amount of time in the actual operation of the business. They are also required to keep complete accounting records and to submit monthly operating reports and sales figures, as well as annual reports to the Sample's Company. As compensation for these services, they will receive a collective general management reimbursement of $2,000 per month beginning at the time the business opens to the public. Their general management reimbursement shall be modified upward each 12-month period thereafter up to a maximum of a ten percent (10%) increase per year.

(2) The General Partners have been and will be intensively involved for months in the design, development, and construction of the business improvements. They also will be coordinating the hiring and training of employees and will be concerned with the myriad of details of opening of the business. As such, they collectively shall be entitled to a nominal project management reimbursement of $5,000.

(Q) THE GENERAL PARTNERS AND THEIR EXPERIENCE

The principals of this project are Brent E. Stace and Patrick

Marris. They have been investigating all aspects of this project for well over two years and have spent considerable time investigating other similar franchises, especially throughout California and Arizona. They are organizing this business enterprise completely, and will carry it through to completion, as well.

Messrs. Stace and Marris have been residents in the City of Elmtown for over ten years. Each of them has had extensive training and experience in the management of personnel and resources. Both are currently employed by the Elmtown County Building Department as Section Managers. As such, they are part of the Department's management team and their responsibilities include staffing, budgeting, planning, scheduling, coordinating, and supervising. They have direct management responsibilities for approximately 160 employees and a budget of over $5.5 million.

Messrs. Stace and Marris also have considerable experience working in management capacities in large restaurants and dinner houses. This direct restaurant experience, as well as flexibility in their present work hours and multiple days off, will help them adequately oversee, manage, and administer the day-to-day operations of this business.

> BRENT E. STACE is a Section Manager with the Elmtown County Building Department, presently responsible for the Operations and Scheduling Sections. At 33 years old, he is the youngest manager in the Department, a position he attained nearly three years ago.
>
> Mr. Stace completed his undergraduate study at California State University, Los Angeles, in 1973, earning a Bachelor's Degree in Political Science and Administration, with a minor in Sociology. He continued his graduate study at University of California at Los Angeles, graduating in 1976 with a Master of Arts Degree in Management and Personnel.
>
> Prior to joining the Elmtown County Building Department, Mr. Stace worked his way through college in the employ of the Reston Unified School District. After graduating, he worked as manager of a large dinner house where he gained valuable insight into the restaurant business. Since moving to Elmtown, Mr. Stace has made several real estate investments which have helped him establish a firm equity base, and which have demonstrated his sound business practices and knowledge.
>
> Mr. Stace is recognized throughout California as a personnel management professional, and he actively participated in the 1983 "Symposium On Professional Issues In

Personnel Management" held in Sacramento. He serves on the Standards and Ethics Committee of the California Personnel Managers' Association, and also instructs on a variety of management subjects through the Elmtown Community College system.

Mr. Stace is actively involved in the community through the Elmtown Presbyterian Church, where he serves as the Usher Coordinator. He is also an active member and past President of the Elmtown chapter of the Fellowship of Christian Public Service Managers. He and his wife of 12 years, Joann, have three children. For recreation, Mr. Stace enjoys running and racquetball. He also is a private pilot and certified scuba diver.

PATRICK MARRIS is Manager of the Safety Enforcement Section of the Elmtown County Building Department. This position includes responsibility for the Department's code enforcement, inspection, and variance activities. He also is responsible for providing staff support to the Director of the Building Department.

Mr. Marris is 38 years old. He received his Associate of Arts Degree from Los Angeles City College in 1967. In 1969, he received a Bachelor of Arts Degree in Marketing from the University of California at Northridge. Mr. Marris received his Master of Science Degree in Marketing Administration from California Lutheran College in 1976. He worked part-time for International Restaurants from 1965 to 1969 to help pay for his college expenses. From 1969 to 1971, he was part of International Restaurant's Regional Management team and was transferred to Elmtown in 1970 to manage one of the Company's largest restaurants on the West Coast.

Mr. Marris is a Commissioned Officer, inactive status, in the California Army National Guard and the United States Army Reserves (1st Lieutenant). His numerous military schools attended include the Army Corps of Engineers School. His last duty assignment was Executive Officer for a company of 160 men. Mr. Marris is very active in the community, serving on the Board of Directors for the Elmtown Boys and Girls Club. He also is a First Vice President on the Advisory Board for the Salvation Army. Mr. Marris, his wife Joy, and their five daughters have lived in the City of Elmtown for 14 years.

(R) INCOME TAX RISK FACTORS

On the basis that the Partnership will be treated as a partnership for income tax purposes, the Partnership will file federal and state partnership information tax returns, reporting its operations on a cash or accrual basis for a calendar taxable year. Each of the Partners will, in general, be entitled to deduct on his individual tax return his distributive share of the Partnership's losses or will be required to include in his reported income his distributive share of the Partnership's profits. Each of the Partners will be advised of the amount to be reported on his individual federal and state income tax return as his distributive share of the Partnership's income, gains, losses, deductions and credits, whether or not actual distribution is made to him for the taxable year of the Partnership ending within or with his taxable year.

The purchase of a limited partnership interest in Sample's Elmtown involves risk. In addition to the general investment risks described throughout this Memorandum, prospective investors should consider the following potential risks with regard to income tax consequences.

It should be recognized that the risk factors set forth below are those which, at the date of the Memorandum, seem to the Partnership the most likely to be significant. Prospective investors should realize, however, that factors other than those set forth below may ultimately affect the investment offered pursuant to this Memorandum in a manner and to a degree which cannot be foreseen at this time.

The General Partners strongly recommend prospective investors to consult with their counsel and/or tax adviser prior to investing in Sample's Elmtown to discuss how the following risk factors may affect them.

Partnership Tax Status - No Request For A Tax Ruling. The Partnership intends to file federal and state Partnership information tax returns. The General Partners have not, however, and do not intend to request a ruling from the Internal Revenue Service (the "IRS") that the Partnership will be treated as a partnership for Federal income tax purposes and not as an association taxable as a corporation. In the absence of such a ruling, there can be no assurance that the Partnership will not be treated as an association taxable as a corporation, and if so treated as a corporation, such treatment will result in the loss of substantially all of the tax benefits that may flow from an investment in the Partnership.

On January 5, 1977, the Commissioner of Internal Revenue proposed Treasury Regulations on the classification of partnerships and associations for tax purposes. The regulations were immediately ordered withdrawn by the Secretary of the Treasury, who subsequently concluded that the proposed Regulations should not be reproposed. The proposed Regulations would have a substantial adverse effect upon the tax status of the Partnership, and there can be no assurance that similar Regulations will not be reproposed in the future.

Risk Of Audit. Information returns filed by the Partnership are subject to audit by the IRS. The IRS is devoting greater attention to the proper application of the tax laws to partnerships. In this connection, the IRS recently issued revised guidelines, procedures and instructions for handling cases under its tax shelter audit program. The Commissioner of Internal Revenue has announced that IRS audits of "tax shelters" will be expanded, and that the IRS plans to examine 25 percent of partnership returns showing losses exceeding $25,000. It is probable that such course will be followed for future years.

While the Partnership's initial returns are not expected to show losses in excess of $25,000, its returns still could be audited. An audit of the Partnership's return may lead to adjustments, in which event the Limited Partners may be required to file amended personal federal and/or state income tax returns, and may be liable for certain interest and penalty payments due to an underpayment of federal and/or state income tax. In addition, any such audit may lead to an audit of a Limited Partner's individual tax return which may lead to adjustments other than those relating to the investment in Sample's Elmtown.

Substantial Underpayment Penalty. A new penalty of ten percent (10%) is imposed by TEFRA, which was adopted in September 1982, on any substantial underpayment of tax. The Partnership strongly advises each potential Limited Partner to consult with his own tax adviser to be sure that he evaluates fully the proposed tax treatment of Partnership items.

Risk Of Loss Of Deductions. The Partnership intends to deduct certain of the cash payments to the General Partners. The interpretation of the Internal Revenue Code and Treasury Regulations to be adopted by the Partnership is that most are favorable to the taxpayer, not the government. There is no assurance that the IRS will not contest the deductibility of some or even most of these or any other items which could result in the disallowance of some or all of the tax benefits.

There is the further risk that even if some deductions or credits are not disallowed entirely, a different tax treatment or allocation may be given various items than that which is contemplated by the Partnership Agreement or reported in the Partnership Information Return. If such challenge were successful, the anticipated deductions would be reduced and the allocations of profits and losses to the Partners for tax purposes could be adversely affected.

Transactions Entered Into For Profit. In order for the Limited Partners to be entitled to all of the anticipated tax losses from the ownership and operation of the Partnership leasehold interest, the transaction must be "engaged in for a profit." While the ultimate resolution of this issue depends upon the facts and circumstances of each case, prospective investors should be aware that as a result of recent developments in this area, deductions attributable to investments producing substantial tax benefits may be disallowed on the grounds that there were insufficient economic benefits to be derived from the investment. Accordingly, while the financial projections of the project may support a basis for the profit motive by the Partnership and the Limited Partners, there can be no assurance that the IRS will not challenge the deductibility of the losses to be incurred by the Partnership on the grounds that there were insufficient economic profits in the transaction, apart from tax consequences.

Taxable Income In Excess Of Cash Receipts. The amount of gain (and possibly the amount of the tax liability on such gain) realized by a Limited Partner by reason of the sale or other disposition (including gifts) by him of his Limited Partnership interest or by reason of a sale (including a sale pursuant to foreclosure proceedings) or other disposition of the Partnership property may, under certain circumstances, exceed the partner's cash, if any, obtained from such sale or other disposition of his Limited Partnership interest or his share of cash, if any, obtained by the Partnership and distributed to him as a Partner as the result of such sale or other disposition of the Partnership property.

In addition, there is a risk that after several years of Partnership operations, an investor's tax liabilities during the tax year may exceed his cash distributions in such year and that, to the extent of such excess, the payment of such taxes will be an additional out-of-pocket expense for the investor.

Depreciation, Other Deductions. The Partnership will elect to depreciate the improvements for federal income tax purposes under the Accelerated Cost Recovery System (ACRS). In addition to depreciation expenses, there may also be an investment tax credit deduction which would be a direct credit against a Partner's personal income tax liability. All depreciation expenses and any investment tax credits shall be passed on to the Limited Partners until they have received an amount equal to their original capital contribution. Thereafter, all such deductions shall be shared by the Limited and General Partners, 65% and 35%, respectively.

Disposition Of Property Or Partnership Interest. Income from certain capital transactions qualifies for preferential tax treatment. The maximum federal tax rate applicable to long-term capital gains after 1981 is applied to 40% of the capital gain. This factor could be advantageous to the Partners in the case of a sale of this project, but again must be discussed with each Partner's adviser for full clarification and impact on the Partner. In the future, it is possible that the Treasury Department may seek to alter some of the existing tax provisions by administrative action. Prospective equity Partners would be ill-advised to rely unduly on the prospect that the tax benefits provided under existing law will continue to be afforded.

Partnership Allocations. The Partnership has not received an IRS ruling that the methods of allocating profits and losses pursuant to the Partnership Agreement will be respected for federal and state income tax purposes. If the IRS should determine, for example, that the allocations under the Partnership Agreement do not have substantial economic affect, the deductions otherwise anticipated by the Limited Partners might not be allowable to them. Any successful challenge to the allocation of Partnership items could adversely affect the tax consequences to the Limited Partners by reducing their share of Partnership profits and losses allocated to them.

Payments To The General Partners. The Partnership will make payments to the General Partners for various services to be rendered and undertakings furnished. The General Partners believe that such payments are deductible. However, there can be no assurance that any or all of such amounts will not be deemed by the IRS to be includible in the costs of organizing the project, or as non-deductible items, in which case the deductions available to the Partnership would be reduced in the early years but possibly increased through additional deductions in the later years.

Possible Future Changes In Tax Laws And In Interpretations Thereof. Various legislative proposals which would affect amendments to the current tax laws have been proposed recently by the Treasury Department and various Congressmen or Congressional committees. Should such legislation be enacted, it could substantially affect the tax treatment currently accorded limited partnerships. Furthermore, no assurance can be given that legislative, judicial, or administrative changes may not be forthcoming which would adversely affect an investor's investment. Any such changes may or may not be retroactive with respect to transactions entered into or contemplated prior to the effective date of such changes. Prospective Limited Partners are urged to consult their own counsel or other personal tax adviser regarding the current status of any such proposals and their potential impact on the Partnership.

Possible Reduction In Partnership Losses. The Financial Projections are based on an assumed opening of the project for business during late 1984. If the event were to occur later than the assumed time period, the amount of the anticipated 1984 Partnership losses, as well as other items in future years allocable to the Limited Partners could be reduced or deferred.

Complex Tax Matters. The foregoing summary is general, is limited in its scope, is approximated, and cannot consider all of the tax considerations or consequences pertinent to each potential Limited Partner. The tax affairs of the Partnership are complex and are subject to varied interpretations. The effect of tax laws on Limited Partners will vary depending on their particular circumstances. There may be tax-related risks which are not listed in this Memorandum. Prospective investors or their advisers should seek the advice of a tax attorney or accountant qualified to discuss other possible tax risks or IRS theories of attack. EACH INVESTOR SHOULD CONSULT WITH AND RELY ON HIS OWN TAX ADVISERS WITH RESPECT TO THE POSSIBLE TAX RESULTS OF THIS INVESTMENT.

(S) PRO FORMA FINANCIAL PROJECTIONS

The following Projected Income Statements contain variable expense and sales data based on information provided by Sample's Company, as well as fixed cost information specific to this Elmtown location. From longtime experience, the Company has been able to break down variable expenses into percentages of sales, and these figures are presented accordingly in the accompanying statements. The gross annual sales projections are derived from the 1983 sales performances of six Sample's locations ranging in size from 1,772 square feet to 3,282 square feet. Because of their range in size, their sales volumes were converted into sales per square foot. The average actual sales per square foot for the six locations, as well as the highest actual sales per square foot were then used to forecast sales for this Elmtown store.

The accompanying projected statements of operations and statements of projected distributions of Sample's Elmtown for three 12-month periods are management's estimates of the results of operations but do not necessarily represent the most probable future financial results. Accordingly, the financial projections reflect management's judgment, based on present circumstances, of the conditions, and its course of action if the sales assumptions are attained. However, even if they were attained, some assumptions inevitably will not materialize and unanticipated events and circumstances may occur; therefore, the actual results achieved during the projection period will vary from the projection, and the variations may be material.

Accountants have compiled the projected financial statements referred to above. A compilation of a projection does not include evaluation of the support for the assumptions underlying the projection. Because a compilation of a projection is limited as described above, no conclusion or any other form of assurance on the accompanying statements of assumptions is expressed.

The objective of a financial projection is to provide management's estimate of the financial results if one or more hypothecated or stipulated events or conditions occur. The American Institute of Certified Public Accountants defines a financial projection as an estimate of financial results based on assumptions that are not necessarily the most likely. This objective is significantly different from the objective of a financial forecast which is defined as an estimate of the most probable financial position for one or more future periods. Accordingly, investors should be aware that the following financial projections are estimates which are not necessarily probable of occurrence.

FUTURE OPERATING RESULTS ARE IMPOSSIBLE TO PREDICT, AND NO REPRESENTATION, GUARANTY OR WARRANTY OF ANY KIND IS MADE BY THE PARTNERSHIP, THE GENERAL PARTNERS OR THEIR AFFILIATES, IF ANY, RESPECTING THE FUTURE ACCURACY OR COMPLETENESS OF, AND NO REPRESENTATION, GUARANTY OR WARRANTY IS TO BE INFERRED FROM THESE PROJECTIONS. PROSPECTIVE INVESTORS ARE URGED, THEREFORE, TO CONSULT THEIR OWN ADVISERS (WHOSE VIEWS MAY DIFFER FROM THOSE DESCRIBED IN THESE PROJECTIONS) WITH RESPECT TO BUSINESS, LEGAL, TAX AND OTHER MATTERS CONCERNING THE FOLLOWING PROJECTIONS.

(S) PROJECTED INCOME STATEMENT
(1st 12 Months of Operation)

	Average Actual Sales	Highest Actual Sales
* Gross Annual Sales Income	$ 687,344	$ 947,264
**Operating Expenses: Variable Costs		
Cost of Sales (29%)	199,330	274,707
Sample's Royalty Fee (5.5%)	37,804	52,100
Wages, incl. all Taxes (23%)	158,089	217,871
Paper Supplies (2%)	13,747	18,945
Clean'g, Office, Rest. Supp. (2%)	13,747	18,945
Repair/Maintenance (.5%)	3,437	4,736
Advertising/Promotion (3%)	20,620	28,418
Outside Services, Other (2%)	13,747	18,945
Lessor % Rental vs. Lease Pymts.	1,444	14,440
Operating Expenses: Fixed Costs		
General Management	24,000	24,000
Leasehold Rent	32,923	32,923
Utilities/Telephone	15,000	15,000
Accounting/Legal	1,800	1,800
Insurance (incl. Work. Comp.)	4,000	4,000
Real Property Taxes (est.)	3,750	3,750
Common Area Maintenance	2,166	2,166
Total Operating Expenses	545,604	732,746
Net Operating Income (Net Cash for Distribution):	$ 141,740	$ 214,518

* The Gross Annual Sales Volume is based upon actual 1983 sales per square feet of six representative Sample's restaurants.

** Operating Expenses are derived from actual expenses experienced by other Sample's stores, as supplied by Sample's Co.

(S) PROJECTED INCOME STATEMENT
(2nd 12 Months of Operation)

	Average Actual Sales	Highest Actual Sales
*Gross Annual Sales Income	$ 756,078	$ 1,041,990
Operating Expenses: Variable Costs		
Cost of Sales (29%)	219,263	302,177
Sample's Royalty Fee (5.5%)	41,584	57,309
Wages, incl. all Taxes (23%)	173,898	239,658
Paper Supplies (2%)	15,122	20,840
Clean'g, Office, Rest. Supp. (2%)	15,122	20,840
Repair/Maintenance (.5%)	3,781	5,210
Advertising/Promotion (3%)	22,682	31,260
Outside Services, Other (2%)	15,122	20,840
Lessor % Rental vs. Lease Pymts.	4,881	19,177
Operating Expenses: Fixed Costs		
General Management	26,400	26,400
Leasehold Rent	32,923	32,923
Utilities/Telephone	16,500	16,500
Accounting/Legal	1,800	1,800
Insurance (incl. Work. Comp.)	4,000	4,000
Real Property Taxes (est.)	3,750	3,750
Common Area Maintenance (est.)	2,166	2,166
Total Operating Expenses	598,994	804,850
Net Operating Income (Net Cash for Distribution):	$ 157,084	$ 237,140

* Sales and applicable variable expenses have been increased ten percent above the 1st 12 months projected operating figures.

(S) PROJECTED INCOME STATEMENT
(3rd 12 Months of Operation)

	Average Actual Sales	Highest Actual Sales
*Gross Annual Sales Income	$ 831,686	$ 1,146,189
Operating Expenses: Variable Costs		
Cost of Sales (29%)	241,189	332,395
Sample's Royalty Fee (5.5%)	45,743	63,040
Wages, incl. all Taxes (23%)	191,288	263,623
Paper Supplies (2%)	16,634	22,924
Clean'g, Office, Rest. Supp. (2%)	16,634	22,924
Repair/Maintenance (.5%)	4,158	5,731
Advertising/Promotion (3%)	24,951	34,386
Outside Services, Other (2%)	16,634	22,924
Lessor % Rental vs. Pymts.	8,661	24,386
Operating Expenses: Fixed Costs		
General Management	29,040	29,040
Leasehold Rent	32,923	32,923
Utilities/Telephone	18,750	18,750
Accounting/Legal	1,800	1,800
Insurance (incl. Work. Comp.)	4,000	4,000
Real Property Taxes (est.)	3,750	3,750
Common Area Maintenance (est.)	2,166	2,166
Total Operating Expenses	658,321	884,762
Net Operating Income (Net Cash for Distribution):	$ 173,365	261,427

* Sales and applicable variable expenses have been increased ten percent above the 2nd 12 months projected operating figures.

(T) PROJECTED LIMITED PARTNER CASH DISTRIBUTION SCHEDULE

Return of Amount Equal to Original Investment ($395,500)

A. If Average Actual Sales level is attained:

Approx. Payout Period	Avg. % Return Per Year
2 years, 7 months	39%

B. If Highest Actual Sales level is attained:

Approx. Payout Period	Avg. % Return Per Year
1 year, 9 months	57%

Based upon projections, all capital should have been returned--if either Average Actual Sales or Highest Actual Sales levels have been reached--prior to the end of the third year of operations. Following years' distributions would be based on 65% of Cash Available for Distribution going directly to Limited Partners.

Cash Distributions After Return of $395,500

The annual cash-on cash return to Limited Partners for the 4th full year of operations is projected below:

	Average Actual Sales Level	Highest Actual Sales Level
Expected cash distribution to limited partners:	$ 124,717	$ 187,682
Cash-on-cash annual return (percent of orig. cash inv.):	31.5%	47.5%

The Cash Distribution figure was generated by increasing the previous year's sales and applicable expense figures by ten percent. Return as a percent of cash investment is referenced for information only. Since all capital would have been returned already, each subsequent year's distribution should equate to a 100% return. The cash distribution should increase each year as fixed expenses become a smaller percentage of annual cost. This return should continue for 15 to 20 years or longer, unless the business and franchise are sold in the interim at which time there could be additional profits (although there could be losses if a sale were unsatisfactory to the Partnership). There should be some tax benefits also although no benefits are shown herein.

The foregoing information has been prepared from the best available estimates and data; however, they are based upon certain assumptions as to future events and, therefore, cannot be considered as completely accurate. These data should be looked upon as an orderly presentation of information and the results to be expected if all assumptions are fulfilled. The Partnership business is competitive and vulnerable to adverse changes in general and local economic conditions, as well as to other unforeseen factors which may be beyond the power of the Partnership to control. Consequently, the expectations shown herein and other data preceding these expectations cannot be guaranteed by the General Partners, nor should they be relied upon for personal income forecasting purposes. (See RISK FACTORS.)

(U) REPRESENTATIONS

Neither the General Partners nor any other person or entity acting in any capacity whatsoever with respect to this private offering has any authority to make any representations or warranties, either express or implied, other than representations or warranties which may be contained in the Confidential Memorandum and the documents attached hereto as exhibits and schedules.

ATTACHMENT I

AGREEMENT OF LIMITED PARTNERSHIP
SAMPLE'S ELMTOWN

This Agreement of Limited Partnership ("Agreement") is entered into by and between the General Partners, BRENT E. STACE and PATRICK E. MARRIS, and the persons whose names and signatures appear at the end of this Agreement and identified as the Limited Partners.

1. <u>GENERAL PROVISIONS.</u>

1.1 FORMATION AND NAME. The Partners hereby form a limited partnership ("Partnership") pursuant to the provisions of the Revised Limited Partnership Act of California as set forth in Title 2, Chapter 3 of the California Corporations Code. The name of the partnership shall be SAMPLE'S ELMTOWN.

1.2 PRINCIPAL PLACE OF BUSINESS. The principal place of business of the Partnership shall be within the Armistice Road Plaza, or such other place or places as the General Partners may from time to time determine after written notice to the Limited Partners of such change.

(A') 1.3 PURPOSE OF PARTNERSHIP BUSINESS. The character of the business to be conducted by the Partnership shall be the lease of real property located within the Armistice Road Plaza, consisting of approximately 2,888 square feet of commercial shop space for the purpose of developing thereon a Restaurant and Ice Cream Main under a franchise from Sample's Ice Cream Company. The Partnership shall thereafter own and operate same for investment and benefit to the Partnership, and in connection therewith cause it to be at all times properly managed, operated and maintained.

2. <u>PARTNERS.</u>

2.1 GENERAL PARTNERS. BRENT E. STACE and PATRICK E. MARRIS shall be the General Partners.

2.2 LIMITED PARTNER. "Limited Partner" shall mean those persons who are admitted to the Partnership who are the owners of an interest in the Partnership. Reference to a "Limited Partner" shall mean any one of the Limited Partners. A Limited Partner shall be deemed to be the owner of Units assigned to him unless and until the assignee of such Units has been admitted to the Partnership as a substituted Limited Partner.

THIS FORM IS FOR ILLUSTRATION PURPOSES ONLY. IT MAY NOT MEET ALL RULES, REGULATIONS, AND PROCEDURES OF YOUR STATE, NOR HAS IT BEEN EDITED FOR SUCH PURPOSES BY THE AUTHOR.

2.3 NONPUBLIC OFFERING. The Partnership intends to make a nonpublic offering of Partnership interests. The Partnership shall admit, as Limited Partners, those persons who have subscribed for the purchase of Partnership interests (by execution of a Subscription Agreement and documents attached thereto) and whose subscriptions for such interests are accepted by the General Partners. Acceptance of any such subscription shall be in the sole discretion of the General Partners. Each such person shall become a Limited Partner in the Partnership when such person has signed, personally or by attorney-in-fact, a copy of the Subscription Agreement, and the General Partners have signed the Certificate required by law to show that such person has become a Limited Partner.

3. DEFINITIONS. Certain terms used in this Agreement of Limited Partnership shall have special meanings as designated in this Paragraph 3.

3.1 "Adjusted Invested Capital" of a Partner shall mean the following: The original Invested Capital attributable to his interest, reduced by the total Distributions of Cash From Sale or Refinancing. Distributions of Cash From Operations shall not reduce Adjusted Invested Capital.

3.2. "Affiliate" An Affiliate of another person or entity is (a) any person directly or indirectly owning, controlling or holding, with a power to vote, ten percent (10%) or more of the outstanding voting securities of such other entity; (b) any entity ten percent (10%) or more of whose outstanding voting securities are directly or indirectly owned, controlled or held with power to vote by such other person; (c) any person directly or indirectly controlling, controlled by or under common control with such other person; (d) any officer, director or partner of such other entity; and (e) if such other person is an officer, director or partner, any entity for which such person acts in any such capacity.

3.3 "Agreement" or "Partnership Agreement" shall mean this Agreement of Limited Partnership.

3.4 "Assignee" shall mean a person who has acquired a beneficial interest in one or more Units from a Limited Partner but who himself has not been admitted to the Partnership as a Limited Partner.

3.5 "Assignee of Record" shall mean an Assignee who has acquired a beneficial interest in one or more Units, as evidenced by a written instrument of assignment the effective date of which has passed, and whose ownership of such

Units has been recorded on the books of the Partnership but who has not been admitted to the Partnership as a Limited Partner.

3.6 "Capital Account", as to any Partner, means the sum of a Partner's Capital Contribution, plus his share of any Partnership income and gain reduced by a Partner's share of any Partnership loss, deductions and expenditures described in Code section 705(a)(2)(B) and by any distributions of Partnership cash and the adjusted tax basis of distributed assets (determined as of the distribution date and net of any liabilities assumed by such Partner and any liabilities to which such distributed property is subject). Investment tax credits shall not be considered in determining the Capital Account of a Partner.

3.7 "Capital Contribution" means the total cash contribution which a Partner makes to the Partnership net of any refunds.

3.8 "Cash From Operations" shall mean the Gross Operating Revenues less all cash funds used to pay the expenses of Partnership, including debt payments, if any, expenses of repair, maintenance, capital improvements and replacements, working capital reserves, management fees, and all other expenses related to the operations of the Partnership business.

3.9 "Cash From Sale or Refinancing" shall mean the net cash realized by the Partnership from the sale, refinancing or other disposition of the Partnership Property after payment of all expenses related to the transaction, and cash from any other source other than Cash From Operations.

3.10 "Closing Date" shall mean the date designated by the General Partners, but no later than January 1, 1985.

3.11 "Code" means the Internal Revenue Code of 1954, as amended (or any corresponding provision of succeeding law).

3.12 "Distributions" shall refer to any cash or other property distributed to Partners or other Holders of Units arising from their interests in the Partnership, but shall not include any payments to the General Partners made under the provisions of Paragraphs 9 or 10 of this Partnership Agreement.

3.13 "General Partners" shall refer collectively to BRENT E. STACE and PATRICK E. MARRIS, as the General

Partners, or to any of them together, or to any other persons or entities who succeed them in such capacities.

3.14 "Gross Operating Revenues" shall mean all revenues derived from the operation of the Partnership Business and any other revenues derived from the operations of the Partnership Business. The term "Gross Operating Revenues" shall not include revenues derived from the sale, refinancing, or other disposition of the Partnership Property.

3.15 "Holders" shall refer to owners of Units who are either Partners, Assignees or Assignees of Record, and reference to a "Holder" shall be to any one of them. The General Partners are not holders except to the extent they own Units.

3.16 "Limited Partners" shall refer to any persons or entities holding Units and who have been admitted to the Partnership as original, additional or substituted Limited Partners. Reference to a "Limited Partner" shall refer to all of them unless the context shall otherwise require.

(B') 3.17 "Majority Vote" shall mean the vote of Limited Partners holding more than 50 percent of the issued and outstanding Units entitled to vote.

3.18 "Net Income" or "Net Loss" shall mean the net income or net loss of the Partnership in accordance with the methods and practices used in the preparation of the tax return of the Partnership for federal income tax purposes.

3.19 "Net Proceeds" shall mean the Gross Proceeds less expenses incurred in connection with the organization and formation of the Partnership and the marketing of Units.

3.20 "Original Invested Capital" of the Partners shall mean the amount contributed to the capital of the Partnership for their Units in cash which amounts shall be attributed to such Units in the hands of subsequent Holders.

3.21 "Partners" shall refer collectively to the General Partners and to the Limited Partners holding Units and reference to a "Partner" shall be to any one of the Partners unless the context shall otherwise require.

3.22 "Partnership" shall refer to the limited partnership created under this Partnership Agreement.

3.23 "Partnership Property" or "Property" shall mean that certain real property leasehold described in Exhibit

"B" attached hereto, as well as improvements located upon said property.

3.24 A "Unit" shall mean an interest in the Partnership representing a contribution of One Thousand Dollars ($1,000.00) to the capital of the Partnership by a Partner. Reference to "Units" shall be to more than one Unit. The authorized number of original units of the Partnership shall be Three Hundred Ninety-Five and one-half (395.5) Units which shall be identified as "Original Units" and are being offered for each cash purchase only. Number of "Original Units" shall mean, with respect to each Partner, those original units set forth opposite his name on Exhibit "A" attached hereto under the caption "Number of Original Units." A Unit shall represent an interest in the Net Income, Net Losses and Distributions without regard to Capital Accounts Balances, subject to the terms of this Partnership Agreement.

4. CAPITAL CONTRIBUTIONS.

4.1 CAPITAL CONTRIBUTION OF THE GENERAL PARTNERS. The General Partners shall not be obligated to contribute to the Partnership any cash or other property.

4.2 The total capital of the Partnership shall be contributed by the Partners in the amount of Three Hundred Ninety-Five Thousand Five Hundred Dollars ($395,500.00) consisting of Three Hundred Ninety-five and One-Half (395.5) Units. If the Partnership is not formed by January 1, 1985, all contributions shall be returned to the person contributing same without deduction or interest.

4.3 CAPITAL CONTRIBUTION OF THE LIMITED PARTNERS.

4.3.1 ORIGINAL INVESTED CAPITAL. Each Limited Partner shall make an initial Capital Contribution to the Partnership in the amount opposite that Limited Partner's name in Exhibit "A" attached hereto. The minimum amount of a Limited Partner's initial Capital Contribution shall be $11,300.00 (provided, however, the General Partners in their discretion, may allow Limited Partners to subscribe to fractional Units). Each Limited Partner's initial Capital Contribution shall be payable in cash on or before the closing date.

The General Partners may purchase Units as a Limited Partner under the same terms and conditions as any other offeree.

(C') 4.3.2 ADDITIONAL CAPITAL CONTRIBUTIONS. The Limited Partners shall not be obligated to contribute additional capital to the Partnership.

4.4 INTEREST ON CAPITAL CONTRIBUTIONS. Partners shall not be paid interest on their initial Capital Contributions or the balances in their Capital Accounts.

4.5 RETURN OF CAPITAL CONTRIBUTIONS. No Partner shall be entitled to the return of his initial Capital Contribution except as otherwise provided in this Agreement, nor shall any Partner have the right to receive property other than cash upon the return of his Capital Contribution.

4.6 TERMINATION OF OFFERING OF UNITS. The offering of Units to Limited Partners shall terminate on January 1, 1985. If subscriptions for 395.5 Units are not accepted by the time the offering is terminated, the General Partners shall return all subscription payments to the prospective Limited Partners without interest.

5. TERM OF THE PARTNERSHIP. The Partnership shall commence as of the date of filing of the Certificate of Limited Partnership (the "Effective Date") and shall terminate forty (40) years from the Effective Date or upon the prior dissolution and winding up of the Partnership pursuant to Paragraph 19.

6. FILING OF THE CERTIFICATE. Upon the execution of this Agreement, the General Partner shall take all actions necessary to assure the prompt filing of a Certificate of Limited Partnership as required by section 15621 of the California Corporations Code and shall take all other necessary actions (if any) required by law to perfect and maintain the Partnership as a limited partnership under the laws of California.

7. <u>STATUS OF LIMITED PARTNERS.</u>

7.1 Limited Partners shall not be bound by, or be personally liable for, the expenses, liabilities or obligations of the Partnership.

7.2 RETURN OF DISTRIBUTIONS OF CAPITAL. A Limited Partner of the Partnership may, under certain circumstances, be required to return to the Partnership, for the benefit of the Partnership's creditors, amounts of capital previously distributed. Distributions of Cash from Operations and Cash from Sales or Refinancings shall not be deemed a return or withdrawal of capital under California Corporations Code Section 15666 of the California Revised Limited Partnership

Act, or any successor statute. No Limited Partner shall be obligated to pay those Distributions to or for the account of the Partnership or any creditor of the Partnership. However, if any court of competent jurisdiction holds that, notwithstanding the provisions of this Partnership Agreement, any Limited Partner is obligated to return or pay over any part of those Distributions, it shall be the obligation of the Limited Partner and not of the General Partner.

8. STATUS OF UNITS.

Each Unit, when issued, shall be fully paid and nonassessable.

(D') 9. COMPENSATION TO GENERAL PARTNERS.

9.1 The General Partners shall receive compensation only as specified in this Partnership Agreement.

9.2 The General Partners will receive collectively as compensation for their organization, development and services rendered to date, including therein the negotiations and finalization of the lease as described in Exhibit "B", preliminary conferences with the Project's designer and general contractor and market and promotional studies for a Sample's Restaurant and Ice Cream Main in the Elmtown area, as well as ongoing direction of the Project's designer and general contractor, continued supervision of the Project site until construction is completed, and the necessary supervision of all matters from the date of the Confidential Memorandum to the date the Project commences to do business, the sum of Five Thousand Dollars ($5,000.00). The expenses described in Section 10.2 and the expenses and fee described herein shall be due and payable on formation of the Partnership. In addition and as compensation for their management of the business and affairs of the Partnership, and as long as they are active in the business and affairs of the Partnership, the General Partners collectively shall be entitled to receive a management fee equal to Two Thousand Dollars ($2,000.00) per month beginning the date the Project commences to do business, payable monthly. The amount of said management fee shall be reviewed at the end of each year of operation and may be adjusted upward a maximum of ten (10%) percent per year as in the opinion of the General Partners said upward adjustment serves the best interests of the Partnership.

9.3 Should the General Partners make loans to the Partnership, they will be entitled to interest on any such loans so made subject to the provisions of this Partnership

Agreement at the prime rate of interest charged by Bank of America, Los Angeles, California, to commercial customers.

10. PARTNERSHIP EXPENSES.

10.1 The General Partners shall, at their own expense and at no expense to the Partnership, pay: (i) all overhead expenses of the General Partners; and (ii) all other expenses which are unrelated to the business of the Partnership.

(E') 10.2 Except as provided in Paragraph 10.1 of this Agreement, the Partnership shall pay or reimburse the General Partners for all expenses of the Partnership, which may include but are not limited to the following: (i) the expenses of organizing and forming the Partnership; (ii) marketing the Units; (iii) all compensation to the General Partners as provided for in paragraph 9 of this Agreement; (iv) all costs of personnel employed by the Partnership and directly involved in the business of the Partnership whether directly employed by the Partnership or by the General Partners; (v) all costs of borrowed money, taxes and assessments on the Partnership Property and other taxes applicable to the Partnership; (vi) legal, accounting, audit, brokerage, and other fees (vii) fees and expenses paid to independent contractors, mortgage bankers, real estate brokers, and other agents; (viii) expenses incurred in connection with the acquisition and disposition of the Partnership Property (including real estate brokerage commissions, if applicable, legal and accounting fees and engineering fees); (ix) expenses incurred in connection with the improvement, repair, maintenance, and operation of the Partnership Property (including but not limited to legal and accounting fees, the costs of any financing incurred by the Partnership, and insurance premiums); (x) all expenses incurred in connection with the maintenance of Partnership books and records, the preparation and dissemination of reports or other information to Limited Partners and the making of Distributions to Limited Partners; (xi) expenses incurred in preparing and filing reports or other information with state or federal regulatory agencies; (xii) expenses of liability insurance for the General Partners and insurance as required in connection with the business of the Partnership; (xiii) costs incurred in connection with litigation in the ordinary and necessary course of business and which is not related to a General Partners' gross negligence, fraud or willful misconduct in which the Partnership may become involved, or any examination, investigation, or other proceedings conducted by any regulatory agency, including legal and accounting fees; (xiv) all other expenses incurred in connection with the ordinary and necessary business of the Partnership;

(xv) the cost of goods, materials and personnel furnished by the General Partners in the ordinary and necessary course of doing business; and (xvi) the cost of a completion and performance bond for the costs of leasehold improvements.

(F') 11. ALLOCATION OF NET INCOME, NET LOSS AND DISTRIBUTIONS.

11.1 DISTRIBUTIONS.

11.1.1 CASH FROM OPERATIONS. The Distributions of Cash From Operations shall be allocated Thirty-Five Percent (35%) to the General Partners, and Sixty-Five Percent (65%) to the Limited Partners, as a group, when and at such time as the Limited Partners have received from distributions from all sources made by the Partnership an aggregate amount equal to 100% of the Adjusted Invested Capital of the Limited Partners without interest.

11.1.2 CASH FROM SALE OR REFINANCING. The Distributions of Cash From Sale or Refinancing of the Property shall be allocated among the Partners in the manner and order of priority set forth below:

11.1.2.1 First, One Hundred Percent (100%) to the Limited Partners holding Units, as a group, less any amount they have received from the Cash From Operations, until the Limited Partners holding Units, as a group, have received aggregate Distributions thereof in an amount equal to One Hundred Percent (100%) of their Adjusted Invested Capital;

11.1.2.2 Thereafter, any remaining Distributions of Cash from Sale or Refinancing shall be allocated as follows: (i) 35% to the General Partners; and, (ii) 65% to the Limited Partners holding Units, as a group.

11.2 NET INCOME AND NET LOSS. For Partnership accounting and tax purposes, the net income and net losses of the Partnership as determined in accordance with generally accepted accounting principles applied on a consistent basis shall be attributed to the Partners as follows:

11.2.1 Net income shall be allocated to the Partners in the same proportion that the entire net income for the taxable year, if fully distributed, would be allocated to the Partners pursuant to the provisions of Section 11.1.1.

11.2.2 All net losses (including but not limited to depreciation expenses and any investment tax credit) shall be allocated to the Limited Partners until the Limited Partners have received distributions from all sources made by the Partnership of an aggregate amount equal to 100% of the initial Capital Contributions of the Limited Partners. Thereafter, all net losses shall be allocated Thirty-Five Percent (35%) to the General Partners and Sixty-Five Percent (65%) to the Limited Partners.

11.3. A partner shall not be required to reimburse in any way the Partnership because of or as a result of a Partner's negative capital account which is caused by allocated net operating losses, or other accounting or bookkeeping causes consistent with generally accepted accounting principles applied on a consistent basis.

11.4 Except as otherwise provided in this Partnership Agreement, all divisions among and allocations of the Net Income, Net Loss and Distributions of the Partnership to the Limited Partners holding Units shall be in the ratio which the number of Units which are held by each such Limited Partners on the date of such allocation (which allocation date shall be selected by the General Partners in their sole discretion), bears to the total number of Units which are issued and outstanding as of such date, without regard to Capital Account Balances and, except as otherwise provided in Paragraph 11.7 of this Partnership Agreement, without regard to the number of days on which each recipient was a Partner or Holder of Units.

11.5 Except as otherwise provided herein, whenever a proportionate part of Net Income or Net Loss is allocated to a Partner, every item of income, gain, loss or deduction entering into the computation of such Net Income or Net Loss shall be considered allocated and every item of credit or tax preference related to such Net Income or Net Loss and applicable to the period during which such Net Income or Net Loss was realized shall be allocated to the Partner in the same proportions.

11.6 In the event of the assignment of a Unit prior to an allocation date, the Net Income, Net Loss and Distributions of the Partnership during the period commencing with the last allocation date before the assignment and ending on the first allocation date after the assignment shall be apportioned as between the Partner and his Assignee based upon the number of days of their respective ownership during such period before and after the date that such Assignee became an Assignee of Record in accordance with

Paragraph 12.3 of this Partnership Agreement, without regard to the results of the Partnership's operations during the period before or after such assignment.

11.7 The Partnership intends to make quarterly Distributions of substantially all Cash from Operations and all Cash from Sale or Refinancing which is available for Distributions as determined by the General Partners, subject to the following: (i) Distributions may be restricted or suspended for limited periods when the General Partners determine in their absolute discretion that it is in the best interests of the Partnership; and (ii) all Distributions are subject to payment of Partnership expenses and to the maintenance of reasonable reserves for debt service, alterations, repairs, improvements, maintenance and replacement of furniture and fixtures. The General Partners may invest undistributed monies in short-term highly liquid investments.

11.8 The methods hereinabove set forth by which the Distributions and allocations of Net Income and Net Loss are made and apportioned are hereby expressly consented to by each Partner as a condition of becoming a Partner.

12. <u>TRANSFER AND OTHER DISPOSITIONS OF PARTNERSHIP INTERESTS.</u>

12.1 TRANSFER OF INTERESTS. The partnership interest of a Partner shall not be sold, assigned, transferred or encumbered, except as provided in this Agreement. Notwithstanding the above, a Limited Partner may transfer any portion of or all of his interest as a Limited Partner to the General Partners, a Limited Partner or by intestacy, testamentary disposition or gift to his spouse and/or issue, or to a trustee for such spouse and/or issue. A Partner's "Interest" shall refer to the entire ownership interest of the Partner in the Partnership, including the right of such Partner to any and all benefits to which such Partner may be entitled as provided in this Agreement, together with the obligations of such Partner to comply with all of the terms hereof; however, such assignee or transferee shall not become a substituted Limited Partner without the consent of the General Partners which consent may be withheld in the absolute discretion of the General Partners. Any purported transfer or assignment made other than in accordance with this Agreement shall be null and void and of no force and effect, at the option of the General Partners. No transfer or assignment to a minor (except in trust or pursuant to the Uniform Gifts to Minors Act) shall be effective.

12.2 DEATH OR INCOMPETENCE OF A LIMITED PARTNER. Subject to the provisions of Section 12.4 and 12.5, the personal representative or other successor of a deceased or incompetent Limited Partner shall succeed to the interest of a Limited Partner after such representative or successor shall have court orders, or other evidence satisfactory to the General Partners, establishing such incompetence or death and the authority of such personal representative or successor; however, such representative or successor shall not become a substituted Limited Partner without the consent of the General Partners, which consent may be withheld in the absolute discretion of the General Partners.

12.3 SALE OR TRANSFER OF INTEREST OF A LIMITED PARTNER.

12.3.1 Subject to any restrictions of transferability required by this Agreement hereof, any Limited Partner may assign or otherwise transfer such Limited Partner's Interest in the Partnership, provided:

12.3.1.1 The Limited Partner must first give the remaining Limited Partners and General Partners the first right of refusal to purchase such Units at the price and on the terms and conditions under which the selling Limited Partner intends to sell, assign or transfer the Units. Before entering into a firm commitment to sell said Units to a third party, the selling Limited Partner shall give written notice to the remaining Partners showing (1) the name and address of the person or firm to whom the Limited Partner intends to sell, assign or transfer the Units or interest in the Units; (2) the number of Units, or the interest in Units, the Limited Partner proposes to sell, assign or transfer; (3) the price or amount per Unit to be paid to the Limited Partner for the proposed sale, assignment or transfer, and (4) all of the terms and conditions of the proposed sale, assignment or transfer. The remaining Limited Partners shall have fifteen (15) days after said notice is given to purchase the Units specified in the notice at the price and on the terms and conditions specified in the notice. In the event any of the remaining Limited Partners fail to elect within the 15-day period to purchase all the Units specified in the notice, the General Partners shall have an additional five (5) days to purchase the Units specified in the notice at the price and on the terms and conditions specified in the notice. In the event the General Partners fail to elect within the additional five-day period to purchase all Units specified in the notice, the selling Limited Partner is under no obligation to sell any of the offered shares to the remaining Partners, but may instead sell them to the person or firm specified in the notice at the price and on the terms and conditions specified in that notice subject to the conditions of Sections 12.4 and 12.5 below. The selling Limited Partner may not, however, without giving a new notice of his intention to do so, sell any or all of the offered Units to any other person or firm or at any other price or on any other terms and conditions than those specified in the notice given pursuant to this paragraph. Any Limited Partner electing to purchase the Units of the selling Limited Partner shall be entitled to purchase the same percentage of the Units being sold as the number of Units owned by the electing Limited Partner bears to the total number of Units owned by all electing Limited Partners. The General Partner electing to purchase the Units shall purchase all the Units offered;

12.3.1.2 The transfer of a Limited Partner's Interest is of its entire Interest;

12.3.1.3 The assignee or transferee meets all requirements set forth in the Confidential Memorandum applicable to additional Limited Partners;

12.3.1.4 The General Partners consent in writing to such assignment or transfer;

12.3.1.5 If requested by the General Partners an opinion from counsel for the Partnership is delivered to the General Partners stating that, in the opinion of such counsel, such transfer or assignment will not violate or cause the Partnership to violate, any applicable law or governmental rule or regulation including, without limitation, any applicable federal or state securities law;

12.3.1.6 The full agreed capital contribution of the assignor or transferor has been paid; and

12.3.1.7 Prior to the transfer or assignment, the assignor or transferor reimburses the

General Partners and the Partnership for their expenses, including attorney's fees, incurred in connection with the transfer or assignment. In the event of any such assignment or transfer, such Limited Partner's assignee or transferee shall be allocated on a prorata basis the same percentage of net income and net losses that the transferring Limited Partner would have been allocated had no such assignment or transfer been made; however, such assignee or transferee shall not become a substituted Limited Partner without the consent of the General Partners, which consent may be withheld in the absolute discretion of the General Partners.

12.3.2 Each Limited Partner shall indemnify and hold harmless the Partnership, the General Partners and any Limited Partner who was or is a party to, or is threatened to be made a party to, any threatened, pending or completed action, suit or proceeding of any kind whatsoever, by reason of or arising from any actual or alleged misrepresentation or misstatement of facts or omission to state facts made or omitted to be made by such Limited Partner in connection with any assignment, transfer, encumbrance or other disposition of all or any part of an interest in the Partnership, or the admission of a substituted Limited Partner to the Partnership, against expenses for which the Partnership, the General Partners or any such Limited Partner has not otherwise been reimbursed including, without limitation, reasonable attorneys' fees, judgments, fines and amounts paid in settlement, actually and reasonably incurred in connection with such action, suit or proceeding.

12.4 ASSIGNEE OR TRANSFEREE BOUND BY THIS AGREEMENT. The assignee or transferee of any Limited Partner's Interest shall be subject to all the terms, conditions, restrictions and obligations of this Agreement. No transfer or assignment shall be recognized until and unless the transferee or assignee shall have so acknowledged in writing to the General Partners in a manner and form reasonably satisfactory to the General Partners.

12.5 EFFECTIVE DATE OF TRANSFER. Any assignment which is permitted hereunder shall be effective as of the close of the calendar month during which all required documentation is received by the General Partners. In addition to the conditions set forth above, an assignee, transferee, heir or legatee of a Limited Partner (to the extent of the Interest acquired from the Limited Partner) shall become a substituted Limited Partner as that term is used in the Act only upon the consent of the General Partners and upon the recording of an amended Certificate of Limited Partnership, if required by the Act.

12.6 NONTRANSFERABILITY OF INTEREST OF GENERAL PARTNER. The General Partners shall not voluntarily resign or withdraw from the Partnership as a General Partner without (i) obtaining the affirmative vote or written consent of the Limited Partners holding a majority of the partnership capital percentages of all Limited Partners, (ii) providing at least one successor general partner (to whom the resigning General Partner shall assign its Interest as General Partner in the Partnership) satisfactory to Limited Partners holding a majority of the partnership capital percentages of all Limited Partners, and (iii) delivering to the Partnership an opinion of the Partnership's counsel that such resignation or withdrawal will not subject the Partnership to federal income taxation as an association taxable as a corporation. Upon said withdrawal or resignation the departing General Partner shall be paid his interest in the Partnership as set forth in Section 17.3 below.

13. <u>SUBSTITUTED LIMITED PARTNERS</u>.

13.1 No Transferee, Assignee or Assignee of Record shall have the right to become a substituted Limited Partner unless all of the following conditions are first satisfied:

> 13.1.1 A duly executed and acknowledged written instrument of transfer or assignment shall have been filed with the Partnership, which instrument shall specify the number of Units being transferred or assigned and set forth in the intention of the transferor/assignor that the Transferee, Assignee or Assignee of Record succeed the transferor's or assignor's interest as a substituted Limited Partner in his place;
>
> 13.1.2 The transferor, assignor and Transferee, Assignee or Assignee of Record shall have executed and acknowledged such other instruments as the General Partners may deem necessary or desirable to effect such substitution, including the written acceptance and adoption by the Transferee, Assignee or Assignee of Record of the provisions of this Partnership Agreement and his execution, acknowledgment and delivery to the General Partners of a special power of attorney, the form and content of which are more fully described herein;

13.1.3 A transfer fee shall have been paid to the Partnership which is sufficient to cover all reasonable expenses connected with such substitution.

13.2 No consent of any of the Limited Partners shall be required to admit a Transferee or Assignee as a substituted Limited Partner. By executing or adopting this Partnership Agreement, each Limited Partner hereby consents to the admission of additional or substituted Limited Partners, and to any Transferee or Assignee of his Units becoming a substituted Limited Partner.

13.3 The General Partners shall cause the Partnership Agreement and any separate Certificate of Limited Partnership to be amended to reflect the substitution of Limited Partners not less frequently than once in each calendar quarter in which any such substitution occurs.

14. BOOKS, RECORDS, ACCOUNTINGS AND REPORTS.

14.1 BOOKS AND RECORDS. The Partnership shall maintain at its principal office all of the following:

14.1.1. A current list of the full name and last known business or residence address of each Partner set forth in alphabetical order together with the contribution and the share in profits and losses of each Partner;

14.1.2. A copy of the Certificate of Limited Partnership and all certificates of amendment, together with executed copies of any powers of attorney pursuant to which any certificate has been executed;

14.1.3. Copies of the Partnership's federal, state, and local income tax or information returns and reports, if any, for the six most recent taxable years;

14.1.4. Copies of the original Partnership Agreement and all amendments;

14.1.5. Financial statements of the limited partnership for the six most recent fiscal years; and

14.1.6. The Partnership's books and records for at least the current and past three fiscal years.

14.2 Upon reasonable request, a Limited Partner or his duly authorized representative shall have the right to inspect and copy any of the foregoing during normal business hours and to obtain, promptly after becoming available, a copy of the Partnership's income tax or information returns for each year. The Partnership shall keep its books, records and tax returns on a fiscal year basis ending December 31 using the cash or accrual basis at the discretion of the General Partners.

(G') 14.3 The General Partners shall have prepared at least once annually, at Partnership expense, financial statements (balance sheet, statement of income or loss, Holders' equity, and changes in financial position) prepared in accordance with generally accepted accounting principles. If requested by Limited Partners holding a majority of the issued and outstanding Units of the Partnership or at the option of the General Partners, such statement shall be accompanied by an auditor's report containing an opinion of an independent certified public accountant. Copies of such statement and any such report shall be distributed to each Limited Partner and Assignee of Record within 120 days after the close of each taxable year of the Partnership.

14.4 The General Partners, at Partnership expense, shall cause income tax returns for the Partnership to be prepared and timely filed with the appropriate authorities.

14.5 The General Partners, at Partnership expense, shall cause to be prepared and timely filed, with appropriate federal and state regulatory and administrative bodies, all reports required to be filed with such entities under then current applicable laws, rules and regulations. Such reports shall be prepared on the accounting or reporting basis required by such regulatory bodies. Any Limited Partners and Assignees of Record shall be provided with a copy of any such report upon request and without expense to him.

(H') 15. <u>RIGHTS, AUTHORITY, POWERS, RESPONSIBILITIES AND DUTIES OF THE GENERAL PARTNERS</u>.

15.1 The General Partners shall have a fiduciary responsibility to the Partnership and the Partners and, in the exercise thereof, shall have all authority, rights and powers conferred by law, those provided to a partner in a partnership without limited partners, and (subject only to the provisions of Paragraph 15.3 following), those required or appropriate to the management of the Partnership business which, by way of illustration but not by way of limitation, shall include the right, authority and power:

15.1.1 To acquire, hold, lease, rent, operate and dispose of the Property;

15.1.2 To borrow money and, if security is required therefor, to mortgage or subject the Property and Partnership personal property to any other security device, to obtain replacements of any mortgage or other security device, and to prepay, in whole or in part, refinance, increase, modify, consolidate, or extend any mortgage or other security device, all of the foregoing at such terms and in such amounts as the General Partners, in their sole discretion, deem to be in the best interests of the Partnership;

15.1.3 To acquire and enter into any contract of insurance which the General Partners deem necessary or appropriate for the protection of the Partnership and the General Partners, for the conservation of Partnership assets, or for any purpose convenient or beneficial to the Partnership;

15.1.4 To employ unaffiliated persons in the operation and management of the business of the Partnership including, but not limited to, supervisory personnel, insurance brokers, real estate brokers and loan brokers, attorneys and accountants, on such terms and for such compensation as the General Partners shall determine to be appropriate and in the best interests of the Partnership;

15.1.5 To prepare or cause to be prepared reports, statements and other relevant information for distribution to Limited Partners and Assignees of Record, including annual and quarterly interim reports;

15.1.6 To open accounts and deposit and maintain funds in the name of the Partnership in banks or savings and loan associations;

15.1.7 To select as its accounting year a calendar year or such fiscal year as may be approved by the Internal Revenue Service;

15.1.8 To determine the appropriate accounting method or methods to be used by the Partnership;

15.1.9 To amend this Partnership Agreement by use of the Special and Limited Power of Attorney set forth in Paragraph 20 without further consent or vote of any of the Limited Partners to reflect the addition or substitution of Limited Partners, changes of address, or the reduction of the capital accounts upon the return of capital to Partners;

15.1.10 To execute, acknowledge and deliver any and all instruments to effectuate the foregoing, and to take all such action in connection therewith as the General Partners shall deem necessary or appropriate. Any and all documents or instruments may be executed on behalf and in the name of the Partnership by the duly authorized signature of any one of the General Partners (the signatures of all General Partners is not required or necessary);

15.1.11 To invest the Gross Proceeds or Net Proceeds temporarily in short-term, highly liquid investments where there is appropriate safety of principal.

15.1.12 Make or arrange long-term and short-term loans to the Partnership, receive interest or other financing charges or fees, provided that the interest charges or fees are not in excess of amounts charged by third party financing institutions on comparable loans for the same purpose, or, if the funds for a loan are obtained by the General Partners from a lending institution, the rate and other fees which the General Partners are required to pay to the lending institution;

15.1.13 Redeem or repurchase Units on behalf of the Partnership as set forth in paragraph 12.3 and 17.3.

15.1.14 Appoint a person, including the General Partners, to act as agent for service of process for the Partnership.

15.2 Except as otherwise provided for herein, the General Partners shall have all rights, powers and authorities permitted partners in partnerships not having limited partners.

15.3 The General Partners unless authorized by a majority of the Limited Partners shall not have the authority to:

15.3.1 Enter into contracts with the Partnership which would bind the Partnership after the expulsion, resignation, adjudication of bankruptcy or insolvency, dissolution or other cessation to exist of the General Partners, or to continue the business with Partnership assets after the occurrence of such event;

15.3.2 Sell or exchange substantially all of the assets of the Partnership in a single sale, or in multiple sales in the same 12-month period, except in the orderly liquidation and winding up of the business of the Partnership upon its termination and dissolution;

15.3.3 Pledge or encumber substantially all of the assets of the Partnership at one time, other than in connection with the acquisition or improvement of assets or the refinancing of previous obligations;

15.3.4 Use or permit any other person to use Partnership funds or assets in any manner except for the exclusive benefit of the Partnership;

15.3.5 Alter the primary purpose of the Partnership as set forth in Paragraph 1.3 of this Partnership Agreement;

15.3.6 Receive any insurance brokerage fee or write any insurance policy governing the General Partners or the Partnership Property;

15.3.7 Receive from the Partnership a rebate or give-up or participate in any reciprocal business arrangements which would enable them to do so;

15.3.8 Sell or lease to the Partnership any real property in which the General Partners have any interest;

15.3.9 Cause the Partnership to invest in any other partnership or other venture;

15.3.10 Purchase or lease real property from the Partnership;

15.3.11 Cause the Partnership to exchange Units for real property;

15.3.12 Make long-term secured loans to the Partnership by the General Partners. On short-term unsecured loans made to the Partnership by the General Partners, receive interest or other financing charges or fees in excess of those amounts which would be charged by third party financing institutions on comparable loans for the same purpose in the same geographic area, or require a prepayment charge or penalty on such loans made to the Partnership by the General Partners;

15.3.13 Except as otherwise provided in this Partnership Agreement, cause the Partnership to redeem or repurchase Units;

15.3.14 Do any act in contravention of this Partnership Agreement or which would make it impossible to carry on the ordinary business of the Partnership;

15.3.15 Confess a judgment against the Partnership in connection with any threatened or pending legal action;

15.3.16 Admit another person or entity as a General Partner except with the consent of the Limited Partners as provided for in this Partnership Agreement;

15.3.17 Perform any act (other than an act required by this Partnership Agreement or any act taken in good faith reliance upon counsel's opinion) which would, at the time such act occurred, subject any Limited Partner to liability as a general partner in any jurisdiction;

15.3.18 Except as otherwise provided in this Partnership Agreement, reinvest Cash from Operations or Cash from Sale or Refinancing in any new or additional Partnership Property;

15.3.19 Cause the Partnership to loan to the General Partners Partnership assets, or employ, or permit to employ, the funds or assets of the Partnership in any manner except for the exclusive benefit of the Partnership;

15.3.20 Commingle the Partnership funds with those of any other person or entity;

15.3.21 Cause the Partnership to enter into any transaction with any other partnership or venture in which the General Partners have any interest, except as provided for in this Partnership Agreement;

15.3.22 Amend this Partnership Agreement without the consent of each Limited Partner who would be adversely affected thereby to: (i) convert a Limited Partner into a General Partner; (ii) adversely affect the limited liability of a Limited Partner; (iii) alter the interests of the Partners in the Net Income, Net Loss, or Distributions of the Partnership; or (iv) adversely affect the status of the Partnership as a partnership for federal income tax purposes; or

15.3.23 Cause the Partnership to invest in trust deeds, or other secured or unsecured obligations.

15.4 Within 90 days after the Limited Partners have voted to remove a General Partner, the General Partners shall have prepared, at Partnership expense, a financial statement (balance sheet, statement of income or loss, Partners' equity, and changes in financial position) prepared in accordance with generally accepted accounting principles and shall cause such statement to be mailed to the Limited Partners and Assignees of Record as soon as possible after receipt thereof.

15.5 The General Partners shall have the duty and responsibility for providing continuing administrative and executive support, advice, consultation, analysis and supervision with respect to the functions of the Partnership as an owner of the Partnership Property, including decisions regarding the sale or refinancing or other disposition of property, and compliance with federal, state and local regulatory requirements and procedures.

15.6 The Partners do hereby appoint the General Partners to act as the "tax matters partner" as defined in Code Section 6231(a)(7). Only one General Partner will act as the "tax matters partner" and the decision as to which General Partner will so act will be made by the General Partners. Said "tax matters partner" shall have the right to represent the Partnership in discussions with the Internal Revenue Service regarding the tax treatment of items of Partnership income, loss, deductions or credits, or any other matter reflected on the Partnership's information returns, and to agree to final Partnership administrative adjustment or file a petition in the appropriate judicial forum for a readjustment of the items in question.

16. <u>RIGHTS, POWERS AND VOTING RIGHTS OF THE LIMITED PARTNERS</u>.

(I') 16.1 No Limited Partner, Assignee or Assignee of Record shall take part in or interfere in any manner with the control, conduct or operation of the Partnership, nor shall they have any right or authority to act for or bind the Partnership.

16.2 Limited Partners (but not Assignees or Assignees of Record) shall have the right to vote only upon the following matters affecting the basic structure of the Partnership:

16.2.1 Removal of General Partners;

16.2.2 Election of successor General Partners;

16.2.3 Termination and Dissolution of the Partnership;

16.2.4 Amendment of this Partnership Agreement, except as otherwise provided by Paragraph 15.1.9 of this Partnership Agreement;

16.2.5 The extension of the term of the Partnership;

16.2.6 The determination of the fair market value of the General Partners' compensation and interest in the Partnership pursuant to Paragraph 17.4 of this Partnership Agreement;

16.2.7 Approval of the terms of the sale or exchange of all or substantially all of the assets of the Partnership in a single sale, or in multiple sales in the same 12-month period, except in the liquidation and winding-up of the business of the Partnership upon its termination and dissolution;

16.2.8 Approval of the terms of any pledge or encumbrance of all or substantially all of the assets of the Partnership at one time, other than in connection with the acquisition, construction or improvement of assets or the refinancing of previous obligations;

16.2.9 Those matters set forth in Paragraph 15 or elsewhere in this Agreement which provide for the vote of the Limited Partners.

16.3 Matters upon which the Limited Partners may vote shall require the Majority Vote or majority written consent, of the Limited Partners entitled to vote to pass and become effective. If by written consent, there shall be no requirement that more than a majority of the Partners sign such consent.

16.4 The General Partners may at any time call for a meeting of the Partners, or for a vote without a meeting, on matters on which the Limited Partners are entitled to vote following receipt of written request therefor of Limited Partners holding 10 percent (10%) or more of the Units entitled to vote as of the date of receipt of such written request ("notice date"). Within 10 days of such notice date, the General Partners shall notify all Limited Partners of record as of the notice date, as to the time and place of the Partnership meeting, if called, and the general nature of the business to be transacted thereat, or if no such meeting has been called, of the matter or matters to be voted upon and the date upon which such votes, without a meeting, will be counted. Any Partnership meeting or the date upon which such votes, without a meeting, will be counted, shall be at a place convenient to the Limited Partners and no less than 15 days nor more than 30 days following mailing of the notice thereof by the General Partners. All expenses of such voting and notification shall be borne by the Partnership.

16.5 A Limited Partner shall be entitled to cast one vote for each Unit owned; (i) at a meeting, in person, by written proxy or by a signed writing directing the manner in which he desires that his vote be cast, which writing must be received by the General Partners prior to such meeting; or (ii) without a meeting, by a signed writing directing the manner in which he desires that his vote be cast, which writing must be received by the General Partners prior to the date upon which the votes of Limited Partners are to be counted. Only the votes of Limited Partners holding Units who are of record on the notice date, whether at a meeting or otherwise, shall be counted. The General Partners as General Partners, shall not be entitled to vote, except that they may vote as Limited Partners with respect to any Units owned by them. Neither Assignees nor Assignees of Record shall be entitled to vote on Partnership matters. The laws of the State of California pertaining to the validity and use of corporate proxies shall govern the validity and use of proxies given by Limited Partners.

16.6 No Limited Partner or Holder shall have the right or power to: (i) withdraw or reduce his contribution to the capital of the Partnership except as a result of the dissolution of the Partnership or as otherwise provided by law, (ii) bring an action for partition against the Partnership, (iii) cause the termination and dissolution of the Partnership by court decree or otherwise, except as set forth in this Partnership Agreement, or (iv) demand or receive property other than cash in return for his contribution. Except as provided in this Partnership Agreement, no Limited Partner or Holder shall have priority over any other Limited Partner or Holder either as to the return of contributions of capital or as to allocations of the Net Income, Net Loss or Distributions of the Partnership. Other than upon the termination and dissolution of the Partnership as provided by this Partnership Agreement, there has been no time agreed upon when the contribution of each Limited Partner or Holder is to be returned.

16.7 AMENDMENTS TO PARTNERSHIP AGREEMENT. Except as provided by this Section 16.6, this Partnership Agreement may be modified or amended only by a Majority Vote of the

Limited Partners conducted in accordance with Sections 16.2 and 16.3; provided, however, this Agreement may be amended from time to time by the General Partners, without the consent of any of the Limited Partners, (i) to add to the representations, duties or obligations of the General Partners or to surrender any right or power granted to the General Partners for the benefit of the business and purpose of the Partnership and for the benefit of the Limited Partners; (ii) to cure any ambiguity, to correct or supplement any provision which may be inconsistent with any other provisions, or to make any other provisions with respect to matters or questions arising under this Agreement which will not be inconsistent with the provisions of this Agreement; (iii) to reflect reductions in the capital contributions of the Limited Partners in accordance with the requirements of this Agreement; (iv) to elect for the Partnership to be governed by an successor California statute governing limited partnerships; and (v) as otherwise provided for pursuant to this Partnership Agreement. The General Partners shall notify the Limited Partners within a reasonable time of the adoption of any amendment. Notwithstanding anything to the contrary contained in this Agreement, this Agreement may not be amended without the consent of all Partners to be adversely affected by the amendment that:

16.7.1 Converts a Limited Partner into a General Partner;

16.7.2 Modifies the limited liability of a Limited Partner;

16.7.3 Alters the interest of the General Partners or Limited Partners in Net Income or Net Loss or Distributions from the Partnership; or

16.7.4 Affects the status of the Partnership as a partnership for federal income tax purposes.

17. <u>EXPULSION, BANKRUPTCY OR DISSOLUTION OF GENERAL PARTNERS</u>.

17.1. Any of the General Partners may be expelled from the Partnership by Majority Vote of the Limited Partners entitled to vote.

17.2 Written notice of the expulsion of any or all of the General Partners shall be served either by certified or registered mail, return receipt requested, or by personal service. Such notice shall set forth the date upon which the expulsion is to become effective.

17.3 Upon the death, retirement, resignation, expulsion, removal pursuant to paragraph 17.4, below, or the dissolution of a General Partner, the interest of such General Partner including the Net Income and Distributions of the Partnership, as set forth in Paragraph 11 of this Partnership Agreement, shall be purchased by the Partnership for a purchase price equal to the aggregate fair market value thereof determined according to the provisions of Paragraph 17.5 following. The purchase price of such interest shall be paid by the Partnership to such General Partner one-third (1/3) in cash, within 60 days of the determination of the aggregate fair market value in accordance with the provisions of Paragraph 17.5 following and the balance shall be evidenced by a promissory note bearing interest at prime as established by Bank of America, Los Angeles, California, secured by the Partnership property. Said note shall provide for the balance of the purchase price to be amortized fully and equally over a 36-month period with payments commencing thirty (30) days after payment of the down payment. Each payment shall include interest. The promissory note shall provide that in the event of default in payment of principal or interest, all unpaid sums in the note shall become due and payable. Said note may be prepaid at any time without penalty and shall contain an attorney's fee provision.

17.4 The relationship between General Partners and the Limited Partners is personal and a relationship of the highest standards of fiduciary relationship. At no time should the Limited Partners be required or forced to have a General Partner who has filed for protection from creditors under any bankruptcy proceeding of any kind or nature without their approval, consent or vote. Therefore, upon the filing of any petition in bankruptcy involving any General Partner, whether voluntary or involuntary, or upon any General Partner being convicted of a felony or who is or has been grossly negligent or willfully participated in misconduct in the operation of the business purpose of the Partnership, the Limited Partners shall have the absolute right to remove such General Partner and may do so by their Majority Vote or written consent.

17.5 The fair market value of the General Partner's interest purchased by the Partnership according to the provisions to Paragraph 17.3 above shall be determined by agreement between the departing General Partner and a majority of the Limited Partners. For this purpose, the fair market value of such interest of the terminated General Partner shall be computed as the present value of the future amount which could reasonably be expected to be realized by such General Partner upon the sale of the Partnership's assets in the ordinary course of its business. If the General Partner and the Partnership cannot agree upon the fair market value of such Partnership interest within 30 days, the fair market value thereof shall be determined in the manner provided by the laws of the State of California for the determination of controversies by arbitration, the General Partner to choose one arbitrator, the Partnership to choose one arbitrator and the two arbitrators so chosen to choose a third arbitrator. The decision of a majority of said arbitrators as to the fair market value of such Partnership interest shall be final and binding and may be enforced by legal proceedings. The General Partner and the Partnership shall each compensate the arbitrator appointed by it and the compensation of the third arbitrator shall be borne equally by such parties.

(J') 18. CERTAIN TRANSACTIONS.

The General Partners, any Limited Partner, Holder, Assignee, Assignee of Record, or any shareholder, officer, director, employee or any person owning a legal or beneficial interest therein, may engage in or possess an interest in any other business or venture of every nature and description, independently or with others which is not detrimental to this Partnership, including, but not limited to, the ownership, financing, leasing, operation, maintenance, brokerage and development of real property, and no Partner, Holder or such other person or entity shall have any interest therein by reason of their interest in the Partnership.

19. TERMINATION AND DISSOLUTION OF THE PARTNERSHIP.

19.1 The Partnership shall be terminated and dissolved upon the earlier to occur of the following:

19.1.1 The death, retirement, resignation, expulsion, or the dissolution of a General Partner unless within 120 days thereafter the remaining General Partner and any successor General Partner which may be elected in place of the terminated General Partner all elect to continue the business of the Partnership.

19.1.2 The filing of any petition in bankruptcy involving any General Partner as set forth in paragraph 17.4, above, unless within 120 days of such filing the remaining General Partner and any successor General Partner which may be elected in place of the terminated General Partner all elect to continue the business of the Partnership.

19.1.3 A Majority Vote in favor of dissolution and termination of the Partnership.

19.1.4 The expiration of the term of the Partnership.

19.1.5 The written decision, subsequent to the Closing Date, of any General Partner to dissolve the Partnership.

19.2 Upon a dissolution and termination of the Partnership for any reason, the General Partner shall take full account of the Partnership assets and liabilities, shall liquidate the assets as promptly as is consistent with obtaining the fair market value thereof, and shall apply and distribute the proceeds therefrom in the following order:

19.2.1 To the payment of creditors of the Partnership, but excluding secured creditors whose obligations will be assumed or otherwise transferred on the liquidation of Partnership assets;

19.2.2 To the repayment of any outstanding loans made by the General Partner to the Partnership;

19.2.3 To the Partners and Assignees of Record pursuant to the provisions of Paragraph 11 of this Partnership Agreement.

19.3 In the event of the death of the General Partner, his heirs, executors and successors shall automatically become Limited Partners and shall be subject to all of the terms and conditions of this Agreement.

20. SPECIAL POWER OF ATTORNEY.

20.1 ATTORNEY-IN-FACT. Each Limited Partner hereby grants to the General Partners a special power of attorney irrevocably making, constituting and appointing the General Partners as the Limited Partner's attorney-in-fact, with power and authority to act in his name with respect to this agreement and on his behalf to execute, acknowledge and swear to in the execution, acknowledgment and filing of documents, which shall include, by way of illustration but not of limitation, the following:

20.1.1 The Agreement, any separate certificates of limited partnership, as well as any amendments to the foregoing which, under the laws of the State of California or the laws of any other state, are required to be filed or which the General Partners shall deem it advisable to file;

20.1.2 Any other instrument or document which may be required to be filed by the Partnership under the laws of any state or by any governmental agency or which the General Partners shall deem it advisable to file; and

20.1.3 Any instrument or document which may be required to effect the continuation of the Partnership, the admission of additional or substituted Limited Partners, or the dissolution and termination of the Partnership (provided such continuation, admission or dissolution and termination are in accordance with the terms of this Partnership Agreement), or to reflect any reductions in amount of contributions of Partners.

The General Partners shall promptly furnish to a Limited Partner a copy of any amendment to this Agreement executed by the General Partners pursuant to a power of attorney from the Limited Partner.

20.2 SPECIAL PROVISIONS. The special power of attorney granted by each Limited Partner:

20.2.1 Is a special power of attorney coupled with an interest, is irrevocable, shall survive the death of the granting Limited Partner, and is limited to those matters herein set forth;

20.2.2 May be exercised by the General Partners for each of the Limited Partners by the signature of one of the General Partners acting as attorney-in-fact for all of the Limited Partners, together with a list of all Limited Partners executing such instrument by their attorney-in-fact; and

20.2.3 Shall survive an assignment by a Limited Partner of all or any portion of his Units except that, where the Assignee of the Units owned by a Limited Partner has been approved by the General Partners for admission to the Partnership as a substituted Limited Partner, the special power of attorney shall survive such assignment for the sole purpose of enabling the General Partners to execute, acknowledge and file any instrument or document necessary to affect such substitution.

21. <u>INDEMNIFICATION</u>.

The Partnership shall indemnify and hold harmless the General Partners, their officers, directors, employees, agents and assigns, from any loss or damage incurred by them in connection with the business of the Partnership, including costs and reasonable attorneys' fees and any amounts expended in the settlement of any claims of loss or damage provided that such loss or damage did not arise as a result of any such person's gross negligence, intentional misconduct or breach of fiduciary duty and, provided further, that any such indemnification shall be recoverable only from the assets of the Partnership and not from the assets of the Limited Partners.

(K') 22. <u>MISCELLANEOUS</u>.

22.1 This Partnership Agreement may be executed in several counterparts, and all so executed shall constitute one Partnership Agreement, binding on all of the parties hereto, notwithstanding that all of the parties are not signatory to the original or the same counterpart.

22.2 The terms and provisions of this Partnership Agreement shall be binding upon and shall inure to the benefit of the successors and assigns of the respective Partners.

22.3 In the event any sentence or paragraph of this Partnership Agreement is declared by a court of competent jurisdiction to be void, such sentence or paragraph shall be deemed severed from the remainder of the Partnership Agreement and the balance of the Partnership Agreement shall remain in full force and effect.

22.4 All notices under this Partnership Agreement shall be in writing and shall be given to the Limited Partner or Assignee of Record entitled thereto, by personal service or by mail, posted to the address maintained by the Partnership for such person or at such other address as he may specify in writing.

22.5 This Partnership Agreement shall be governed by and construed in accordance with the laws of the State of California, the state where the Partnership maintains its principal place of business and the state where this Partnership Agreement is made and entered into.

22.6 Paragraph titles or captions contained in this Partnership Agreement are inserted only as a matter of convenience and for reference. Such titles and captions in no way define, limit, extend or describe the scope of this Partnership Agreement nor the intent of any provision hereof.

22.7 Whenever required by the context hereof, the singular shall include the plural, and vice versa; the masculine gender shall include the feminine and neuter genders, and vice versa; and the word "person" shall include a corporation, partnership, firm or other form of association.

22.8. The names and addresses of the General Partners are as follows:

Brent E. Stace ____________________
Patrick E. Marris ____________________

22.9. The names, addresses and capital contributions of the Limited Partners shall be set forth on Exhibit "A" to this Partnership Agreement, which exhibit shall be separately recorded and a copy thereof maintained at the principal place of business of the Partnership.

IN WITNESS WHEREOF, the undersigned have set their hands to this Agreement of Limited Partnership on the __________ day of __________________, 1984.

GENERAL PARTNERS	LIMITED PARTNER
____________________ BRENT E. STACE	Name (Sign) ____________________ (Print) ____________________
____________________ PATRICK E. MARRIS	Name (Sign) ____________________ (Print) ____________________
	Address ____________________ ____________________
	Social Security No: __________
	or Tax I.D. No: __________
	Social Security No: __________
	or Tax I.D. No: __________

(L') EXHIBIT "A"

AGREEMENT OF LIMITED PARTNERSHIP

SAMPLE'S ELMTOWN

LIMITED PARTNERS

CAPITAL CONTRIBUTIONS

Limited Partners Name and Address:	Number of Original Units	Amount of Original Invested Capital

NOTE: This Exhibit "A" will be used to list all limited partners and their individual investment amounts.

EXHIBIT "B"

PARTNERSHIP PROPERTY

That certain tenant space located within Armistice Road Plaza in the County of Elmtown, State of California containing approximately 2,888 square feet of Floor Space with a frontage of approximately 40 feet 8 inches and a depth of approximately 70 feet. Said tenant space is located in the Building labelled Shop Building and identified as Space F on on Exhibit "A" to the Lease Agreement dated June 9, 1984, with the approximate location of the premises crosshatched thereon.

ATTACHMENT II

STATEMENT OF SUITABILITY
AND SUBSCRIPTION AGREEMENT
SAMPLE'S ELMTOWN
a California limited partnership

The undersigned hereby purchase a limited partnership interest in SAMPLE'S ELMTOWN, a California limited partnership (the "Partnership") and in connection therewith, make the following representations:

(A") (1) I acknowledge that I received the Confidential Memorandum dated July 1, 1984, and all exhibits to the foregoing and the Agreement of Limited Partnership in connection with SAMPLE'S ELMTOWN prior to the execution of this Statement of Suitability, and I understand and agree to all of the terms, conditions and provisions contained in said Confidential Memorandum and Limited Partnership Agreement.

(B") (2) I understand that the interests in SAMPLE'S ELMTOWN are being sold under the exemption provided by Section 25102 of the California Corporations Code for non-public offerings and sales. I further understand that the Partnership and Partnership Interests have not been registered or qualified with any federal, state or local governmental agency or commission. I am buying my Limited Partnership interest for my own account, or for the account and benefit of a member or members of my immediate family, for investment. I agree that my interest in the Limited Partnership shall not be sold or otherwise transferred contrary to the terms of the Limited Partnership Agreement. I agree that a legend may be placed on the certificate(s) representing my Limited Partnership interest to reflect the substance of said Agreement.

(C") (3) The following information may be relied upon by you in connection with my investment as a Limited Partner in the above-named Limited Partnership:

(a) That I am a resident of the State of California, or if an entity, it has a permanent office in California, is doing business in California and was formed for purposes other than investing in these Units.

(b) I have not borrowed sums of money to purchase the interest as a Limited Partner of SAMPLE'S ELMTOWN without having a source of repayment other than the interest being purchased.

THIS FORM IS FOR ILLUSTRATION PURPOSES ONLY. IT MAY NOT MEET ALL RULES, REGULATIONS, AND PROCEDURES OF YOUR STATE, NOR HAS IT BEEN EDITED FOR SUCH PURPOSES BY THE AUTHOR.

(c) That the offer to sell these Units, and the payment for my Units was made in the State of California, and, this Statement signed in the State of California.

(d) I have resided in California since 19__, and I am employed at (city)_____________, (state)______________.

(e) I am a registered California voter ( ) yes, ( ) no; I have a current California Driver's License ( ) yes, ( ) no.

(f) I have relied solely upon the Confidential Memorandum and an independent investigation made by me or my representatives in making my decision to purchase an interest as a Limited Partner of SAMPLE'S ELMTOWN.

(g) I have the following pre-existing business or personal relationship with one or more of the General Partners:

____

____

____

(h) I have business or financial experience which qualifies me as a person who is able to understand the nature of this investment and as a person who is able to protect my own interests in connection therewith; and the following information is true and correct: (1) my overall commitment to investments which are not readily marketable is not disproportionate to my net worth, and my investment in the Units will not cause such overall commitment to become excessive; (2) I have substantial knowledge and experience in making investment decisions of this type or I am relying on my own Purchaser Representative (as defined in the Selection of Purchaser Representative form which is attached hereto as an exhibit) in evaluating the merits and risks of this investment and in making this investment decision; (3) that I have adequate means of providing for my current needs and possible personal contingencies; (4) that I am able to hold the investment for an indefinite period of time and have no need for liquidity of my investment in the Partnership; (5) that I can bear the economic risk of losing my entire investment herein.

(i) The information contained in the Questionnaire (Exhibit 1) is true and correct and may be used by the Partnership to meet the investor standards imposed by laws and regulations of the State of California relating to Private Placement Offerings.

(D") (4) I understand that neither SAMPLE'S ELMTOWN nor the General Partners can guarantee as to the accuracy of any statement made by the General Partners with respect to the tax consequences to SAMPLE'S ELMTOWN or to me as a Limited Partner, under the laws of the United States, the State of California, or any other jurisdiction. Furthermore, I realize that the laws of the United States, the State of California, or any other jurisdiction, and any regulations which may affect tax consequences with respect to SAMPLE'S ELMTOWN or with respect to me as a Limited Partner, may be amended in such a manner as to deprive SAMPLE'S ELMTOWN and/or me as a Limited Partner of any or all tax benefits that it or I might now otherwise receive. I ACKNOWLEDGE THAT I HAVE BEEN ADVISED TO CONSULT WITH MY OWN ATTORNEY AND/OR ACCOUNTANT CONCERNING THE TAX ASPECTS OF THE PURCHASE, OWNERSHIP AND SALE OF INTERESTS AS A LIMITED PARTNER IN SAMPLE'S ELMTOWN AS THE SAME RELATES TO ME, INDIVIDUALLY.

(E") (5) I recognize that SAMPLE'S ELMTOWN will be a newly formed entity that has no operating history. I further recognize that the purchase of Units is a financial investment which involves a degree of risk of loss by me, and I could lose the entire amount of my investment. I also recognize that neither SAMPLE'S ELMTOWN nor the General Partners give any guarantee or assurance that any revenue will be realized by the Partnership from its activities.

(E") (6) I further realize that there is no ready market for the sale of interests as Limited Partners in SAMPLE'S ELMTOWN and I may be unable to sell my interest in the event of an emergency. In addition, I realize the marketability and profitability of the Partnership assets may be adversely affected by a variety of economic conditions with respect to which the Partnership has no control and that even in the most favorable marketing atmosphere there is no guarantee that the assets of the Partnership could be sold, or if sold, that such sale would be made upon terms favorable to me as a Limited Partner. I also understand that subject to certain rights that I may have as a Limited Partner as provided by the Limited Partnership Agreement, the business operations of the Partnership are under the exclusive control of the General Partners.

(F") (7) I have been advised that the following person will receive from the Partnership compensation as a broker or finder in connection with my purchase of Units (if none, so indicate): ______________________________.

(8) In consideration of other individuals agreeing to make contributions and agreeing to form the above-named Limited Partnership, and in consideration of the General Partners' activities on behalf of the Partnership, I hereby agree, upon acceptance by them, to become a Limited Partner and to contribute as payment for the investment in Units in the Partnership, the sum of ONE THOUSAND DOLLARS ($1,000.00) per Unit herewith.

Number of Units Subscribed for	Total Capital Contribution
______________	______________

Make check payable to SAMPLE'S ELMTOWN.

I understand and agree that in the event the interests of the Partnership are not fully subscribed for and purchased by January 1, 1985, that the offering may be terminated without liability and that all monies paid by me will promptly be refunded in full without interest.

(9) The undersigned desires to take title to the Units as follows:

Initial one:

___ INDIVIDUAL OWNERSHIP AS A SINGLE PERSON (one signature required)

___ JOINT TENANTS WITH RIGHT OF SURVIVORSHIP (both signatures required)

___ HUSBAND AND WIFE AS COMMUNITY PROPERTY (both signatures required)

___ TENANTS-IN-COMMON (both signatures required)

___ SEPARATE PROPERTY

___ INDIVIDUAL RETIREMENT ACCOUNT

___ PENSION OR PROFIT SHARING TRUST

___ CUSTODIAN UNDER UNIFORM GIFT MINORS ACT, as custodian of ______________________

___ TRUST

___ OTHER ____
(specify)

PLEASE TYPE OR PRINT THE FOLLOWING INFORMATION:

LIMITED PARTNER

____
Full name(s) of subscriber as they should appear on schedule of limited partners

If subscriber is an IRA, Keogh or Trust this form must be signed by the Trustee(s)

Signature______________________

Signature______________________

____
Title or capacity of signing party if the subscriber is a partnership, corporation, trust or other non individual entity.

Address______________________
(Street)

____
(City) (State) (Zip)

Business Phone:(___)__________

Home Phone:(___)______________

____
Social Security or employer ID number(s) of subscriber

I CERTIFY THAT THE FOREGOING IS TRUE AND CORRECT.

DATED: ________________198_, at ________________________.

____
Signature of Limited Partner

____
Signature of Limited Partner

STATEMENT OF SUITABILITY
SAMPLE'S ELMTOWN
a California Limited Partnership

(G")

EXHIBIT 1

QUESTIONNAIRE

This Questionnaire must be completed in full and delivered to the Partnership with the Statement of Suitability. Interests in the Partnership will not be registered under the Securities Act of 1933, as amended (the "Act"), or the California Corporate Securities Law and other applicable state securities laws (the "State Laws"). The following information is provided to assure you, the issuer, that the offering (the "offering") will be exempt from registration under the Act and the State Laws, and the purchaser has such knowledge and experience in financial and business matters that he is capable of evaluating the merits and risks of the investment.

The information contained herein will be kept strictly confidential. It will be disclosed to no one other than the issuer or to counsel or accountants for the issuer unless it is necessary for the issuer to use such information to support the exemption from registration under the Act and the state acts, which it claims for this offering.

Name:* ______________________ ______________________
(Print)

Residence Address ______________________________
Telephone Number

____

Occupation ______________________________

Business Address ______________________________

____

Business Telephone ______________________________

____

*If the purchaser is a partnership, it must furnish such information as may be required to satisfy the General Partner that the purchasing partnership is a preexisting business entity which has not been formed for the purpose of making this investment. If the purchaser is a trust, a Confidential Prospective Offeree Questionnaire must be completed by or on behalf of each of the beneficiaries of the trust.

1. In which states have you maintained your principal residence during the past two years and the dates during which you resided in each state?

   State:__________________ Date:__________________

   State:__________________ Date:__________________

   State:__________________ Date:__________________

2. Do you maintain a residence in any other state? If so, in which state(s)?

   ____

3. In which state, if any, do you pay state income taxes?

   ____

4. In which state, if any, are you registered to vote?

   ____

5. Please describe your education background, indicating dates of attendance and degrees obtained.

   ____

   ____

   ____

   ____

6. Please describe briefly the principal positions you have held during the last five years or since graduation from college. What is sought is a sufficient description to enable the Partnership to determine the extent of your vocationally related experience in financial and business matters.

FROM	TO	POSITION	BRIEF DESCRIPTION OF POSITION

7. Real estate holdings, including personal residence (other than Limited Partnerships).

Description (type)	Date Purchased	Purchase Price

8. Are you a Trustee of a Pension or Profit Sharing Plan? ( ) Yes, ( ) No. If yes, please describe and set forth the value of the assets of the Plan:
$______________________________

____

9. Do you believe that you are capable of evaluating the merits and risks of this investment? ( ) Yes, ( ) No. If yes, please describe and set forth the reasons.

____

____

10. Do you intend to use a Purchaser Representative to assist you in your understanding of this investment? ( ) Yes, ( ) No.
If you use a Purchaser Representative, fill out the enclosed Selection of Purchaser Representative form.

11. Have you previously purchased Private Limited Partnership investments which were sold in reliance upon the non-public offering exemption from registration under the Securities Act of 1933 and State Law? ( ) Yes, ( ) No.

12. Do you own tax-shelter investment holdings? ( ) Yes, ( ) No.
If yes, please describe (a) name of investment, (b) date purchased, (c) purchase price.

____

____

13. Please indicate the frequency of your investment in marketable securities:
( ) Often, ( ) Occasionally, ( ) Never.

14. (a) Estimated net worth (exclusive of home, home furnishings and automobiles) at present time (check one):

Under $100,000	$100,000- $150,000	$150,000- $250,000	$250,000- $500,000	$500,000 and over
( )	( )	( )	( )	( )

(b) Liquid Assets (check one):

Under $35,000	$35,000- $75,000	$75,000- $150,000	$150,000 and over
( )	( )	( )	( )

(c) Non-liquid assets (check one):

$50,000- $100,000	$100,000- $150,000	$150,000 and over
( )	( )	( )

15. Is your net worth $1,000,000 or more? (For purposes of this question, you may <u>include</u> your spouse's net worth and may <u>include</u> the value of your home, home furnishings and automobiles). ( ) Yes, ( ) No.

16. Was your individual adjusted gross income (not joint with spouse) during the past two years at least $200,000 and do you anticipate that in the current year it will be at least $200,000? ( ) Yes, ( ) No.

17. $150,000 Purchasers only. Does the investment exceed 10 percent of your net worth? ( ) Yes, ( ) No.

18. (a) Gross income during 1983 (check one):

Under $40,000	$40,000- $60,000	$60,000- $100,000	$100,000- $150,000	$150,000 and over
( )	( )	( )	( )	( )

(b) Taxable income during 1983 (check one):

Under $35,000	$35,000- $60,000	$60,000- $100,000	$100,000- $150,000	$150,000 and over
( )	( )	( )	( )	( )

19. (a) Estimated gross income for 1984 (check one):

Under $50,000	$50,000-$70,000	$70,000-$100,000	$100,000-$150,000	$150,000 and over
( )	( )	( )	( )	( )

(b) Estimated taxable income for 1984 (check one):

$50,000-$100,000	$100,000-$150,000	$150,000 and over
( )	( )	( )

20. I understand that the Partnership will be relying on the accuracy and completeness of my responses to the foregoing and I therefore represent and warrant to the Partnership the following:

(a) The answers to the above questions are complete and correct and may be relied upon by the Partnership in determining whether the offering in which I propose to participate is exempt from registration under the Securities Act of 1933 and the California Corporate Securities Act or any other similar state act;

(b) I will notify the Partnership immediately of any material change in any statement made herein occurring prior to the closing of any purchase by me of an interest in the proposed investment; and

(c) I personally have sufficient knowledge and experience in financial and business matters to evaluate the merits and risks of the prospective investment, and I am able to bear the economic risk of the investment and, at the present time, could afford a complete loss of such investment.

____
Date

____
Signature

____
Social Security No.

____
Print Name

(H") EXHIBIT 2.

TO: BRENT E. STACE and PATRICK E. MARRIS

RE: SELECTION OF PURCHASER REPRESENTATIVE

This is to inform you that I have selected the individual(s) indicated below as my proposed Purchaser Representative(s) for the offering of the securities of the above issuer. I will pay any and all fees, compensation or costs payable to such individual, at no cost to the Partnership, the General Partners, or their Affiliates. I understand that you will contact this individual to assess his qualifications to serve as my Purchaser Representative and may communicate with me again on this matter.

NAME OF PROPOSED PURCHASER REPRESENTATIVE

____

ADDRESS OF PROPOSED PURCHASER REPRESENTATIVE

____

____

Sincerely,

____
Signature

____
Print Name

____
Date

NOTE: If the prospective investor chooses to use a Purchaser Representative, you will need to qualify such person to ensure yourself that he is knowledgeable enough to investigate the project on behalf of the prospective investor.

Appendix II

MODEL MINI-PACKAGE

THIS MINI-PACKAGE is an example for illustrative purposes only. It possibly could be expanded to cover some additional details (e.g., income tax risk factors), but it should not be any shorter than it is now. It assumes that you are the syndicator (general partner), performing all of the syndication functions. As such, you would be entitled to all the fees, commissions, and the promotional ownership percentage involved. In fact, you also would receive a commission upon the purchase of the duplex (from the seller) which does not show up in this package.

Names, places, and facts used are fictitious. As with the full package, however, you can use this as a working document after marking it up to suit your needs. I use a mini-package only when I have a short time fuse, say two or three weeks, because it is less than one-third as long as a full-length document. And, I use it only when I know all the prospective investors well. If you use a mini-package, I again recommend that you make certain that an attorney reviews it to ensure that all applicable state and federal guidelines are met.

NOTE: The following mini-package form is for illustration purposes only. It may not meet all rules, regulations, and procedures of your state, nor has it been edited for such purposes by the author.

CONFIDENTIAL MEMORANDUM

July 1, 1983

MAPLE PROPERTIES, a California Limited Partnership

Short-Term Residential Rental Property Investment

This Confidential Memorandum describes ownership interests (Units) in Maple Properties, a proposed limited partnership. This is a private offering and the sale of these ownership interests has not been qualified, recommended or endorsed by any federal, state, or local governmental commission or agency.

PURPOSE

To complete the acquisition of a residential duplex in a prime area of Elmtown, California. The Partnership will operate this duplex as a rental for approximately two years, then sell it and distribute the proceeds. Projected tax benefits, and capital growth through debt reduction and appreciation, are expected to produce profits for the Partners.

The Partnership's General Partner is JOHN B. READER. Mr. READER is a real estate broker with considerable experience in rental properties and other real estate transactions. He also has a substantial background in the legal, financial, and practical application of operating new business opportunities successfully.

OFFERING INFORMATION

Referencing Summary Of Cash Requirements below, total capital required to purchase and operate this rental is $44,000. This offering consists of 44 ownership Units at $1,000 per Unit with a minimum purchase of 1.5 Units ($1,500) required. A participant may purchase any amount desired above the minimum up to a total of ten Units. Limited Partners shall receive all operating profits, if any, and all sale profits until an amount equal to their investment has been received; thereafter, they shall receive 75% and the General Partner 25% of distributions. The Limited Partners shall receive all net losses including depreciation and investment tax credit.

The Partnership will be organized pursuant to the Agreement of Limited Partnership attached to this Memorandum. All proceeds from this offering will be deposited into Maple Properties account to be utilized at escrow close on August 1 for payment of the down payment and other costs referenced in the Summary Of Cash Requirements.

RISK FACTORS

Investment in Partnership Units involves a degree of risk and is suitable only for persons who have no need for liquidity of their investment. The business is speculative and competitive, it is unlikely that a public market will develop for purchase and sale of these Units, and anticipated tax benefits cannot be guaranteed. In addition, changes in local and general economic conditions may adversely affect the Partnership business. Prospective purchasers are advised that except for certain matters described in the partnership agreement, the Limited Partners will not participate in decisions made by the General Partner.

PROJECT BACKGROUND

Three years of unprecedented high mortgage loan interest rates have caused a slowdown of home and apartment construction, and have forced many would-be home owners into a rental situation. This steadily has forced up rent levels. Recently, however, the high interest rates have been dropping, and home buying as well as home building have increased dramatically. Market experts expect the housing market to explode as interest rates stabilize and the pent-up demand for housing is released.

The General Partner has been evaluating the real estate market very carefully for several months. To take advantage of the expected seller's market, he has negotiated very favorable price and terms, and has opened escrow on the subject duplex. Continuing high rents should enable this duplex to carry itself on close to a break-even basis until it is sold. At that time, the anticipated surge in prices should produce the profits expected.

THE PROPERTY; PURCHASE TERMS AND CONDITIONS

This large duplex is in excellent condition, requiring no refurbishment of any kind. Each unit is unfurnished with three bedrooms, two full baths, and two-car garage. Landscaping is immaculate, and the location is ideal. The duplex is in Shaker Heights, a high density/demand area conducive to rentals, close to schools, transportation, and shopping. Its address is 12 Mapl

The purchase price, $120,000, is well below the average market for duplexes in the area. Financing is unusually good. The cash down payment is $30,000, with the seller taking back a second note and trust deed of $17,850, interest only at 10% per annum for five years. The balance of approximately $72,150 is a VA first loan at 9.25%; it is being taken over on a "subject to" basis by the Partnership.

The first loan monthly payment of $767.29 includes principal, interest, taxes, and insurance. This payment, together with the $148.75 second loan interest payment, is less than current rents of $950.00 per month. After allowing for property management, vacancy factor, and other expenses, there should be only a very small negative cash flow which is provided for in the Summary of Cash Requirements below.

SUMMARY OF CASH REQUIREMENTS

Purchase Price of Duplex	$120,000
Less 1st and 2nd Trust Deeds	90,000
Cash Down Payment	30,000
Other Cash Required (detail below)	14,000
TOTAL CAPITALIZATION	$ 44,000

Detail of Other Cash Required:

Legal, Accounting Expense	$ 3,000
Gen. Partner Administrative Fee (5% of Purchase Price)	6,000
Negative Cash Flow Reserve	1,000
Reserve For Unforeseen Contingencies	4,000
Total	$ 14,000

TWO YEAR PROJECTED OPERATING STATEMENT

	1983	1984	1985
Duplex Purchase Price $120,000			
Total Partnership Capitalization	$44,000		(To Aug. 1)
Operating Data			
Income:	(5 Mos.)		(7 Mos.)
Gross Rents	$4,750	$12,600	$7,700
Net Rents (After 5% Vac. Allow.)	4,513	11,970	7,315
Expenses:			
Real Estate Taxes	600	1,440	840
Legal, Accounting	*3,000	350	350
Property Mgmt. (5% Gross)	226	599	366
Maintenance/Repair	250	660	450
Interest Expense	3,522	8,453	4,931
Misc. Oper. Expenses	350	840	490
Total Expenses	$7,948	$12,342	$7,427
Income/(Loss) Before Depreciation	($3,435)	($ 372)	($ 112)
Depreciation	2,667	6,400	3,733
Net Income/(Loss)	($6,102)	($ 6,772)	($3,845)
*Plus: 2,855 Leg/Actg cap'tlzn=Net	($3,247)		
Tax Write-Off	7.4%	15.4%	8.7%
Equity Accumulation	440	1,056	616

PROJECTED LIMITED PARTNER PROFIT SCHEDULE

Duplex scheduled for sale end of July, 1985 (24 months after close of purchase escrow).

Projected Sales Price			$156,000
Less:	Mortgage Notes - 1st	$70,038	
	- 2nd	17,850	
	Closing Costs, 6% Commission -	9,900	
	Total Costs		97,788
	Partnership Equity		58,212
Plus:	Contingency Reserve		4,000
	Total Partnership Equity		62,212
Less:	Return of Lim. Partners' Capital		44,000
	Profit For Distrib. (Cash/Notes)		18,212
Limited Partners' 75% of Profits			13,659
Plus:	Cumulative Tax Savings (50% Bracket)		6,932
	Total Profit		$ 20,591
Total % Return Per Year (Two Years)			23.4%

NOTE: The profit from the sale of this duplex should qualify for capital gain tax treatment, further benefiting each Limited Partner. As a real estate broker, the General Partner may receive a real estate commission on the purchase and the sale of this duplex. Such commission shall not be deemed a Partnership asset.

It is noted that these statements have been prepared from the best available estimates and data, but are based upon certain assumptions as to future events and, therefore, may not be completely accurate. They should be looked upon as an orderly presentation of the results to be expected if those assumptions are fulfilled. The Partnership business is and will be competitive and vulnerable to adverse changes in general and local economic conditions, as well as to other unforeseen factors which may be beyond the power of the Partnership to control. Consequently, the results shown above and other data preceding these results cannot be guaranteed, and should not be relied on for personal income forecasting purposes.

ATTACHMENT I

AGREEMENT OF LIMITED PARTNERSHIP
OF
MAPLE PROPERTIES

This Agreement of Limited Partnership ("Agreement") is made and entered into by and among JOHN B. READER as initial "General Partner" and the persons whose names, signatures and addresses appear at the end of the Agreement and identified as initial "Limited Partners."

In consideration of the mutual covenants and conditions contained herein, it is agreed:

1. FORMATION AND NAME. The Partners hereby form a limited partnership ("Partnership") pursuant to the provisions of the Revised Limited Partnership Act of California as set forth in Title 2, Chapter 3 of the California Corporations Code. The name of the partnership shall be MAPLE PROPERTIES.

2. PARTNERSHIP BUSINESS. The business of the Partnership shall be the purchasing, owning, renting, and future selling of the duplex real property located at 12 Maple, Elmtown, California, described in Exhibit "B" attached hereto, and doing and engaging in any and all activities reasonably related or incidental thereto. The Partnership shall maintain an office at 2033 Jensen Boulevard, Elmtown, California, or at such other place as the General Partner may hereafter determine.

3. TERM. The term for which the Partnership is to exist is from the date the Certificate is filed and shall terminate fifteen (15) years from the filing date.

4. TERMINATION AND DISSOLUTION.

4.1 The Partnership shall be terminated and dissolved upon the earlier to occur of the following:

4.1.1 The death, retirement, resignation, expulsion, or the dissolution of a General Partner unless within 120 days thereafter the remaining General Partner and any successor General Partner which may be elected in place of the terminated General Partner all elect to continue the business of the Partnership.

4.1.2 The filing of any petition in bankruptcy involving any General Partner unless within 120 days of such filing the remaining General Partner and any successor General Partner which may be elected in place of the terminated General Partner all elect to continue the business of the Partnership.

4.1.3 A Majority Vote in favor of dissolution and termination of the Partnership.

4.1.4 The expiration of the term of the Partnership.

4.1.5 The written decision, subsequent to the filing date, of any General Partner to dissolve the Partnership.

4.2 Upon a dissolution and termination of the Partnership for any reason, the General Partner shall take full account of the Partnership assets and liabilities, shall liquidate the assets as promptly as is consistent with obtaining the fair market value thereof, and shall apply and distribute the proceeds therefrom in the following order:

4.2.1 To the payment of creditors of the Partnership, but excluding secured creditors whose obligations will be assumed or otherwise transferred on the liquidation of Partnership assets;

4.2.2 To the repayment of any outstanding loans made by the General Partner to the Partnership;

4.2.3 To the Partners and Assignees of Record.

4.3 In the event of the death of the General Partner, his heirs, executors and successors shall automatically become Limited Partners and shall be subject to all of the terms and conditions of this Agreement.

5. FILING OF THE CERTIFICATE. Upon the execution of this Agreement, the General Partner shall take all actions necessary to assure the prompt filing of a Certificate of Limited Partnership as required by section 15621 of the California Corporations Code and shall take all other necessary actions (if any) required by law to perfect and maintain the Partnership as a limited partnership under the laws of California.

6. <u>TRANSFER OF PARTNERSHIP INTERESTS</u>.

6.1 A Limited Partner may, at any time, within the limitations set forth in subparagraphs 6.2, 6.3, 6.4 and 6.5 below, transfer his interest to the General Partner, another Limited Partner or by intestacy, testamentary disposition or gift to his spouse or children, or to a trustee for such spouse or children.

6.2 If a Limited Partner wishes to transfer his interest during his lifetime except as permitted in subparagraph 6.1 above, said Limited Partner shall first offer, in writing, to transfer said interest to the Partners, stating the terms and conditions of such transfer. Such offer shall be delivered to the General Partner to be communicated to the Partners. For thirty (30) days following the receipt of the notice of the proposed transfer, the Partners shall have the right to purchase such interest at the price stated in the notice. If said right is exercised within that thirty-day period, the Partners or any combination of the Partners shall give notice of that fact to the offering Limited Partner. Payment for the interest to be purchased shall be made pursuant to the terms of the notice of the proposed transfer.

6.3 Any such offer not accepted in full by the Partners within the time period stated above shall, at the option of the offering Limited Partner, be deemed to have been rejected. In the event the Limited Partner making said offer desires to transfer his interest to a person or persons other than his spouse, children or a trustee for such spouse or children, he shall first obtain the written consent of the General Partner prior to making any such offer. The General Partner shall not unreasonably withhold his consent to a transfer to a third person if in the opinion of legal counsel for the Partnership or the General Partner, said transfer would not be in violation of the regulations and guidelines established by federal, state or local governmental agencies as related to "nonpublic offerings." In the event the General Partner gives his consent to a Limited Partner to transfer his interest to a third person or persons, the terms and conditions of a proposed transfer shall not be more favorable to the transferee than were contained in the offer to the other Partners. Any such transfer shall be subject to the limitations set forth in paragraphs 6.4 and 6.5 below. The Limited Partner shall have sixty (60) days from the receipt of the written consent of the General Partner to transfer his interest in compliance with this paragraph, and after the expiration of such sixty-day period said Limited Partner may not transfer his interest without first reoffering it to the Partners in compliance with provisions of this paragraph.

6.4 The transferor Limited Partner shall cause a duly executed and acknowledged instrument of assignment to be filed with the General Partner which shall be in compliance with the terms hereof. The transferee shall pay a transfer fee to the Partnership which amount shall be set by the General Partner and shall cover all costs and expenses including attorneys' fees.

6.5 No Limited Partner shall transfer his interest to a minor or to any person who for any reason lacks the capacity to contract for himself under applicable laws, provided that this limitation shall not restrict the right of any Limited Partner to transfer his interest to a custodian, guardian, or trustee for a person who would, for such reason, be ineligible to become a transferee hereunder.

6.6 The General Partner may not sell, transfer, assign, pledge, hypothecate or otherwise transfer his interest as General Partner of the Partnership except to a successor General Partner.

6.7 It is contemplated that the General Partner may desire to give, from time to time, without consideration, as yet unspecified percentage interests in his share of the Partnership to members of his immediate family. Upon making such gift or gifts, the respective donees of such percentage interests shall automatically become substituted Limited Partners herein and as such subject to all of the terms and conditions hereof and entitled to their respective percentage interests in Partnership distribution.

7. CAPITAL.

7.1 The total capital of the Partnership to be contributed by the Partners is the amount of $44,000.00 and shall be contributed by the Limited Partners as set forth below:

> 7.1.1 Limited Partners may purchase up to 44 initial Units for a purchase price of $1,000.00 per Unit with a minimum purchase of 1.5 Units, or $1,500.00 per Limited Partner.

7.2 WITHDRAWAL OF CAPITAL. No Limited Partner has the right, during the term of the Partnership, to require the return of his capital contribution or of any interest in Partnership property.

7.3 INTEREST ON CAPITAL CONTRIBUTIONS. No interest shall be payable on the capital contributions of the Limited Partners.

8. ALLOCATION OF NET PROFITS AND NET LOSSES.

8.1 NET PROFITS. Until the Limited Partners have received distributions from all sources made by the Partnership of an aggregate amount equal to 100% of the Capital Contributions of the Limited Partners, all of the Net Profits or Cash Available for Distribution shall be distributed to the Limited Partners. Following receipt by the Limited Partners of an aggregate amount equal to 100% of their Capital Contributions, 25% of the Net Profits shall be distributed to the General Partner, and the balance of the Net Profits shall be distributed to the Limited Partners.

8.2 NET LOSSES. Net Losses of the Partnership shall be shown in the Partnership Information Tax Return filed in accordance with the Internal Revenue Code, using generally accepted tax basis accounting principles. All net losses (including but not limited to depreciation expenses and any investment tax credit) shall be allocated 100% to the Limited Partners.

9. MANAGEMENT. The General Partner shall have exclusive management and control over the business of the Partnership. Except as specifically limited herein, in addition to those powers granted to the General Partner by law, the General Partner shall have the right to:

9.1 Borrow money on behalf of the Partnership in the ordinary course of business and, as security therefor, encumber all or any of the Partnership assets.

9.2 In the ordinary course of business, prepay in whole or in part, refinance, increase, modify or extend any obligations affecting the Partnership assets.

9.3 Employ as required at the expense of the Partnership other persons for the operation and management of the Partnership business, including insurance brokers, real estate brokers, appraisers, accountants and attorneys for such compensation as the General Partner shall deem to be reasonable.

9.4 Prepare annual reports to Limited Partners summarizing the operating results of the Partnership.

10. COMPENSATION. The General Partner will receive as compensation for the organization, investigation, and services rendered to date, including therein the negotiations and finalization of the duplex purchase terms and conditions, and market and promotional studies for this Project, as well as ongoing direction of the Project and supervision of all matters from the date of the Confidential Memorandum to the date the Project commences to do business, the sum of Six Thousand Dollars ($6,000.00). The expenses described in paragraph 16 and the expenses and fee described herein shall be due and payable on formation of the Partnership. In addition and as compensation for his property management of the duplex operations, and as long as he is active in the business and affairs of the Partnership, the General Partner shall be entitled to receive a property management fee equal to 5% of the gross monthly revenues beginning the date the Project commences to do business, payable monthly.

11. CASH AVAILABLE FOR DISTRIBUTION. Cash Available for distribution shall be such sums from the excess of cash receipts derived from the day-to-day operations over cash disbursements, including payments on debts and obligations of the Partnership or its property and the creation of reasonable reserves, as the General Partner shall determine, from time to time.

12. DISTRIBUTION OF CAPITAL. Distribution of Capital shall mean the aggregate amount of any cash or other property distributions, which are received by the Partners upon liquidation, termination, refinancing, or sale of the Partnership assets.

13. COMPETING BUSINESSES. The General Partner may engage for his own account and for the account of others in any business ventures and employments, including ventures and employments having a business similar or identical or competitive with the business of the Partnership, without having or incurring any obligation to offer any interest in such activities to the Partnership or any other Partner. JOHN B. READER is a licensed real estate broker under the laws of the State of California. As such, the General Partner may receive or share in a real estate commission upon the purchase or sale of the Project in an amount which he would be entitled to in the event of a purchase or sale were he not General Partner. Any such commission shall not be deemed a Partnership asset.

14. INDEMNIFICATION OF GENERAL PARTNER. The General Partner (including any of his employees) shall not be liable for, and to the extent of its assets the Partnership shall indemnify the General Partner or such other persons against, liability arising out of their activities as or for the General Partner resulting from errors in judgment or any acts or omissions, whether or not disclosed, unless caused by willful misconduct or bad faith.

15. LIMITATIONS ON PARTNERS. No Partner shall have the right to demand or receive property other than cash where distribution is made pursuant to the terms hereof in return for his capital interest or otherwise, nor shall any Partner have the right to cause partition of any real property owned or leased by the Partnership. Nothing herein contained shall be construed to limit the power of the Partners to contract with the Partnership or have business relations with the Partnership to the fullest extent authorized by law. Nothing herein contained shall limit the right of the Limited Partners, upon demand, to receive full and true information at all reasonable times concerning all things affecting the Partnership or any other rights conferred on them as Limited Partners by law.

16. REIMBURSEMENTS. The General Partner shall be entitled to reimbursement for all advances or expenses incurred by him for the benefit of the Partnership, whether made or incurred prior to or subsequent to the date hereof, and such amounts shall be deemed expenses of the Partnership and shall be repaid on demand to the General Partner without regard to the income of the Partnership.

17. TAX RETURNS; STATEMENTS. The General Partner shall cause information and other tax returns for the Partnership to be prepared and filed with the appropriate authorities and shall furnish each Partner a statement of the distributive share of the Partnership income, gain, loss, deduction or credit which is allocable to each Partner in accordance with the terms of this Agreement.

18. <u>SPECIAL POWER OF ATTORNEY.</u>

18.1 ATTORNEY-IN-FACT. Each Limited Partner hereby grants to the General Partner a special power of attorney irrevocably making, constituting and appointing the General Partner as the Limited Partner's attorney-in-fact, with power and authority to act in his name with respect to this Agreement and on his behalf to execute, acknowledge and swear to in the execution, acknowledgment and filing of documents, which shall include, by way of illustration but not of limitation, the following:

18.1.1 The Agreement, any separate certificates of limited partnership, as well as any amendments to the foregoing which, under the laws of the State of California or the laws of any other state, are required to be filed or which the General Partner shall deem it advisable to file;

18.1.2 Any other instrument or document which may be required to be filed by the Partnership under the laws of any state or by any governmental agency or which the General Partner shall deem it advisable to file; and

18.1.3 Any instrument or document which may be required to effect the continuation of the Partnership, the admission of additional or substituted Limited Partners, or the dissolution and termination of the Partnership (provided such continuation, admission or dissolution and termination are in accordance with the terms of this Partnership Agreement), or to reflect any reductions in amount of contributions of Partners.

The General Partner shall promptly furnish to a Limited Partner a copy of any amendment to this Agreement executed by the General Partner pursuant to a power of attorney from the Limited Partner.

19. NOTICES. All notices under this Partnership Agreement shall be in writing and shall be given to the Limited Partner or Assignee of Record entitled thereto, by personal service or by mail, posted to the address maintained by the Partnership for such person or at such other address as he may specify in writing.

20. COUNTERPARTS. This Agreement may be executed in any number of counterparts with the same effect as if all parties hereto have signed the same document. All counterparts shall be construed together and shall constitute one Agreement.

21. BINDING EFFECT. This Agreement shall be binding upon and inure to the benefit of the parties hereto and their respective heirs, representatives, executors, administrators, successors and permitted assigns.

IN WITNESS WHEREOF, the undersigned have executed this Agreement as of the ______ day of ____________________, 1983.

Name (Sign) ______________________
(Print)

Name (Sign) ______________________
(Print)

Address ______________________

____

Social Security or Tax I.D. Number ______________________

____
JOHN B. READER

GENERAL PARTNER

LIMITED PARTNER

EXHIBIT "A"

AGREEMENT OF LIMITED PARTNERSHIP

MAPLE PROPERTIES

LIMITED PARTNERS

CAPITAL CONTRIBUTIONS

Limited Partners Name and Address:	Number of Initial Cash Units	Amount of Initial Capital Contribution

NOTE: This Exhibit "A" will be used to list all limited partners and their individual investment amounts.

EXHIBIT "B"

PARTNERSHIP PROPERTY

NOTE: This Exhibit "B" will be used to state the legal description of the Partnership Property.

ATTACHMENT II

STATEMENT OF SUITABILITY
AND SUBSCRIPTION AGREEMENT
MAPLE PROPERTIES
a California limited partnership

TO: JOHN B. READER

The undersigned hereby purchase a limited partnership interest in MAPLE PROPERTIES, a California limited partnership (the "Partnership") and in connection therewith, make the following representations:

(1) I acknowledge that I received the Confidential Memorandum dated July 1, 1983, and all exhibits to the foregoing and the Agreement of Limited Partnership in connection with MAPLE PROPERTIES prior to the execution of this Statement of Suitability, and I understand and agree to all of the terms, conditions and provisions contained in said Confidential Memorandum and Limited Partnership Agreement.

(2) I understand that the interests in MAPLE PROPERTIES are being sold under the exemption provided by Section 25102 of the California Corporations Code for non-public offerings and sales. I further understand that the Partnership and Partnership Interests have not been registered or qualified with any federal, state or local governmental agency or commission. I am buying my Limited Partnership interest for my own account, or for the account and benefit of a member or members of my immediate family, for investment. I agree that my interest in the Limited Partnership shall not be sold or otherwise transferred contrary to the terms of the Limited Partnership Agreement. I agree that a legend may be placed on the certificate(s) representing my Limited Partnership interest to reflect the substance of said Agreement.

(3) The following information may be relied upon by you in connection with my investment as a Limited Partner in the above-named Limited Partnership:

(a) That I am a resident of the State of California, or if an entity, it has a permanent office in California, is doing business in California and was formed for purposes other than investing in these Units.

(b) I have not borrowed sums of money to purchase the interest as a Limited Partner of MAPLE PROPERTIES without having a source of repayment other than the interest being purchased.

(c) That the offer to sell these Units, and the payment for my Units was made in the State of California, and this Statement signed in the State of California.

(d) I have resided in California since 19__, and I am employed at (city)_____________, (state)_____________.

(e) I am a registered California voter ( ) yes, ( ) no; I have a current California Driver's License ( ) yes, ( ) no.

(f) I have relied solely upon the Confidential Memorandum and an independent investigation made by me or my representatives in making my decision to purchase an interest as a Limited Partner of MAPLE PROPERTIES.

(g) I have the following pre-existing business or personal relationship with the General Partner:

____

____

____

(h) I have business or financial experience which qualifies me as a person who is able to understand the nature of this investment and as a person who is able to protect my own interests in connection therewith; and the following information is true and correct: (1) my overall commitment to investments which are not readily marketable is not disproportionate to my net worth, and my investment in the Units will not cause such overall commitment to become excessive; (2) I have substantial knowledge and experience in making investment decisions of this type or I am relying on my own Purchaser Representative (as defined in the Selection of Purchaser Representative form which is attached hereto as an exhibit) in evaluating the merits and risks of this investment and in making this investment decision; (3) that I have adequate means of providing for my current needs and possible personal contingencies; (4) that I am able to hold the investment for an indefinite period of time and have no need for liquidity of my investment in the Partnership; (5) that I can bear the economic risk of losing my entire investment herein.

(i) The information contained in the Questionnaire (Exhibit 1) is true and correct and may be used by the Partnership to meet the investor standards imposed by laws and regulations of the State of California relating to Private Placement Offerings.

(4) I understand that neither MAPLE PROPERTIES nor the General Partner can guarantee as to the accuracy of any statement made by the General Partner with respect to the tax consequences to MAPLE PROPERTIES or to me as a Limited Partner, under the laws of the United States, the State of California, or any other jurisdiction. Furthermore, I realize that the laws of the United States, the State of California, or any other jurisdiction, and any regulations which may affect tax consequences with respect to MAPLE PROPERTIES or with respect

to me as a Limited Partner, may be amended in such a manner as to deprive MAPLE PROPERTIES and/or me as a Limited Partner of any or all tax benefits that it or I might now otherwise receive. I ACKNOWLEDGE THAT I HAVE BEEN ADVISED TO CONSULT WITH MY OWN ATTORNEY AND/OR ACCOUNTANT CONCERNING THE TAX ASPECTS OF THE PURCHASE, OWNERSHIP AND SALE OF INTERESTS AS A LIMITED PARTNER IN MAPLE PROPERTIES AS THE SAME RELATES TO ME, INDIVIDUALLY.

(5) I recognize that MAPLE PROPERTIES will be a newly formed entity that has no operating history. I further recognize that the purchase of Units is a financial investment which involves a degree of risk of loss by me, and I could lose the entire amount of my investment. I also recognize that neither MAPLE PROPERTIES nor the General Partner gives any guarantee or assurance that any revenue will be realized by the Partnership from its activities.

(6) I further realize that there is no ready market for the sale of interests as Limited Partners in MAPLE PROPERTIES and I may be unable to sell my interest in the event of an emergency. In addition, I realize the marketability and profitability of the Partnership assets may be adversely affected by a variety of economic conditions with respect to which the Partnership has no control and that even in the most favorable marketing atmosphere there is no guarantee that the assets of the Partnership could be sold, or if sold, that such sale would be made upon terms favorable to me as a Limited Partner. I also understand that subject to certain rights that I may have as a Limited Partner as provided by the Limited Partnership Agreement, the business operations of the Partnership are under the exclusive control of the General Partner.

(7) I have been advised that the following person will receive from the Partnership compensation as a broker or finder in connection with my purchase of Units (if none, so indicate):

______________________________________.

(8) In consideration of other individuals agreeing to make contributions and agreeing to form the above-named Limited Partnership, and in consideration of the General Partner's activities on behalf of the Partnership, I hereby agree, upon acceptance by him, to become a Limited Partner and to contribute as payment for the investment in Units in the Partnership, the sum of ONE THOUSAND DOLLARS ($1,000.00) per Unit herewith.

Number of Units Subscribed for	Total Capital Contribution
______________	______________

Make check payable to MAPLE PROPERTIES.

I understand and agree that in the event the interests of the Partnership are not fully subscribed for and purchased by

January 1, 1984, that the offering may be terminated without liability and that all monies paid by me will promptly be refunded in full without interest.

(9) The undersigned desires to take title to the Units as follows:

Initial one:

___ INDIVIDUAL OWNERSHIP AS A SINGLE PERSON (one signature required)

___ JOINT TENANTS WITH RIGHT OF SURVIVORSHIP (both signatures required)

___ HUSBAND AND WIFE AS COMMUNITY PROPERTY (both signatures required)

___ TENANTS-IN-COMMON (both signatures required)

___ SEPARATE PROPERTY

___ INDIVIDUAL RETIREMENT ACCOUNT

___ PENSION OR PROFIT SHARING TRUST

___ CUSTODIAN UNDER UNIFORM GIFT MINORS ACT, as custodian of ____________________

___ TRUST

___ OTHER ______________________________________
(specify)

PLEASE TYPE OR PRINT THE FOLLOWING INFORMATION:

LIMITED PARTNER

____
Full name(s) of subscriber as they should appear on schedule of limited partners

If subscriber is an IRA, Keogh or Trust this form must be signed by the Trustee(s)

Signature____________________

Signature____________________

____
Title or capacity of signing party if the subscriber is a partnership, corporation, trust or other non individual entity.

Address____________________
(Street)

____
(City) (State) (Zip)

Business Phone: (___)__________

Home Phone: (___)__________

____
Social Security or employer ID number(s) of subscriber

I CERTIFY THAT THE FOREGOING IS TRUE AND CORRECT.

DATED: ______________198_, at ____________________.

____
Signature of Limited Partner

____
Signature of Limited Partner

STATEMENT OF SUITABILITY
MAPLE PROPERTIES
a California Limited Partnership

EXHIBIT 1

QUESTIONNAIRE

This Questionnaire must be completed in full and delivered to the Partnership with the Statement of Suitability. Interests in the Partnership will not be registered under the Securities Act of 1933, as amended (the "Act"), or the California Corporate Securities Law and other applicable state securities laws (the "State Laws"). The following information is provided to assure you, the issuer, that the offering (the "offering") will be exempt from registration under the Act and the State Laws, and the purchaser has such knowledge and experience in financial and business matters that he is capable of evaluating the merits and risks of the investment.

The information contained herein will be kept strictly confidential. It will be disclosed to no one other than the issuer or to counsel or accountants for the issuer unless it is necessary for the issuer to use such information to support the exemption from registration under the Act and the state acts, which it claims for this offering.

Name:* ______________________________ ______________________________
(Print)

Residence Address ____
Telephone Number

____

Occupation ____

Business Address ____

____

Business Telephone ____

---

*If the purchaser is a partnership, it must furnish such information as may be required to satisfy the General Partner that the purchasing partnership is a preexisting business entity which has not been formed for the purpose of making this investment. If the purchaser is a trust, a Confidential Prospective Offeree Questionnaire must be completed by or on behalf of each of the beneficiaries of the trust.

1. In which states have you maintained your principal residence during the past two years and the dates during which you resided in each state?

   State:__________________ Date:__________________

   State:__________________ Date:__________________

   State:__________________ Date:__________________

2. Do you maintain a residence in any other state? If so, in which state(s)?

   ____

3. In which state, if any, do you pay state income taxes?

   ____

4. In which state, if any, are you registered to vote?

   ____

5. Please describe your education background, indicating dates of attendance and degrees obtained.

   ____

   ____

   ____

   ____

6. Please describe briefly the principal positions you have held during the last five years or since graduation from college. What is sought is a sufficient description to enable the Partnership to determine the extent of your vocationally related experience in financial and business matters.

FROM	TO	POSITION	BRIEF DESCRIPTION OF POSITION

7. Real estate holdings, including personal residence (other than Limited Partnerships).

Description (type)	Date Purchased	Purchase Price

8. Are you a Trustee of a Pension or Profit Sharing Plan? ( ) Yes, ( ) No. If yes, please describe and set forth the value of the assets of the Plan:
$________________________

9. Do you believe that you are capable of evaluating the merits and risks of this investment? ( ) Yes, ( ) No. If yes, please describe and set forth the reasons.

10. Do you intend to use a Purchaser Representative to assist you in your understanding of this investment?
( ) Yes, ( ) No.
If you use a Purchaser Representative, fill out the enclosed Selection of Purchaser Representative form.

11. Have you previously purchased Private Limited Partnership investments which were sold in reliance upon the non-public offering exemption from registration under the Securities Act of 1933 and State Law? ( ) Yes, ( ) No.

12. Do you own tax-shelter investment holdings? ( ) Yes, ( ) No.
If yes, please describe (a) name of investment, (b) date purchased, (c) purchase price.

13. Please indicate the frequency of your investment in marketable securities:
( ) Often, ( ) Occasionally, ( ) Never.

14. (a) Estimated net worth (exclusive of home, home furnishings and automobiles) at present time (check one):

Under $100,000	$100,000-$150,000	$150,000-$250,000	$250,000-$500,000	$500,000 and over
( )	( )	( )	( )	( )

(b) Liquid Assets (check one):

Under $35,000	$35,000-$75,000	$75,000-$150,000	$150,000 and over
( )	( )	( )	( )

(c) Non-liquid assets (check one):

$50,000- $100,000	$100,000- $150,000	$150,000 and over
( )	( )	( )

15. Is your net worth $1,000,000 or more? (For purposes of this question, you may include your spouse's net worth and may include the value of your home, home furnishings and automobiles). ( ) Yes, ( ) No.

16. Was your individual adjusted gross income (not joint with spouse) during the past two years at least $200,000 and do you anticipate that in the current year it will be at least $200,000? ( ) Yes, ( ) No.

17. $150,000 Purchasers only. Does the investment exceed 10 percent of your net worth? ( ) Yes, ( ) No.

18. (a) Gross income during 1982 (check one):

Under $40,000	$40,000- $60,000	$60,000- $100,000	$100,000- $150,000	$150,000 and over
( )	( )	( )	( )	( )

(b) Taxable income during 1982 (check one):

Under $35,000	$35,000- $60,000	$60,000- $100,000	$100,000- $150,000	$150,000 and over
( )	( )	( )	( )	( )

19. (a) Estimated gross income for 1983 (check one):

Under $50,000	$50,000- $70,000	$70,000- $100,000	$100,000- $150,000	$150,000 and over
( )	( )	( )	( )	( )

(b) Estimated taxable income for 1983 (check one):

$50,000- $100,000	$100,000- $150,000	$150,000 and over
( )	( )	( )

20. I understand that the Partnership will be relying on the accuracy and completeness of my responses to the foregoing and I therefore represent and warrant to the Partnership the following:

(a) The answers to the above questions are complete and correct and may be relied upon by the Partnership in determining whether the offering in which I propose to participate is exempt from registration under the Securities Act of 1933 and the California Corporate Securities Act or any other similar state act;

(b) I will notify the Partnership immediately of any material change in any statement made herein occurring prior to the closing of any purchase by me of an interest in the proposed investment; and

(c) I personally have sufficient knowledge and experience in financial and business matters to evaluate the merits and risks of the prospective investment, and I am able to bear the economic risk of the investment and, at the present time, could afford a complete loss of such investment.

______________________	______________________
Date	Signature
______________________	______________________
Social Security No.	Print Name

EXHIBIT 2

TO: JOHN B. READER

RE: SELECTION OF PURCHASER REPRESENTATIVE

This is to inform you that I have selected the individual(s) indicated below as my proposed Purchaser Representative(s) for the offering of the securities of the above issuer. I will pay any and all fees, compensation or costs payable to such individual, at no cost to the Partnership, the General Partners, or their Affiliates. I understand that you will contact this individual to assess his qualifications to serve as my Purchaser Representative and may communicate with me again on this matter.

NAME OF PROPOSED PURCHASER REPRESENTATIVE

____

ADDRESS OF PROPOSED PURCHASER REPRESENTATIVE

____

____

Sincerely,

____
Signature

____
Print Name

____
Date

NOTE: If the prospective investor chooses to use a Purchaser Representative, you will need to qualify such person to ensure yourself that he is knowledgeable enough to investigate the project on behalf of the prospective investor.

Index

Index

Index